Sue Lawrence

ON BAKING

Sue Lawrence is a former BBC Masterchef and appears regularly on television as a cookery presenter. She is now a well-established food writer, featuring in national publications from *The Sunday Times* and *Country Living* to *Woman & Home* and *Sainsbury Magazine*. *On Baking* is her fifth book.

Sue Lawrence

ON BAKING

with photographs by
Jean Cazals

KYLE CATHIE LIMITED

First published in paperback in Great Britain 1998 by
Kyle Cathie Limited
20 Vauxhall Bridge Road, London SW1V 2SA

Hardcover edition published 1996
Reprinted 1997

ISBN 1 85626 266 9

A Cataloguing in Publication record for this title is
available from the British Library

Book Design by Kit Johnson
Typeset by Dorchester Typesetting, Dorset
Printed and bound in Singapore by Kyodo Printing Co Pte Ltd

The publishers wish to thank food stylist Liz Trigg, assisted by Clare Breen;
Helen Trent for the loan of props used in the photographs;
and the Chocolate Society for their donation of Valrhona white chocolate.

Cover food photographs by Jean Cazals
Cover photograph of Sue Lawrence by Karl Grant

Photograph on pages 2/3: Rum, Raisin and Rye Scone Ring (see page 104).

CONTENTS

Introduction 7

SWEET BREADS 11

BREADS 33

CAKES TO EAT FRESH 57

CAKES WHICH KEEP 79

SCONES 101

GRIDDLE COOKERY 117

BISCUITS 139

BROWNIES, FLAPJACKS & TIFFIN 161

FRUIT LOAVES 181

TARTS & PASTRIES 199

Index 222

Bibliography 224

FOR ANNA, MY MOTHER,
WITH LOVE

I have lived and breathed baking since early childhood.
I recall so vividly the rich aroma of my mother's warm
treacle scones, the sight of Scotch pancakes being
flipped over, the taste of sticky jam tarts and the crunch
of sugar-topped shortbread. For me, home-baking was
a way of life.

INTRODUCTION

High tea in my Scottish home seemed to revolve around the contents of the cake and biscuit tins,
neatly decanted on to serving plates each afternoon. I learned the basics of baking in
my kitchen at home, and it was also there that I intuitively discovered that there is absolutely no
substitute for home-baking.

Even for those who, unlike me, did not grow up on home-baking, there is something about the therapeutic activity involved – the alluring aromas wafting from the oven and the comforting taste of freshly-baked cakes or buns – which evokes atavistic feelings in all of us. While other forms of cooking go through trends and fashions, baking has remained essentially the same over the years. When I read Enid Blyton stories with my children, they marvel at the description of the tables groaning with cherry cake, macaroons and fruit cake. We could continue back through history, chewing over Proust's madeleines, 19th-century Bakewell pudding, 16th-century Richmond maids of honour, medieval mince pies or 9th-century Alfred the Great's bakestone cakes, precursors to our much-loved Welsh cakes. The trail would lead back through all the biblical stories of bread or famine, such as Ruth being allowed to glean corn in Boaz's fields and Jacob sending his sons to Egypt to buy corn during the famine in Canaan.

The first flour production is believed to date back about 6,000 years, when grains from wild grasses were ground by stones to make 'meal'. This meal produced a type of porridge that was baked on heated stones to make unleavened cakes. These were the forerunners of bread. The next important step was the Ancient Egyptians' discovery of natural fermentation – natural airborne yeasts, reacting on dough that had been allowed to stand for some time, made the dough expand, producing a lighter, airier loaf. This was the origin of bread as we know it.

This book is not only about breads. It is also about scones, cakes, pies and pancakes. Some recipes are traditional, some regional, some from abroad, some from a nearby village. Baking can play a role in our lives, however busy and health-conscious we are. There is, admittedly, a relatively high fat and sugar content in many recipes, but at least you – the baker – are the arbiter of how much butter, sugar and salt go in. Not only do home-baked goods taste far better than commercial substitutes, they are also completely devoid of additives and preservatives. They are packed full of 2 precious things: quality ingredients and effort.

It is this factor – effort – which many people would argue gives baking no role in our hectic lives. I strongly disagree on many counts. As I have just explained, home-baked goods are healthier than shop-bought ones. They can be incorporated into meals, or eaten in conjunction with fresh fruit for dessert. In the days of microwave-pinging 'oven-ready' meals for those without inclination to cook, surely there is time during weekends or holidays for a spot of recreational baking to rekindle the family's belief in the old-fashioned creed that home-made is best. Do we really want our children to grow up with culinary memories of unwrapping silver foil from chocolate bars each day, instead of delighting in the anticipatory smells, the warm touch, the magnificent appearance of a perfectly risen loaf and, above all, the unforgettable taste of home-baking? I, for one, do not.

I must stress the therapeutic value of baking for those unfamiliar with kneading dough. It is the best way to eradicate stress and aggression. Even those more delicate skills such as scone or pastry-making are therapeutic, for they involve concentration on things other than domestic tedium or problems at work. I like to equate the deft manipulative finger movements of rubbing fat into flour with playing the piano. (Or, in my case, listening to Chopin on tape and wishing my fingers could emulate the experts!) It is worth noting that baking is intrinsically a selfless act. Do you know many people who would bake a whole cake all for themselves? Precisely. Whereas many cooks cook for themselves, I would suggest that all bakers bake for others.

Baking is not, as is so often suggested, an anachronism. With the added emphasis on leisure in our lives, there is surely more time to enjoy a cup of tea and a slice of something home-baked. We can also enjoy the much wider variety of ingredients in our shops nowadays – particularly the choice of flours, from barley and buckwheat to millet and spelt. There is the most wonderful choice of foodstuffs from all over the world at our fingertips. Why should we follow popular trends in cookery? Why not follow our hearts and dust off our mixing bowls?

One attempt at home-baking and I believe you will be converted to its virtues. You will also come to appreciate why home-baking has endured over the centuries. Simply, it tastes so good.

Sue Lawrence
November 1995

Author's Note on Measurements and Freezing

I have always worked in imperial measurements primarily, so I have given my recipes in both imperial (pounds and ounces) and metric. The metric conversions are – unlike in any of my other books – not approximate conversions, but precise ones.

Baking, unlike many other types of cooking, requires exact measurements. The exact metric equivalents are therefore given alongside the imperial ones.

There are, however, a few exceptions to this rule – namely specific tin, packet or carton sizes, as indicated for certain ingredients.

$1 \times 7g/\frac{1}{4}oz$ sachet of easy-blend yeast is equivalent to $14g/\frac{1}{2}oz$ fresh yeast.

All eggs are size 3 (medium) unless otherwise stated. All tablespoons and teaspoons are level unless otherwise specified.

All recipes marked ❄ freeze well; I would not recommend freezing those without ❄.

SWEET BREADS

Not all bread is for toasting. In this first chapter are enriched loaves and buns which will emerge from the oven bulging, hot, sweet and crusty. Here are cardamom buns from Finland, saffron rolls from Sweden and Easter bread from Greece. From the modern (banana pizza) to the traditional (Sally Lunn), these are the ultimate treats for breakfast, tea – or in-between.

CHELSEA BUNS

Makes 9 buns

The Chelsea bun differs from other British buns because of its shape: no other traditional bun is coiled up. The name Chelsea bun originates from the famous Chelsea Bun House, situated in the borough of Chelsea, London. For about 100 years, until its demise in 1839, it sold all sorts of buns. It is recorded that on Good Friday in 1829, 240,000 buns were sold at the Chelsea Bun House. It does not indicate which type of buns, but these were surely hot cross buns. More importantly, the Bun House also sold the coiled, fruity, sticky Chelsea bun in some form or other. There are many different recipes: some include peel, some grated lemon zest, some mixed spice. I like the addition of mixed spice – just a hint – although if you want them to have a decidedly spicy edge, then increase the amount of spice given to 2 teaspoons. I think Chelsea buns are best served freshly baked for breakfast, so I have given a recipe which necessitates an overnight rising. If you want to make them for another time, however, simply allow them to rise in a warm place for 1½–2 hours.

BUNS

■ 454 g / 1 lb strong white flour ■ 1 heaped teaspoon ground mixed spice ■ ½ teaspoon salt
■ 57 g / 2 oz butter, cut into cubes ■ 1 sachet easy-blend dried yeast ■ 28 g / 1 oz caster sugar
■ 1 egg ■ 227 ml / 8 fl oz warm milk

TOPPING

■ 43 g / 1½ oz butter ■ 57 g / 2 oz raisins ■ 57 g / 2 oz currants ■ 57 g / 2 oz sultanas
■ 57 g / 2 oz soft light brown sugar ■ 2 teaspoons runny honey

Sift the flour, spice and salt into a large mixing bowl. Rub in the butter with your fingertips, until the mixture resembles breadcrumbs, then stir in the yeast, combining well.

In a separate bowl, whisk together the caster sugar and egg, then stir in the warm milk. Pour into the dry ingredients and mix to a soft dough.

Turn on to a lightly floured board and knead for 10 minutes, or until smooth. Then place in a lightly oiled bowl, cover with clingfilm and leave to rise in the refrigerator overnight – or place somewhere warm for 1½–2 hours.

Turn on to a floured board and knock back with your fists. Then, pressing gently, roll into a rectangle about 36 cm / 14 in by 25 cm / 10 in.

For the topping, melt the butter in a small saucepan and brush all over the dough, using a pastry brush. Mix the 3 dried fruits with the brown sugar and sprinkle evenly over the melted butter, leaving a 1 cm / ½ in border all round. Place both hands at the long side of the rectangle and very carefully roll the dough towards you – just as if you were rolling a swiss-roll. If any fruit tries to escape, poke it back with your fingers. Press the joins together to seal.

Using a sharp knife, cut the roll into 9 even pieces. Butter a 23 cm / 9 in square baking tin and arrange the pieces, cut-side up, so you can see the pin-wheels of fruit. They should be touching, but not squashed.

Gently warm 1 teaspoon honey and brush over the buns. Cover loosely with buttered clingfilm and leave to prove in a warm place for 35–40 minutes, or until slightly puffy. Pre-heat the oven to 200°C/400°F/Gas mark 6. Bake in the oven for 35 minutes, or until golden brown.

Remove the rolls from the oven and brush with the remaining warmed honey. Leave to cool in the tin for 3–4 minutes before transferring to a wire rack.

Pull the buns apart after they have cooled for 10–15 minutes. Serve warm. ❋

GREEK EASTER BREAD

Makes 1 loaf

This festive bread or 'Tsoureki' is eaten on special occasions and, in particular, forms part of the celebrations that mark the end of the 40-day Lenten fast in Greece. Some are so highly decorated that they are displayed on the walls on Easter Sunday before being eaten.
The basic tsoureki is a sweet, enriched, plaited bread with red-dyed hard-boiled eggs nestling among the plaits. You need a strong red food colouring to dye the eggs. I use about 3 tablespoons to 1.136 litres/2 pints of water. The eggs are hard-boiled in the coloured water, then left in the water to cool. They are then removed from the water and allowed to dry, before brushing with olive oil until they shine. For the best texture, leave the dough to rise 3 times, not the usual 2. An optional topping is a sprinkling of split, blanched almonds or a glaze of warmed runny honey.

■ 57 g / 2 oz butter, softened ■ 57 g / 2 oz caster sugar ■ 2 eggs, beaten ■ 1 sachet easy-blend dried yeast
■ 511 g / 1 lb 2 oz strong white flour, sifted ■ 199 ml / 7 fl oz warm milk
■ 3 hard-boiled, red-dyed eggs ■ beaten egg, to glaze

Beat together the butter, sugar and eggs until light and creamy.

Combine the yeast with the flour in a large bowl, then make a well in the middle. Stir in the warm milk and butter mixture and combine to a softish dough with a wooden spoon.

Turn on to a floured board and knead for about 10 minutes, or until smooth and silky.

Place in a lightly oiled bowl, cover with clingfilm and allow to rise somewhere warm for about 1½ hours, or until well-risen. Knock back with your fists, knead briefly and return to the bowl. Cover and leave to rise for a further hour.

Divide into 3 pieces. Roll each piece into a sausage shape, then pinch the ends together and plait fairly loosely to allow room for the dough to expand. Transfer to a baking sheet, then press the 3 hard-boiled eggs deep into the loaf. Brush with beaten egg and place somewhere warm for about 35–45 minutes, or until puffed up. Pre-heat the oven to 200°C/400°F/Gas mark 6.

Bake in the oven for about 25–30 minutes, or until well-risen and golden brown. Gently tap the base of the bread to make sure it is cooked – it should sound hollow. Transfer to a wire rack to cool. Remove the eggs and cut into slices.

CHOCOLATE BREAD ROLLS

Makes 10 rolls

My first experience of eating chocolate with bread was at an informal bread-based meal with Danish friends. A chocolate spread which, although common in this country now, was a novelty some 30 years ago, intrigued me, but I was not sure whether I liked it. Then, as an au pair in Provence in the late 1970s, my duties included giving my charges 'goûter' at 5 o'clock. They always had hunks of baguette and squares of plain chocolate. Again, I was not totally convinced about the combination. Some years later, when 'pains au chocolat' became much more prevalent in Britain, I saw the light. I loved the contrast of warm, melting chocolate and the light buttery bread roll. The following recipe is not like the French creation, which is usually made from croissant dough. Instead it resembles the pains au chocolat of pre World War II France; bread rolls baked around some good couverture chocolate. This is also much easier to make. I have used a basic bread dough, with just a hint of fat and sugar. Since they are at their absolute best warm for breakfast, I have given timings for an overnight proving in the refrigerator. If you prefer milk chocolate (and my children certainly do), buy some with a high percentage of cocoa solids that is not so sweet. Otherwise, use a plain chocolate with 50–60 per cent cocoa solids. It should not be too bitter at breakfast time. Chocolate bread rolls can be reheated successfully on the following day. The best way is to pop them in the microwave: regular oven heat dries them out.

■ 624 g / 1 lb 6 oz strong white flour ■ 2 teaspoons salt ■ 1 sachet easy-blend dried yeast
■ 28 g / 1 oz butter, cut into cubes ■ 28 g / 1 oz caster sugar
■ about 341 ml / 12 fl oz semi-skimmed or skimmed milk, warmed
■ 113–142 g / 4–5 oz plain chocolate, chopped ■ milk, to glaze

Combine the flour, salt and yeast in a large bowl, then rub in the butter. Stir in the sugar, then make a well in the centre.

Add enough warm milk to combine to a fairly stiff dough. Turn on to a floured board and knead for about 10 minutes. Place in an oiled bowl, cover tightly with clingfilm and place in the refrigerator overnight.

Next morning, knock back the dough with your fists, then divide into 10 pieces. Roll into rectangles about 10 × 15 cm / 4 × 6 in. Place the chopped chocolate down the middle, then roll up, swiss-roll style, tucking in the ends.

Place on a baking tray, cover loosely with clingfilm and leave to rise somewhere warm for about 30–40 minutes. Pre-heat the oven to 220°C/425°F/Gas mark 7.

Bake in the oven for about 15 minutes, or until risen and golden brown. Cool on a wire rack for about 5 minutes. Serve warm.

CHOCOLATE BREAD ROLLS

BARM BRACK

Makes 1 loaf

I love this Irish loaf – but then I also adore Scotland's Selkirk Bannock and Welsh Bara Brith, which are both rather similar. Ireland's Barm Brack is a spicy loaf, traditionally baked for Hallowe'en in a cast-iron pot (a bastible) hung over an open fire. 'Barm', which is literally the froth that collects on fermenting malt liquor, was traditionally used to leaven the dough before compressed baker's yeast was introduced. 'Brack', from the Irish word *brac*, means speckled. As with all regional breads, there are endless variations: some contain ground ginger, some include sultanas as well as currants, and some use muscovado sugar instead of caster. After baking, the barm brack is glazed to give it a lovely sweet sheen. It can be eaten fresh in slices, spread with butter, or toasted the next day.

BARM BRACK

■ 14 g / ½ oz fresh yeast ■ ½ teaspoon sugar ■ 256 ml / 9 fl oz half milk, half water, warm
■ 454 g / 1 lb strong white flour ■ 28 g / 1 oz butter ■ 1 teaspoon mixed spice ■ whole nutmeg, to grate
■ 57 g / 2 oz caster sugar ■ 227 g / 8 oz currants ■ 57 g / 2 oz mixed peel

GLAZE

■ 1 tablespoon sugar ■ 1 tablespoon water

Combine the yeast, sugar and warmed liquids in a small mixing bowl, stir well and leave to stand for 10 minutes.

Place the flour in a bowl and then rub in the butter with your fingertips. Stir in the mixed spice and about ⅛ teaspoon grated nutmeg, then add the caster sugar, currants and peel. Make a well in the centre.

Pour in the yeast liquid and combine to a firm – not crumbly – dough. Add a further 1–2 tablespoons warm water if necessary.

Turn on to a floured board and knead for 10 minutes, or until smooth.

Place in a buttered bowl, cover with clingfilm and leave to rise in a warm place for 2 hours, or until well-risen.

Knock back the dough with your fists, then shape into a buttered 18 cm / 7 in deep cake tin.

Cover and leave somewhere warm for 1 hour, or until the dough has risen nearly to the top of the tin. Pre-heat the oven to 220°C / 425°F / Gas mark 7.

Bake in the oven for 15 minutes, then reduce the temperature to 200°C / 400°F / Gas mark 6 and cook for a further 20–25 minutes.

Meanwhile, make the glaze. Bring the water to the boil in a small saucepan, add the sugar and dissolve over a low heat. Brush over the top of the bread and return to the oven for 2 minutes.

Transfer the cake to a wire rack. Allow to become cold before cutting into slices. ✳

---

1 × 7 g / ¼ oz sachet of easy-blend dried yeast is equivalent to 14 g / ½ oz fresh yeast.

SALLY LUNN

Makes 1 cake

There are two explanations about the delightful name of this cake. Some believe it was named after a pretty young girl called Sally Lunn who sold hot, golden-brown, dome-shaped cakes in the streets of Bath during the 19th century. Others believe the name to be a corruption of the French words *soleil lune* or sun and moon, since the cake has a shiny, golden appearance. I certainly prefer the former theory, but I have a sneaking suspicion that the French one is correct, most significantly because there is a cake made in the Alsace region of France called 'Solilem'. This has very similar ingredients and is shaped in the same round, deep mould. It is also served in the same manner as a Sally Lunn, being split horizontally into 2 or 3 layers and spread with butter.
There are also several theories as to the authentic ingredients: some recipes are enriched with milk and butter, others with double cream; some include strands of saffron, which are infused with the milk or cream, others add grated lemon zest or mixed spice. My recipe is for a deep cake which can be split into 3. I like to fill the layers while still warm with clotted cream, which dribbles appealingly down the sides. It is delicious with quince or damson cheese.

■ 454 g / 1 lb strong white flour ■ ¼ teaspoon salt ■ 28 g / 1 oz caster sugar
■ 1 sachet easy-blend dried yeast ■ 284 ml / ½ pint double cream ■ 2 eggs ■ 1 egg yolk, to glaze
■ butter or clotted cream, to serve

Combine the flour, salt, sugar and yeast in a large mixing bowl. Make a well in the centre.

Warm the cream over a very gentle heat then add the eggs and beat well. Pour into the centre of the well and combine to a soft dough.

Turn the dough on to a floured board and knead for about 10 minutes, or until smooth and satiny and no longer sticky. Place in a lightly buttered bowl, cover with clingfilm and leave to rise in a warm place for about 2½ hours, or until well-risen.

Knock back with your fists, then shape into a ball. Place in a buttered 18 cm/7 in deep cake tin, cover loosely with clingfilm and leave to rise in a warm place for about 1½ hours, or until the dough almost reaches the top of the tin. Pre-heat the oven to 200°C/400°F/Gas mark 6.

Brush the cake with beaten egg yolk, then bake in the oven for about 25 minutes, or until golden brown.

Transfer to a wire rack to cool for at least 30 minutes. Split into 3 layers and spread with softened butter or clotted cream.

❇ To freeze: cool first, then wrap tightly with clingfilm; defrost at room temperature for about 6 hours before warming in a medium oven for about 5 minutes.

When 'flouring' your work surface to knead on, or to roll out pastry, use a flour shaker, rather than a handful of flour – otherwise, too much flour will be absorbed into your dough or pastry.

SELKIRK BANNOCK

Makes 1 bannock

The Selkirk Bannock developed from the idea of a canny Scots baker in Selkirk who was looking for a use for his spare bread dough. Although there is no exact date given for its inception, we do know that Queen Victoria adored it. Catherine Brown writes in her book *Scottish Cookery* that when Queen Victoria visited Sir Walter Scott's grand-daughter at Abbotsford, she refused to eat anything other than Selkirk Bannock with her tea.

The traditional recipe, baked by most Borders bakers, is a bread dough enriched with fruit, butter and sugar. Many use a combination of lard and butter, and many use a high proportion of sugar. I prefer to use only a little sugar, since the richness of the bannock comes from all the dried fruit. Eat the bannock in slices, either freshly baked or toasted, spread with butter.

■ 907 g / 2 lb strong white flour ■ a pinch of salt ■ 57 g / 2 oz caster sugar ■ 35 g / 1¼ oz fresh yeast
■ 170 g / 6 oz unsalted butter ■ 341 ml / 12 fl oz milk ■ 340 g / 12 oz sultanas
■ 113 g / 4 oz mixed peel, chopped ■ beaten egg, to glaze

Place the flour and salt in a bowl, then make a well in the centre. Combine the yeast with 1 teaspoon of sugar and mix to a paste, then stir in the rest of the sugar.

Place the butter and milk in a small saucepan and heat together until the butter has melted, then allow to cool until lukewarm. Combine with the yeast mixture.

Pour the liquid ingredients into the well and combine to a soft – but not sticky – dough, adding more warm milk if you feel the dough is too dry.

Turn on to a floured board and knead for at least 10 minutes, or until smooth and elastic. If you do not knead thoroughly at this stage, the bannock will be heavy and dense.

Place the kneaded dough in a lightly oiled bowl, cover with clingfilm and leave to rise in a warm place for about 2 hours, or until well-risen.

On a floured board work in the sultanas and peel, a third at a time, using well-floured hands. Knead until the fruit is evenly distributed.

Shape like a bannock – that is, a round dome 25 cm / 10 in in diameter.

Brush the top and sides with beaten egg, then leave somewhere warm for about 1 hour, or until well-risen. Pre-heat the oven to 220°C / 425°F / Gas mark 7.

Bake in the oven for 15 minutes, then lower the heat to 190°C / 375°F / Gas mark 5 and bake for a further 20–25 minutes. If necessary, cover with foil after about 10 minutes to prevent the fruit from burning.

Remove from the oven, tap the base to make sure it is cooked – the bannock should sound hollow – then transfer to a wire rack to cool completely before slicing. ❄

The easiest way to incorporate liquids into dry ingredients is to make a 'well' in their centre, then gradually pour the liquids into the well with one hand, while 'drawing in' the flour with the other.

SELKIRK BANNOCK PUDDING
WITH SHORTBREAD ICE-CREAM

Serves 4–6

This stunning recipe was given to me by Gary Moore, chef at Burt's Hotel, Melrose, in the heart of the Borders. He is passionate about using local ingredients and Selkirk Bannock is one of his favourites. Use the best and most buttery shortbread for the ice-cream.

I have reduced the quantities in Gary's ice-cream recipe to suit my ice-cream machine. I have also added some natural yoghurt, which gives a tangy edge to the otherwise very sweet ice-cream. If you prefer to use lime curd instead of lemon for the pudding, this also works very well.

If you have no Selkirk Bannock, then the Barm Brack on page 16 also works well in this pudding.

ICE-CREAM
■ 1 × 400 g / 14 oz tin condensed milk ■ 284 ml / ½ pint double cream
■ 426 ml / ¾ pint crème anglaise ('real' custard), cooled ■ 340 g / 12 oz shortbread
■ 284 ml / ½ pint natural yoghurt

PUDDING
■ 1 small Selkirk Bannock (about 6 good slices) ■ 113 g / 4 oz unsalted butter
■ 1 small jar lemon curd, see page 88 ■ 284 ml / ½ pint double cream
■ 3 eggs

For the ice-cream, place the unopened tin of condensed milk in a pan of water. Cover, then bring to the boil and simmer for 3 hours, checking the water level regularly. Remove from the pan, taking care not to burn your fingers, and allow to cool.

Lightly whip the double cream. Open the tin of condensed milk (which looks like toffee) and mix with the whipped cream and crème anglaise. Continue to whisk together until thoroughly combined and smooth.

Pour into an ice-cream machine and churn for about 20 minutes.

Roughly chop the shortbread and stir into the ice-cream, along with the yoghurt. Turn into a freezer container and freeze until firm.

For the pudding, cut the bannock into thin slices, then spread with butter and lemon curd.

Butter a rectangular oven dish and line with some of the buttered bannock. Join the remainder together, as if you were making sandwiches, then cut into small 2 cm / ¾ in cubes. Place in the dish. Pre-heat the oven to 180°C / 350°F / Gas mark 4.

To make the custard for the pudding, beat together the double cream and eggs, then pour over bannock until completely covered.

Cover with foil and cook in the oven for about 15–20 minutes, or until the custard is just about set.

To serve, spoon a portion of the pudding on to a plate and top with a dollop of ice-cream.

LUCIA ROLLS

Makes 12 rolls

In Sweden, on St Lucia Day – December 13th –
there are great festivities. Children dress
up in white and wear great towering crowns of
glowing, lighted candles. In Britain,
there is enough of a song and dance when
children have to carry turnip or
pumpkin lanterns containing one little night-
light, so it would be unthinkable to
imagine this delightful custom catching on here.
Those Swedes obviously live more
dangerously than we imagine!
One of the traditional dishes made for
the special Swedish celebration of light is saffron
buns. There are, of course, many
variations of the basic recipe but this is one I
love. It is made with fresh yeast, but if
you have difficulty finding it, then use dried
yeast instead, altering the amount
according to the packet instructions.
Less than 1 teaspoon of saffron threads is
required, which is enough to impart the most
wonderfully spicy, exotic aroma to these
buns. It also gives them a lovely pale golden
colour. Saffron is the most expensive
spice to buy anywhere in the world. Do not be
tempted by very cheap packets which
are bound to be fake – there are many rogue
saffrons around. Spain and the Middle
East both produce excellent and very
reliable saffron.

PULLA (page 22)
LUCIA ROLLS

- ¾ teaspoon saffron threads ■ 1 tablespoon brandy ■ 14 g / ½ oz fresh yeast ■ 1 teaspoon sugar
- 227 ml / 8 fl oz lukewarm milk ■ 454 g / 1 lb strong white flour ■ a pinch of salt
- 57 g / 2 oz caster sugar ■ 57 g / 2 oz butter, melted ■ 1 egg, beaten
- 1 egg yolk ■ caster sugar, to dust ■ a handful of raisins

First toast the saffron. Pre-heat the grill, spread the saffron on a small grill tray and set under the grill for 1–2 minutes, depending on how near to your grill the dish is. Equally, you can toast the strands in a medium oven for 3–5 minutes. This releases some of the aroma – take care not to burn the saffron. Stir the toasted saffron into the brandy and leave to infuse for about 10 minutes.

Meanwhile, place the yeast in a small dish with 1 teaspoon sugar. Add 2 tablespoons of the lukewarm milk and stir well with a fork to dissolve the yeast. Leave to stand for 5–10 minutes.

Combine the flour, salt and remaining sugar in a large mixing bowl, then make a well in the centre. Stir the saffron and melted butter into the milk, then check the temperature is still only lukewarm. (If it is too hot, wait.) Stir in the beaten egg and yeast mixture, then pour into the well. Combine all the ingredients with a wooden spoon and mix to a softish dough.

Turn on to a floured board and knead for about 10 minutes, or until smooth. (You will need to add quite a lot of flour, as you knead, because the dough is rather soft. Only add little by little, however, as you require it.)

Place in a lightly oiled bowl, cover with clingfilm and allow to rise in a warm place for about 1½–2 hours, or until the dough has risen to about 1½ times its original volume.

Turn on to a floured board, knock back with your fists, then divide into 12 pieces. Roll each piece into a rectangle about 20 cm/8 in long. Twist into an 'S' shape, making it as tight as possible since the rolls loosen as they prove. Place on a lightly greased baking tray, cover loosely with clingfilm and place somewhere warm for 30–40 minutes, or until puffed up.

Pre-heat the oven to 220°C/425°F/Gas mark 7. Brush with beaten egg yolk to glaze, then sprinkle with caster sugar. Place one raisin in the centre of each 'S' curl – so that you have 2 per bun. (Tighten up the curls, if necessary.)

Bake in the oven for about 10–15 minutes, or until well-risen and golden brown.

Transfer to a wire rack to cool. Serve warm with a cup of coffee or a glass of cold milk. ❈

PULLA

Makes about 15 buns

'Pulla' is a generic term in Finland for coffee bread – that is, sweetened bread to be served with coffee, not coffee-flavoured bread. There are many varieties, but the most common is 'Korvapuustit', buns flavoured with brown sugar, cinnamon and butter. This is the recipe given below. While I was teaching in northern Finland, I was given many lessons in how to make the best pulla. The basic ingredients are flour, sugar, yeast, butter and milk. In Finland, the dough rises very quickly indeed, for the houses are all centrally-heated and triple-glazed to make them wonderfully warm and snug. In this country, however, I leave the dough to rise in the airing cupboard to hasten the process along, but you can simply leave it at room temperature for a few hours.

Once the basic pulla dough is made, it is flavoured with crushed cardamom – a popular ingredient in many Finnish recipes. Cardamom is Finland's oldest imported spice: records of its use date back as far as the 16th century. Do not use ready-ground cardamom for this recipe.

'Isoaidin Pulla' – Grandmother's Pulla – is another great favourite. Here the basic pulla dough is spread out in a large flat ovenproof dish, then filled with berries which have been mixed with a little cornflour and sugar. The berries most commonly used in Finnish cookery are blueberries, cloudberries, lingonberries, cranberries and arctic brambles. Another variation of pulla is 'Munkit' or Finnish Doughnuts, made with slightly less flour. The dough is formed into rolls, allowed to rise, then fried for 15 minutes in vegetable oil before being rolled in sugar and served warm. Pulla are best served straight from the oven, with a long glass of ice-cold, creamy milk.

PULLA
■ 28 g / 1 oz fresh yeast ■ 1 teaspoon sugar ■ 199 ml / 7 fl oz warm milk
■ 454 g / 1 lb strong white flour, sifted ■ 85 g / 3 oz butter, cut into cubes ■ 28 g / 1 oz caster sugar
■ 1 teaspoon salt ■ 2 teaspoons crushed (not ready-ground) cardamom seeds

FILLING
■ 57 g / 2 oz butter, softened ■ 57 g / 2 oz soft light brown sugar ■ 2–3 teaspoons ground cinnamon

GLAZE
■ beaten egg

Combine the yeast, sugar and warm milk in a small bowl and allow to stand for 5–10 minutes.

Place the flour in a large mixing bowl, rub in the butter with your fingertips, then add the caster sugar, salt and cardamom. Make a well in the centre and stir in the yeast mixture. Combine to a dough with your hands, then turn on to a floured board. Knead for about 10 minutes, or until smooth and elastic.

Place in a lightly oiled bowl, cover with clingfilm and leave to rise in a warm place for 1–1½ hours, or at room temperature for 4–5 hours.

Roll out the dough to a large rectangle, about 25 × 36 cm / 10 × 14 in. Spread with softened butter, then top with sugar and cinnamon. Roll up swiss-roll style, then cut into about 15 slices.

Place cut-side up in paper cases on a baking sheet. Cover loosely with clingfilm and leave to rise somewhere warm for about 30 minutes. Preheat the oven to 220°C/425°F/Gas mark 7.

Gently press down on the centre of each bun, using your finger or the handle of a knife, so that the spiral-like filling bulges out upwards. Brush with beaten egg and bake for about 10 minutes, or until puffed up and golden brown. Transfer to a wire rack to cool. ❄

Only use green cardamom pods for baking. First snip off the outer pod, then remove the tiny black seeds and crush them in a pestle and mortar.

KULICH AND PASKHA

Makes 1 kulich and 1 paskha

In Russia, Easter is synonymous with feasting. Kulich, or Easter cake, and paskha are two very significant parts of the celebrations. On Easter Saturday evening, the kulich (and sometimes the paskha) is taken to church to be blessed. Then on Easter Sunday, tables groaning with food are prepared and painted eggs handed out as an Easter greeting.

Paskha is, in fact, the Russian word for Easter. It is made from curd cheese ('tvorog') which has been pressed for 24 hours to extract the whey, before being mixed with the other ingredients on Good Friday. The resulting mixture is like an unbaked cheesecake mix, a slice of kulich serving as its base once spread with it. The paskha is flavoured with lemon and vanilla, and filled with dried and candied fruits, mixed peel and nuts – usually almonds. The traditional mould for the paskha is a wooden pyramid-shape, carved inside with decorations and lined with muslin, which is weighted down for at least 24 hours. A terracotta flowerpot can be used instead. Once unmoulded, the paskha is decorated with raisins to form the symbolic letters XB, the Cyrillic for 'Christ is Risen'.

The kulich should be baked in a tall cylindrical mould or a round cake tin which is deep enough for the dough to rise. The kulich can be flavoured with cardamom, cinnamon, saffron, lemon peel, or dried fruits and nuts. Often a white candle is placed in the middle, on top of the icing. The kulich is traditionally cut horizontally into slices, but you might find it easier to cut it into wedges. Although it is authentic to ice and decorate the kulich, I prefer to leave it un-iced. Instead I like to top it with the paskha and a spoonful of home-made lemon curd – even more ambrosial!

KULICH

■ 454 g / 1 lb strong white flour, sifted ■ ¼ teaspoon salt ■ 1 sachet easy-blend dried yeast
■ 284 ml / ½ pint warm milk ■ 113 g / 4 oz unsalted butter, softened
■ 85 g / 3 oz caster sugar ■ 3 eggs ■ 6 cardamom pods ■ 57 g / 2 oz blanched almonds, roughly chopped
■ 57 g / 2 oz raisins ■ beaten egg, to glaze

TO DECORATE

■ 113 g / 4 oz icing sugar, sifted ■ 3–4 tablespoons cold water or lemon juice
■ candied and glacé fruit and peel, chopped ■ blanched almonds

Combine the flour, salt and yeast in a large mixing bowl and then stir in the warm milk. Using your hands, knead for a couple of minutes in the bowl to form a fairly dry dough, then cover with clingfilm and leave at room temperature for at least 1 hour.

In a separate bowl, cream together the butter and sugar until light and fluffy. Then beat in the eggs, one at a time. Remove the seeds from the cardamom pods and grind together in a pestle and mortar. Stir into the butter mixture, along with the almonds and raisins.

Stir the butter and fruit mixture into the risen flour mix. The best way to do this is to start with a wooden spoon, then finish with your hands: the mixture is very soft and sticky, so use both hands to squeeze the 2 mixtures together for about 5–10 minutes. It will look a real mess – but do not despair. There is plenty of time left for the dough to become more manageable! Cover the dough again and place somewhere warm for 1½ hours, or until risen by about half.

Then, using a wooden spoon, beat the mixture really well for about 5 minutes. This is very hard work, but it is instead of kneading, which is difficult to do with such a soft mixture. The texture will become slightly smoother and thicker after it has been beaten well.

Pour the mixture into a buttered 18 cm/7 in loose-bottomed cake tin. Cover with clingfilm and place somewhere warm for about 1¼–1½

hours, or until the dough reaches the top of the tin. Keep checking on it, for there is a danger of it spilling over the edge if it rises too much. Preheat the oven to 190°C/375°F/Gas mark 5.

Brush the top with beaten egg, then bake in the oven for about 35–40 minutes, or until the top forms a rounded, golden-brown dome. Do not open the oven door during the cooking time. Only open it after 35 minutes, to test. Once cooked, the cake should feel quite firm to the touch. To doublecheck, a fine skewer should come out clean when inserted into the middle.

Loosen the sides of the tin with a knife, then leave to cool for about 5 minutes before transferring to a wire rack to cool.

To make the icing, combine the icing sugar and water or lemon juice in a small bowl. Spoon over the top of the kulich and decorate with fruit and nuts. ✳

PASKHA

■ 567 g / 1¼ lb curd cheese ■ 85 g / 3 oz unsalted butter, softened ■ 2 egg yolks ■ 113 g / 4 oz caster sugar
■ 1 teaspoon vanilla essence ■ the grated zest and juice of 1 lemon ■ 142 ml / ¼ pint soured cream
■ 57 g / 2 oz blanched almonds, roughly chopped ■ 57 g / 2 oz raisins
■ 57 g / 2 oz candied fruit and peel, chopped

TO DECORATE
■ candied fruits and peel ■ raisins ■ blanched almonds

Place the curd cheese and butter in a mixing bowl and beat together until thoroughly mixed.

In a separate bowl, whisk the egg yolks with the sugar and vanilla, then add the lemon zest and juice and whisk again.

Beat in the soured cream, then add the almonds, raisins, candied fruits and peel. Stir in the curd cheese mixture and beat together until thoroughly mixed.

Now line a medium-sized flowerpot (mine is 14 cm/5 in across the top and 13 cm/5½ in

high) with muslin, leaving some hanging over the edges to cover the top. Pour in the mixture, pressing down well. Cover with the extra muslin, then place a weight on top. Place the weighted flowerpot over a bowl (or deep saucer) and leave to stand in the refrigerator overnight.

Next day, remove the weight, discard the whey (the liquid that collects in the bowl or saucer) and invert the paskha on to a serving plate. Carefully remove the muslin.

Decorate with nuts, dried and candied fruit.

PRUNE, LEMON AND HAZELNUT BREAD

Makes 1 loaf

The idea of combining prunes with anything other than lumpy custard is perhaps alien to some diners in Britain. Like rhubarb, the two are inextricably linked. However, prunes work well with many other ingredients, so it is a shame to confine them to that dreadful pudding. Try them with lemon, chocolate, vanilla or cinnamon. They also work beautifully with Armagnac or whisky. This sweet bread is full of contrasting flavours and textures. It is important to knead the prune, butter and sugar mixture really well into the already-risen dough. This is a sticky process, so have the flour shaker at the ready. It bulges rather voluptuously out of the tin, but will not collapse, so do not worry! After baking, it should have a firm, crisp crust and a soft, lemony fruit and nut interior. Eat in thick slices on its own, or toast on the following day and spread with butter.

■ 680 g / 1½ lb strong white flour ■ 2 teaspoons salt ■ 14 g / ½ oz butter, cut into cubes
■ 1 sachet easy-blend dried yeast ■ 426 ml / ¾ pint warm water
■ 170 g / 6 oz pitted prunes, chopped ■ 57 g / 2 oz blanched hazelnuts, roughly chopped
■ 57 g / 2 oz butter, melted ■ 85 g / 3 oz soft light brown sugar ■ the grated zest and juice of 1 lemon
■ 1 teaspoon runny honey, to glaze

Place the flour and salt in a large mixing bowl, then rub in the butter. Stir in the yeast, then make a well in the centre. Pour in the warm water and combine with a wooden spoon. Turn on to a floured board and knead for about 10 minutes, or until smooth.

Place in an oiled bowl, cover with clingfilm and allow to rise in a warm place for about 1½ hours, or until well-risen.

In a separate bowl, combine the prunes, nuts, melted butter, sugar and lemon zest and juice.

Knock back the dough with your fists and push out with the heel of your hands to form a large square. Then tip the prune mixture into the centre of the dough square and fold up the edges to enclose the filling. Gently knead the prune mixture into the dough, adding more flour if necessary to prevent the dough from becoming too sticky.

Form into a loaf shape, tucking under the ends, and place in a buttered 1 kg / 2 lb loaf tin, making sure it fills into all the corners. Cover very loosely with oiled clingfilm and place somewhere warm for about 45 minutes, or until the dough starts to bulge out of the tin. Pre-heat the oven to 200°C/400°F/Gas mark 6.

Bake in the oven for about 30 minutes, then cover loosely with foil to prevent the crust from burning, reduce the heat to 180°C/350°F/Gas mark 4 and bake for a further 15 minutes.

Carefully remove from the tin: since the top crust is so large, the best way to do this is to slide a knife carefully around all the sides before inverting on to a wire rack. Turn the right way up, then brush the top with warmed honey.

Leave to cool completely before cutting into thick slices. Serve cold with a mug of tea or toasted, spread with unsalted butter. ❋

LEMON BRIOCHE

Makes 1 brioche

If you do not have a brioche mould, do not overlook this recipe. I often make up this recipe in a
1 kg/2 lb loaf tin and use it in bread and butter or summer pudding 'with a difference',
instead of pappy, sliced white bread. However, if you are serving it for breakfast with butter and preserves,
or as an adjunct to poached peaches or quince, or even with a dollop of rich
chocolate mousse, then try to get hold of the real mould, for it looks sensational when it emerges
from the oven with its golden brown top-knot.
Brioche dough requires very little yeast, so it takes longer to make than most breads. There are
3 risings in all – 2 at room temperature and one in the refrigerator – which ensures a light and finely
crumbed texture. The taste, naturally, is wonderfully buttery, although I have reduced the
normal amount of butter – which can be anything from 227–340 g/8–12 oz per 454 g/1 lb flour!
I love the addition of grated lemon zest, which makes the brioche delightfully fragrant.

■ 14 g / ½ oz fresh yeast ■ 85 ml / 3 fl oz warm milk ■ 454 g / 1 lb strong white flour
■ the grated zest of 1 large lemon ■ 1 teaspoon salt ■ 28 g / 1 oz caster sugar
■ 3 eggs, beaten ■ 170 g / 6 oz butter, softened ■ beaten egg, to glaze

Dissolve the yeast in the warm milk, then leave to stand for 5 minutes.

Sift the flour into a large mixing bowl, stir in the lemon zest, salt and sugar, then make a well in the centre.

Pour the yeast mixture into the well, along with the eggs, and stir well to combine.

Cut the softened butter into small pieces and stir into the mixture. Using your hands, incorporate the butter into the flour mixture using a squeezing action.

Knead to a smooth dough for a couple of minutes, then place in a clean bowl, cover with clingfilm and leave to rise at room temperature for about 2½–3 hours.

Turn on to a floured board and knock back the dough with your fists, then knead for another couple of minutes. Return to the bowl, cover tightly with clingfilm and refrigerate for at least 8 hours (or overnight, if possible).

Turn on to a floured board and divide into 2 pieces, one twice the size of the other. Roll the large piece into a ball and place in a well-buttered 1.36 litre/2 pint brioche mould. Shape the small piece into another ball and gently press on top. Lightly brush the top with beaten egg, taking care it does not spill down the sides.

Cover loosely with clingfilm and leave to rise at room temperature for 2–3 hours, or until well-risen. Pre-heat the oven to 220°C/425°F/Gas mark 7.

Glaze the brioche again with beaten egg, then make 4–5 cuts all around the edge with kitchen scissors, to form the characteristic bubble shapes.

Bake in the oven for 20 minutes, then reduce the heat to 190°C/375°F/Gas mark 5. Continue to cook for a further 15–20 minutes. If necessary, cover loosely with foil so the crust doesn't burn. Remove the mould at once and cool completely on a wire rack before slicing. ❋

POPPY SEED BREAD RING

Makes 1 large ring

This recipe is inspired by the many poppy seed cakes, buns, breads and tarts found in
Eastern Europe and Russia. Although poppy seeds combine very well with other flavourings,
such as chocolate, vanilla or lemon, I think one of the most complementary flavours
is honey, as in this recipe.
Some recipes for poppy seeds involve the seeds being boiled, toasted or ground. In my recipe, they are
soaked in boiling water, then drained before being mixed with the other ingredients.
Serve this bread in slices – either warm with some Greek yoghurt for dessert, or with a cup of Russian
tea . . . freshly made in a samovar would be ideal!

■ 567 g / 1¼ lb strong white flour ■ ½ teaspoon salt ■ 1 sachet easy-blend dried yeast
■ 57 g / 2 oz caster sugar ■ 2 eggs, beaten
■ 57 g / 2 oz butter, melted and cooled for 5 minutes ■ the grated zest of ½ lemon
■ 2 tablespoons Greek yoghurt (at room temperature) ■ 284 ml / ½ pint warm water
■ 170 g / 6 oz poppy seeds ■ 43 g / 1½ oz ground almonds ■ 57 g / 2 oz caster sugar
■ 2 tablespoons (for the filling), plus 2 teaspoons (for the glaze) runny honey

Combine the flour, salt, yeast and sugar in a bowl, make a well in the centre and pour in the eggs, butter, lemon zest and yoghurt. Combine with a wooden spoon, adding just enough warm water to form a softish dough.

Turn on to a floured board and knead for about 8–10 minutes, or until smooth. Place in a lightly oiled bowl, cover with clingfilm and allow to rise in a warm place for about 2 hours, or until well-risen.

For the filling, measure the poppy seeds into a bowl and cover with boiling water. Leave to stand for about 1 hour, then drain thoroughly – either through a fine sieve or over a regular one lined with 4–5 sheets of kitchen paper. Try to ensure there is no surplus liquid. Mix the drained poppy seeds with the almonds, sugar and honey.

Once the dough is ready, knock it back with your fists and roll out – using the heel of your hands – into a fairly large rectangle, about 46 × 25 cm / 18 × 10 in. Spread the poppy seed mixture over the dough using a spatula, leaving a margin all round of about 2.5 cm / 1 in.

Carefully roll up the bread, swiss-roll style, taking care the filling does not escape. Then bring the 2 ends together, to form a ring. Using a large cake slice or 2 large fish slices, transfer to a buttered baking sheet. Brush with 2 teaspoons warmed honey, then place somewhere warm for 30 minutes. Pre-heat the oven to 200°C/400°F/ Gas mark 6.

Bake in the oven for about 25 minutes, or until puffed up and golden brown. Very gently transfer to a wire rack to cool.

POPPY SEED BREAD RING

BATH BUNS

Makes 12 buns

The original characteristic of Bath buns – a scattering of 'caraway comfits' – has long gone. Caraway comfits were caraway seeds thickly coated in boiled sugar and were used to flavour buns and wiggs (spiced tea-cakes) up until the 18th century. Nowadays, we strew the tops of the buns with either roughly crushed lump sugar or crystalised sugar, which is usually sold in its dark brown state. I like this dark colour on top of the buns – and the crunch is excellent. The technique for Bath buns is a little different from other buns, as there is a ferment (a liquid batter) and a dough mix. Altogether there are 3 rising periods, so don't contemplate making these unless you have time. I have given the minimum rising times. Add an extra 30–45 minutes for the second rising, if time permits.

FERMENT

■ 113 g / 4 oz strong white flour ■ 1 sachet easy-blend dried yeast ■ 1 teaspoon sugar
■ 199 ml / 7 fl oz warm milk

DOUGH MIX

■ 340 g / 12 oz strong white flour ■ 1 teaspoon salt ■ 57 g / 2 oz butter, cut into cubes
■ 85 g / 3 oz caster sugar ■ 57 g / 2 oz sultanas or currants
■ 28 g / 1 oz chopped mixed peel ■ 2 eggs, beaten

TOPPING

■ 1 tablespoon caster sugar ■ ½ tablespoon milk
■ about 3 teaspoons crushed sugar lumps, or sugar crystals

First prepare the ferment. Combine the flour, yeast and sugar in a large mixing bowl, then stir in the milk. Cover with clingfilm and leave to rise in a warm place for about 25–30 minutes, or until soft and spongey.

Now prepare the dough mix. Place the remaining flour and salt in a bowl, rub in the butter and stir in the sugar, dried fruit and mixed peel.

Stir the dry ingredients, with the beaten eggs, into the ferment and mix to a dough. Flour your hands, gather up the dough and transfer to a floured board. Knead for 8–10 minutes, or until silky. Since the dough is fairly soft, you will have to flour your board often – but only sprinkle lightly with flour. Place in a lightly oiled bowl, cover with clingfilm and allow to rise in a warm place for about 1½–2 hours, or until well-risen.

Knock back the dough with your fists, then divide into 12 pieces. Roll into balls and place on a buttered baking sheet.

For the topping, dissolve the sugar and milk in a small saucepan over a very low heat. Then, using a pastry brush, brush over the buns. Cover loosely with oiled clingfilm and leave to rise again in a warm place for 30 minutes. Pre-heat the oven to 230°C/450°F/Gas mark 8.

Sprinkle the buns with crushed or crystalised sugar and bake in the oven for 14–15 minutes, or until golden brown. Allow to cool on a wire rack for at least 20 minutes. Serve warm. ✳

BANANA PIZZA

Makes 1 pizza

This sweet pizza is topped with thickly sliced bananas and a sticky, toffee-like crust of brown sugar and lemon juice. Serve it in wedges with thick clotted cream.

BASE

■ 454 g / 1 lb strong white flour ■ 1 sachet easy-blend dried yeast ■ ½ teaspoon salt
■ 28 g / 1 oz caster sugar ■ 2 tablespoons sunflower oil ■ 199–227 ml / 7–8 fl oz warm water

TOPPING

■ 3 large or 4 medium bananas ■ the juice of 1 lemon ■ 57 g / 2 oz soft dark brown sugar

For the base, combine the flour, yeast, salt and caster sugar in a large mixing bowl. Make a well in the centre and pour in the oil. Now add just enough warm water to combine to a softish but not sticky dough. Turn on to a floured board and knead for about 10 minutes.

Place in a lightly oiled bowl, cover with clingfilm and leave to rise in a warm place for about 1½ hours, or until well-risen.

Knock back the dough with your fists, then press into an oiled 23 × 33 cm / 9 × 13 in swissroll tin. Make the dough base as thin as possible, pressing it up the sides of the tin to form a rim.

Lightly cover with clingfilm and place somewhere warm for about 25–30 minutes. Pre-heat the oven to 220°C / 425°F / Gas mark 7.

Just before baking, peel the bananas and cut on the diagonal into thick slices. Arrange on top of the dough base, then sprinkle with lemon juice and dark brown sugar.

Now bake the pizza in the oven for about 25 minutes, or until the bread rim is puffed up and a golden brown and the bananas are nicely glazed.

Cool for about 10 minutes, then cut into wedges. Serve with clotted cream.

To 'knock down' or 'knock back' means to knead lightly in order to deflate any air bubbles in the dough, after it has risen.

BREADS

Baking bread is truly a labour of love. But it is not an arduous chore: the satisfaction of kneading the dough, the seemingly magical way it rises, the eager anticipation of waiting for it to cool, its comforting aromas and, finally, its heavenly taste make it all worth while. Experiment with the variety of loaves given here, whether pecan, olive, leek or soda . . .

COTTAGE LOAF

Makes 1 loaf

I was relieved to hear my son remarking that the term 'cottage loaf' surely derived from its shape resembling a thatched cottage, with a small round loaf baked on top of a larger round. I too had suffered the same delusion for many years! Elizabeth David, in her *English Bread and Yeast Cookery Book*, explains that the shape was in fact due to the need to economise on baking space in a small cottage oven; 2 smaller loaves, joined together, could fit better than one large one.

For the best shaped loaf, it is essential that the dough is fairly firm and the second rising (once the bread is shaped into 2 rounds, then into the classic top-knot) is done at room temperature. This ensures the dough will not rise too quickly and consequently collapse. Elizabeth David describes how the indentation in the top was sometimes made by the baker's elbow to save time; I recommend cooks at home use their thumb and 2 fingers. The loaf should always be allowed to cool for at least half an hour before slicing. If you cut into it at once (tempted by the aroma), its texture might be rather 'doughy', rather than soft and light.

I like to have everything at the same temperature before preparing the dough. In order for the yeast to rise efficiently, it is a good idea to warm the mixing bowl slightly and to use tepid or lukewarm water. Try measuring out one-third boiling water to two-thirds cold water, then test. It should feel warm, but not uncomfortable. Finally, although cottage loaves are often made from pure white flour, I like to use a third wholemeal for added depth of flavour.

- 454 g / 1 lb strong white flour ■ 227 g / 8 oz strong stoneground wholemeal flour
- 2 teaspoons salt ■ 28 g / 1 oz butter, cut into cubes ■ 1 sachet easy-blend dried yeast
- 369–398 ml / 13–14 fl oz tepid water ■ 1 small beaten egg, to glaze

Sift the flours and salt into a large mixing bowl. Rub in the butter with your fingertips, until the mixture resembles breadcrumbs.

Stir in the yeast, then make a well in the centre. Pour in a sufficient amount of hand-hot water to combine to a fairly stiff dough.

Turn on to a lightly floured board and knead for at least 10 minutes, or until the dough is smooth and elastic, and no longer feels rough and bitty. (It is a good idea to time yourself since you have to knead for a long time in order to produce a light, airy loaf.) The easiest kneading action is to stretch the dough by pushing it away from you with the heel of your hand, then to fold it towards you, turn and push again. Keep turning as you knead as this distributes the yeast throughout the dough.

Place the dough in a lightly greased bowl, then cover with clingfilm or a damp tea-towel, leaving plenty of room for the dough to rise. Place the bowl in a barely warm place, such as an airing cupboard, for at least 1½–2 hours.

After this time, the dough should have risen to about 1½ times its original bulk.

Turn on to a floured board and knock back with your fists – that is, punch it all over in order to deflate any air bubbles. Divide into 2 pieces, one twice the size of the other. Shape into balls and place on a greased baking tray. Cover loosely with clingfilm and leave at room temperature – somewhere that is draught-free – for about 40 minutes. Pre-heat the oven now to 230°C/450°F/Gas mark 8.

Gently flatten the balls of dough and place the small one on top of the large one. Using your thumb and 2 fingers, press the 2 balls together, making an imprint that extends about half-way through the whole loaf. Now leave again at room temperature for about 10 minutes.

Glaze the loaf all over with beaten egg. Place in the pre-heated oven for 15 minutes, then reduce the heat to 200°C/400°F/Gas mark 6 and bake for a further 25–30 minutes, or until well-risen and golden brown. Once perfectly cooked, the loaf should sound hollow when tapped underneath.

Turn on to a wire rack to cool completely before cutting. Serve with butter. ✳

KENTISH HUFFKINS

Makes 12 rolls

Although it is virtually impossible to find these bread rolls in commercial bakers in Kent nowadays, the baking of huffkins goes back a long way. They are soft, oval-shaped rolls with a characteristic dent in the middle. They are meant to be kept soft, and not allowed to crisp up after coming out of the oven. The best way to keep them soft is to wrap them in a tea-cloth after removing them from the oven. They can be eaten with butter and jam or, for a typically Kentish touch, fill the dent in the middle with hot cherries and serve as an unusual dessert.

■ 14g/½oz fresh yeast ■ 1 teaspoon sugar ■ 227ml/8floz milk and water, mixed
■ 454g/1lb strong white flour ■ 1 teaspoon salt ■ 57g/2oz butter, cut into cubes

Place the yeast and sugar in a small bowl. Warm the milk/water, pour over the yeast and combine to a paste. Leave to stand for about 10 minutes.

Place the flour and salt in a large bowl, then rub in the butter. Make a well in the middle and pour in the yeast mixture, stirring to combine. Turn on to a floured board and knead for about 10 minutes, or until smooth and elastic.

Place the dough in a lightly oiled bowl, cover with clingfilm and leave to rise in a warm place for 1–1½ hours, or until well-risen.

Knock back with your fists and divide into 12 pieces. Shape into oval rolls (do not worry if the shape is not exact – they will still taste good!) and place on a greased baking sheet. Make a small dent in each roll with your finger, then cover loosely and leave to prove in a warm place for about 30 minutes. Pre-heat the oven to 220°C/425°F/Gas mark 7.

Bake in the oven for about 15 minutes, or until golden brown. Eat straight from the oven, or wrap in a clean tea-cloth to keep soft. ✳

FLOWERPOT BREAD

Makes 1 loaf

Terracotta flowerpots are not only much cheaper than the average metal bread tin, they also give the loaf a wonderful shape. I bought one specifically for baking bread, but you can use one from the greenhouse as long as you give it a good scrub first. You have to 'season' the pot beforehand to ensure that the bread does not stick. To do this, coat the pot liberally outside and inside with oil – sunflower or groundnut oil is fine. Then pop it in a hot oven for 20 minutes or so, remove and allow to cool. Do this a couple of times if you have time. When you oil the pot prior to proving and baking, you only need to oil the inside, not the outside.

If the pot is well-seasoned, the bread will slip out easily. Should you have difficulty on the first go, however, wait for a few minutes to allow the bread to shrink slightly, then gently ease a knife around the edges and carefully prise out the loaf.

My Flowerpot Loaf is baked with the pot the right way up, so it has a slightly mushrooming top which swells up from the tapering shape of the base. Elizabeth David, in her *English Bread and Yeast Cookery Book*, recommends baking flowerpot bread upside down, giving, she claims, a more perfect shape. During the first few minutes of baking, the dough springs up to fill the pot. Once the perfect form is achieved, the pot is removed and the last 10–15 minutes of baking takes place pot-less.

However, I prefer to bake it upright for 2 reasons: firstly, unless you have exactly the right amount of dough for your pot, there is the danger of it being compressed. Also, I rather like the slightly imperfect shape of the loaf – with its billowing, crusty top – that my recipe produces. But then, I have always preferred the home-made look!

The pot I use is 14 cm/5½ in across the top and 13 cm/5 in deep. You can use one slightly bigger, but I do not recommend you try any smaller.

■ 397 g / 14 oz strong white bread flour ■ 113 g / 4 oz granary flour ■ 1 heaped teaspoon salt
■ 2 teaspoons easy-blend dried yeast (about ¾ of a sachet) ■ 1 tablespoon black treacle
■ 1 tablespoon sunflower oil ■ 312–341 ml / 11–12 fl oz tepid water

Combine the flours and salt in a large mixing bowl, then stir in the yeast.

Gently heat together the treacle and oil until tepid. Make a well in the middle of the flour and pour in the treacle mixture, together with just enough water to form a manageable dough. Turn on to a lightly floured board and knead for at least 10 minutes, or until smooth.

Place in a lightly oiled bowl and cover with clingfilm. Leave to rise in a warm place (an airing cupboard is ideal) for 1½–2 hours. Meanwhile grease the pot with oil and pre-heat the oven to 220°C/425°F/Gas mark 7. Place the pot in the oven for 5 minutes or so to warm it.

Once the dough has risen well, turn it on to a floured board and knock back with your fists. Oil the pot again. Roll the dough into a ball and push it gently into the base of the pot. Cover with oiled clingfilm and allow to prove in a warm place for about 30 minutes, or until the dough has risen nearly to the top of the pot.

Set the pot on a baking tray and bake in the pre-heated oven for 15 minutes, before reducing the heat to 190°C/375°F/Gas mark 5 and baking for a further 15 minutes. Slip the loaf out of its pot and set on a wire rack to cool. ❋

PECAN BREAD

Makes 1 loaf

There are many types of nut bread. Although walnut bread is perhaps a little more common than pecan bread, I like the slightly sweeter flavour of the pecan nut. If you only have walnuts in the larder, however, then use those instead. Whichever nuts you use, you should toast or grill them first, since this greatly enhances their flavour. This bread can be served with a cheese course – it is particularly good with an unpressed, soft goat's cheese such as Blunt's 'Chabis' or 'Golden Cross'; or a tangy blue such as Lanark Blue – or with soup at lunchtime. It is also tasty when toasted on the next day and spread with butter and lemon curd or honey, or crunchy peanut butter.

■ 28 g / 1 oz fresh yeast   ■ ½ teaspoon caster sugar   ■ 256–284 ml / 9–10 fl oz warm water
■ 113 g / 4 oz strong wholemeal flour   ■ 454 g / 1 lb strong white flour   ■ 1½ teaspoons salt
■ 2 tablespoons walnut or hazelnut oil   ■ 113 g / 4 oz pecan nuts, lightly toasted and roughly chopped

Place the yeast and sugar in a bowl and combine to a paste with a third of the warm water. Leave to stand for about 5 minutes.

Combine the flours and salt in a large mixing bowl, then form a well in the centre. Pour in the oil, then stir in enough of the remaining water to combine to a stiff dough.

Turn the dough on to a floured surface and knead for about 10 minutes. Add the toasted pecan nuts and continue to knead for a couple of minutes, or until they are evenly distributed.

Place in a lightly oiled bowl, cover with clingfilm and leave to rise in a warm place for about 2 hours, or until well-risen.

Knock back the dough with your fists, then knead for 1 minute more. Shape into a long oval, set on an oiled baking tray and cover loosely with clingfilm. Leave to prove in a warm place for about 45 minutes. Pre-heat the oven to 220°C/425°F/Gas mark 7.

Make 3 slashes along the length of the bread with a knife. Bake in the oven for 15 minutes, then reduce the heat to 190°C/375°F/Gas mark 5 and continue to cook for a further 20–25 minutes, or until the bread sounds hollow when tapped underneath.

Transfer to a wire rack to cool completely before cutting. ❋

BAGUETTES

Makes 2 loaves

I used to wonder why no French woman – no matter how talented she was at cooking – made her own baguettes. She would always go to the boulangerie, often twice a day, to buy fresh bread.
Having worked out how long a truly great baguette with a deep flavour takes to prepare, I understood why. You also need exactly the right ingredients. French flour is softer than ours. So try to overcome this problem by mixing soft (plain) flour into hard (strong) flour. Then there is the steam factor: in boulangeries, the bread is sprayed with water as it bakes. This helps create the characteristic shiny, crisp crust, formed by the starch on the loaf's surface gelatinising in the dry heat which follows the damp heat from the injection of steam. Then there is the question of time: in the best boulangeries, the maturing of the dough is a lengthy but worthwhile process. It takes long because cold water is used to activate the yeast. Cold is probably not the right word: it must be the same temperature as the flour. I suggest removing the flour from the cupboard, placing it in the mixing bowl and at the same time measuring out the water, cold from the tap. Leave them both for an hour, so they reach the same temperature. Once the yeast is added, the dough should be left to rise for a minimum of 4 hours before kneading and leaving to prove. I prefer to leave it overnight. If you want the bread for lunch on a Saturday or Sunday, start preparing on the Friday or Saturday night. If it is winter, leave the well-covered dough in a cold room, such as a larder, or even a garage (I did say well-covered!). In summer, place it in the refrigerator.
I do urge you to try this loaf – it is not any more difficult than baking regular bread. All you need is a little more time. The result – I hope you'll agree – is formidable!

■ 511 g / 1 lb 2 oz strong white bread flour (unbleached, if possible) ■ 113 g / 4 oz plain flour
■ 1½ teaspoons salt ■ 1 sachet easy-blend dried yeast ■ 454 ml / 16 fl oz cold water

Sift the flours and salt into a mixing bowl. Pour the water into a measuring jug and leave both to stand for about an hour at room temperature.

Remove 4 tablespoons of the flour and set side. Add the sachet of yeast to the mixing bowl and mix thoroughly. Make a well in the centre, then pour in the water and combine with a wooden spoon to a soft batter. Cover the bowl with a damp tea-towel and place somewhere cold overnight, or for a minimum of 4–5 hours.

Next day, add the remaining flour to the slightly frothy dough and stir well. Then, using your hands, combine to a soft, sticky dough. Turn on to a floured board and knead for about 10 minutes, or until smooth. Set in an oiled bowl, cover with clingfilm or a damp tea-towel and leave at room temperature for 2 hours.

Knock back the dough with your fists and divide into 2 equal pieces. Roll each one into a long sausage-shape about 30 cm / 12 in long. Flour a clean tea-towel and lay out on the table. Place one of the loaves across it and push it up against a wall so it is supported on one side. Then make a deep pleat along the middle of the tea-towel and place the second loaf on the other side of the pleat so the loaves of bread are not touching. Place something against this, to support the other side – I use a heavy rolling pin. Now cover loosely and leave for 1 hour, at room temperature. Pre-heat the oven to 230°C/450°F/Gas mark 8.

Carefully roll the loaves on to a greased baking tray. Using a sharp knife, make 4 diagonal slashes along the length of each loaf. Set the tray in the pre-heated oven, then quickly spray the loaves and the inside of the oven with water, using a household-plant water spray (make sure it has never been used for chemicals!). Bake in the oven for 15 minutes, spraying with water again after 10 minutes. After the initial 15 minutes, reduce the heat to 200°C/400°F/Gas mark 6, spray one last time and bake at this lower heat for a further 10 minutes.

Remove the loaves from the oven and allow to cool on a wire rack for at least 20 minutes before devouring. ❄

PORTUGUESE CORN BREAD

Makes 1 loaf

This recipe is based very loosely on a recipe for 'broa', a dense cornmeal loaf from the north of Portugal. Although broa is usually made in a round baking tin, I like to bake it in a rectangular loaf tin so that it can be cut into slices easily. This recipe makes a loaf with a good rough texture, a delicate cornmeal flavour and a pale golden colour. I like to spread it with unsalted butter and serve it with thick vegetable soup or a hearty main-course salad.

■ 170 g / 6 oz maizemeal (cornmeal) ■ 1 heaped teaspoon salt ■ 284 g / 10 oz strong white flour
■ 1 teaspoon sugar ■ 1 sachet easy-blend dried yeast ■ 284 ml / ½ pint warm water
■ 1 tablespoon olive oil

Combine the maizemeal, salt, flour and sugar in a large mixing bowl, then stir in the yeast.

Make a well in the centre, then pour in the water and oil. Stir well to combine.

Turn on to a floured board and knead for about 10 minutes, or until smooth.

Place in a lightly oiled bowl, cover with clingfilm and leave to rise in a warm place for about 1 hour, or until well-risen.

Knock back the dough with your fists, then shape into a lightly buttered 1 kg/2 lb loaf tin. To do this, use your hands to roll the dough into a square the length of the loaf tin, then roll up the sides to make a rectangle, tucking the ends underneath. Cover loosely with clingfilm and leave to prove in a warm place for 40–45 minutes, or until the dough reaches the top of the tin.

Pre-heat the oven to 220°C/425°F/Gas mark 7.

Bake in the oven for about 30 minutes, or until golden brown and cooked through – that is, when the loaf sounds hollow when tapped underneath.

Transfer to a wire rack to cool completely before cutting. ❄

OLIVE BREAD

Makes 1 loaf

I once had the privilege of attending a wedding in Provence. The number of courses and the quality of the food – and wine – impressed me greatly. With each course, different breads were served. There was a rough, almost chewy 'pain de campagne', a baguette-type loaf studded with tiny pieces of fried bacon; a glorious walnut bread to go with the local goat's cheese; and there was olive bread, which was quite delicious. The basic bread, a mixture of pain de campagne and baguette, was full of flavour and this was enhanced by the addition of roughly chopped olives – both green and black. It was moister than the other loaves, so I presume there was also olive oil in the dough.

The memory of this nuptial loaf inspired me to create an olive bread. I have used a little rye flour, a popular ingredient in many French country breads, for added texture and a good colour. Try to use a mixture of green and black olives and do not chop them too finely.

■ 567 g / 1¼ lb unbleached strong white flour ■ 113 g / 4 oz rye flour ■ 2 teaspoons salt
■ 1 sachet easy-blend dried yeast ■ 2 tablespoons olive oil ■ 369–398 ml / 13–14 fl oz warm water
■ 85 g / 3 oz green and black olives, pitted and chopped ■ olive oil, to glaze

Combine the flours and salt in a mixing bowl, then stir in the yeast.

Make a well in the centre and pour in the oil, along with just enough warm water to combine to a firm dough. Then turn on to a lightly floured board.

Knead for about 10 minutes, or until smooth. Then place in a lightly oiled bowl, cover with clingfilm and leave to rise in a warm place for about 2 hours, or until doubled in volume.

Knock back the dough with your fists and sprinkle with olives. Knead well to incorporate them into the dough.

Shape into a large ball and place on an oiled baking sheet. Brush lightly with olive oil, cover loosely with clingfilm and leave to prove in a warm place for 45 minutes. After proving, the dough should not spring back when pressed with 2 fingers – instead, they should leave an indentation. Pre-heat the oven to 230°C/450°F/Gas mark 8.

Using a sharp knife, score the top of the loaf with 3 diagonal slashes.

Bake in the pre-heated oven for 15 minutes, then reduce the heat to 200°C/400°F/Gas mark 6 and cook for a further 20 minutes, or until the loaf sounds hollow when tapped on the base.

Transfer to a wire rack to cool. Serve warm, with or without butter. ❋

To pit olives easily, lay them on a board, then roll over them with a heavy rolling pin.

OLIVE BREAD

RYE BREAD

Makes 1 loaf

This bread is based on a Scandinavian rye bread recipe. In Scandinavia, buttermilk or sour milk is often used instead of ordinary milk. Sometimes fennel seeds are used instead of caraway. The loaf is a round ring shape, which is typical throughout Scandinavia where they are often sold on wooden stands – like rings at the hoop-la stalls. Long ago, they were hung on poles above the oven, to dry off. It became a hard bread which dried out as it hung – the predecessor of all the crispbreads and rusks which are so popular now. While you are kneading the dough, it will feel much heavier than, say, a cottage loaf or a French loaf – but, provided your yeast is fresh and the liquids are the correct temperature, it will rise well and have a close, rough texture. It keeps well and is superb toasted, with a smear of good butter and some honey or a slice of cheese.

■ 284g / 10oz strong brown flour ■ 227g / 8oz rye flour ■ 1½ teaspoons salt
■ 1 heaped teaspoon caraway seeds ■ 14g / ½oz fresh yeast ■ ½ teaspoon caster sugar
■ 142ml / 5floz warm water ■ 85ml / 3floz milk ■ 2 tablespoons black treacle ■ 28g / 1oz butter

Combine the flours, salt and caraway seeds in a mixing bowl.

Mix the yeast with the caster sugar, then combine to a paste with 2 tablespoons of the warm water. Leave to stand for 5 minutes.

Heat together the milk, treacle and butter until warm.

Make a well in the centre of the flours, then pour in the treacly liquid, the remaining warm water and the yeast mixture. Combine the ingredients to a dough.

Turn on to a floured board and knead for 10 minutes, or until smooth. Place in an oiled bowl, cover with clingfilm and leave to rise in a warm place for about 1½–2 hours.

Turn on to a floured board, knock back with your fists and shape into a ring or hoop, ensuring it is an even height all round. Set on a greased baking tray, loosely cover with clingfilm and place somewhere warm for an hour, or until slightly puffy. Pre-heat the oven to 200°C/ 400°F/Gas mark 6.

Brush all over with a little warm water, then bake in the pre-heated oven for about 25 minutes, or until well-risen and dark brown. Transfer to a wire rack to cool completely. Serve in thin slices, and toast if desired. ✳

Although most recipes advise that dough should rise by double the bulk in the first rising, in fact one and a half times the original bulk is usually adequate. To test whether it has risen properly, try gently pressing with your finger. If the dough is ready, it should not spring back.

POTATO AND TARRAGON RIESKA

Makes 4 rieska

The name 'rieska' is Finnish, but this recipe is not from Finland. Rieska are small, flat bread rounds, which are made with mashed potatoes, salt and flour. Often barley flour is used instead of wheat flour. They are quite delicious – the potatoes make them very moist inside – but since they have no yeast, they are fairly flat.

I have added 2 extra ingredients to my rieska recipe – yeast, to give a better rise, and finely chopped tarragon. Like many herbs, tarragon complements potato dishes very well. It also gives the finished bread a lovely speckled green appearance. It is important to use freshly mashed – and still warm – potatoes for this recipe. Yesterday's left-over mash will not do!

Although this recipe is based on one from Finland, the idea of a potato bread is not unknown in this country. Most of the Celtic fringe of Britain have their own variations on potato scones and cakes. One of my favourites is Boxty Bread, an Irish bread made from a mixture of freshly grated raw potato and cooked, mashed potato, which is either fried in a frying pan, boiled in a saucepan or baked in an oven.

Serve the rieska with a bowl of thick pea soup in winter or a fresh herby salad in summer.

- 397 g / 14 oz strong white flour ■ 2 heaped tablespoons fresh tarragon, chopped
- 1 sachet easy-blend dried yeast ■ 14 g / ½ oz caster sugar ■ 2 heaped teaspoons salt
- 227 g / 8 oz potatoes (this is the peeled weight) ■ 28 g / 1 oz unsalted butter
- 199–227 ml / 7–8 fl oz warm milk

Combine the flour, tarragon, yeast, sugar and salt in a large mixing bowl.

Boil the potatoes in unsalted water until just tender, then drain very well. Using a potato masher, mash with the butter until smooth.

While the mashed potatoes are still very warm, stir into the flour mixture with just enough warm milk to combine to a softish – but not sticky – dough.

Using well-floured hands, turn the mixture on to a floured board and knead for about 5 minutes, or until fairly smooth. Then place in a clean bowl and cover with clingfilm. Leave to rise in a warm place for about 1 hour, or until well-risen.

Then, using floured hands, divide the mixture into 4 pieces and shape each into a round. Place these on a lightly buttered baking tray and shape again into rounds about 4 cm / 1½ in high.

Sprinkle very lightly with flour and leave to prove in a warm place for about 30 minutes, or until puffed up. Pre-heat the oven to 220°C/425°F/Gas mark 7.

Bake in the pre-heated oven for about 20 minutes, or until golden brown. Transfer to a wire rack to cool. Serve warm. ❉

MEALIE BREAD

Makes 1 loaf

It is rather difficult to make truly authentic mealie bread in Britain because the flour – mealie meal – is not readily available, but this recipe is a good substitute. If you can find mealie meal, your bread should taste similar to the mealie bread so much loved in many of the African countries. My recipe is based on one from my friend Isabelle, who lives in Zimbabwe.

Traditionally, mealie bread is made by mixing regular wheat flour with 'mealies', which are immature corn on the cob. The corn kernels are cut off the cob and minced before being added to the flour. The whole mixture is then steamed. The mealie bread is usually served sliced and buttered, often accompanying a meat dish or any barbecue food.

For my recipe, I often use maizemeal (corn meal – not cornflour), which is available from health-food shops or South American food stores. Although the bread's texture is rougher and the taste not quite as delicate as when made with mealie meal, the only really noticeable difference is the colour. In general, mealie-meal bread is a pale golden colour, whereas most maizemeals make a brighter yellow loaf. An alternative topping is to sprinkle with caraway seeds prior to baking.

■ 227 g / 8 oz mealie meal or maizemeal ■ ½ teaspoon salt ■ 1 teaspoon sugar
■ 2 teaspoons baking powder ■ 43 g / 1½ oz butter ■ 2 eggs, beaten ■ 142 ml / 5 fl oz milk

Pre-heat the oven to 220°C/425°F/Gas mark 7. Combine the meal, salt, sugar and baking powder in a large mixing bowl.

Melt the butter and add to the bowl while still warm. Stir in the eggs and milk and beat together until light and creamy.

Spoon the mixture into a buttered 454 g / 1 lb loaf tin and smooth the top. Bake in the pre-heated oven for about 30 minutes, or until firm and well-risen.

Turn on to a wire rack to cool before slicing. Serve with butter. ✳

To test whether bread is cooked, use oven gloves to remove it from the tin. Then turn it upside down and tap the underside. If it is ready, it should sound hollow, like a drum; if it sounds heavy or dense, return it to the oven for a few more minutes.

MEALIE BREAD

BARLEY AND SUNFLOWER BREAD

Makes 1 loaf

If you have never tasted barley bread before, you will perhaps be surprised by its distinctive flavour.
I use beremeal, a stoneground barley flour from Orkney. The barley for beremeal
comes from the 'bigg' variety, which is only grown in the north of Scotland. If you cannot buy beremeal,
however, I suggest you use regular barley flour which has a similar earthy, slightly nutty
flavour. In addition to this, beremeal has a distinctly smoky taste – one slice of this bread and you
could be sitting in a peat-fired croft in Orkney! This quality is also found in some
Islay malt whiskies, such as Laphroaig.
This bread recipe combines 2 cultures. The Scots have used barley since Neolithic times, while the
Finns have also used barley considerably over the years. Today, rye bread is more popular
than barley bread in Finland, but traditional 'ohraleipa' is still made and sold for special occasions.
My recipe uses sunflower seeds, which give the bread a welcome crunch, and sunflower oil to
make it moist. It should be eaten in thick slices, spread with butter and a slice of cheese or meat. Try
some smoked cheese or sausage to accentuate the smoky flavour of the bread.

■ 170 g / 6 oz beremeal or barley flour ■ 397 g / 14 oz strong white flour ■ 1 sachet easy-blend dried yeast
■ 2 teaspoons salt ■ 28 g / 1 oz sunflower seeds ■ 1 tablespoon sunflower oil
■ 284 ml / 10 fl oz warm water ■ sunflower oil, to glaze

Place the flours in a bowl, then stir in the yeast, salt and sunflower seeds. Make a well in the middle of the dry ingredients.

Pour in the oil, then the water, and combine to a soft dough first with a spoon, then with your hands. Turn on to a floured board and knead for 8–10 minutes.

Lightly oil a bowl, place the dough inside and cover with clingfilm. Leave to rise in a warm place for about 2–2½ hours, or until well-risen.

Knock back the dough with your fists, shape into a round and place on an oiled baking sheet. Using the back of a knife, score the shape of a cross in the top, then lightly brush with oil. Cover loosely and leave in a warm place for 45–50 minutes, or until slightly puffy. Pre-heat the oven to 230°C/450°F/Gas mark 8.

Bake in the pre-heated oven for 10 minutes, then reduce the temperature to 200°C/400°F/Gas mark 6 and bake for a further 20 minutes, or until the bread sounds hollow when tapped underneath. Transfer to a wire rack to cool before serving. ✳

To knead, stretch the dough away from you with the heel of your hand, then turn and repeat the movement. Involve the children in bread-making: their table-bashing kneading skills are ideal!

RICE AND LEEK BREAD

Makes 1 loaf

The first time I came across a recipe for rice bread was in Australia, home of weird and wonderful combinations. However, when I noticed that the recipe came from Elizabeth David, I felt justified in developing a recipe of my own. Elizabeth David, in *English Bread and Yeast Cookery*, cites Eliza Acton as baking rice bread. She added rice to bread dough when flour was expensive, but kept on using it because she felt it improved the flavour and prevented the crust becoming too hard. Nowadays, rice is far more expensive than flour, but I would still recommend baking this bread for special occasions, as it is moist and full of flavour.

When you bake it as suggested, you will have a nicely textured round loaf with a buttery leek filling. Eaten warm, it is the most perfect bread to serve with soups of all description. Otherwise, I like to serve it with antipasti such as salami, parma ham, olives and capers. It also makes excellent sandwiches when the leek filling is omitted.

■ 85 g / 3 oz long-grain rice ■ 567 g / 1¼ lb strong white flour ■ 3 teaspoons salt
■ 1 packet easy-blend dried yeast ■ 1 medium leek ■ 25 g / 1 oz butter

First cook the rice: place in a saucepan with approximately double the amount of water (I use about 227 ml / 8 fl oz to 85 g / 3 oz rice). Bring slowly to the boil, then cover and simmer over a low heat for about 20 minutes, or until just cooked. Leave to cool, covered, for about 30 minutes, or until still warm.

Combine the flour, salt and yeast in a bowl. Stir in the warm rice and mix to a soft – but not sticky – dough with 312–341 ml / 11–12 fl oz warm water.

Turn on to a floured board and knead for about 10 minutes, or until smooth. Then place in a lightly oiled bowl, cover with clingfilm and leave to rise in a warm place for about 1 hour.

Wash and trim the leek, then cut into thin slices. Place in a small saucepan with the butter and soften over a low heat. Leave to cool for about 10 minutes.

Knock back the dough with your fists, then shape into a large round. Place the leeks in the middle, then fold up the sides over the leeks to create a parcel. Do not knead the leek-filled dough; you want a thick layer of filling, not interspersed leeky patches.

Turn the parcel the right-way up, with the untidy edges underneath, and place on a lightly oiled baking tray. Cover loosely with clingfilm and leave to prove in a warm place for about 45 minutes, or until well-risen. Pre-heat the oven to 220°C / 425°F / Gas mark 7.

Bake in the oven for about 30 minutes, or until golden brown on top. When the loaf is perfectly cooked, it should sound hollow when tapped underneath. Transfer to a wire rack to cool for at least 20 minutes. Serve warm.

For all bread-making, ensure both bowls and flours are at room temperature. If baking in winter, warm them slightly in a very low oven before use.

CHOLLA

Makes 1 loaf

This Jewish bread is also known as 'Challah', pronounced 'Hala'. It is traditionally eaten on Friday night, at the start of Shabbat (the Sabbath). It is served either plaited or round, and is invariably rather sweet. The crust is glazed with egg to give it a deep golden colour, and the top is strewn with poppy seeds. My recipe is based on the one in Florence Greenberg's *Jewish Cookery Book*, first published in 1947. I like the recipe for cholla in this book, as it is far less sweet than many breads found in Jewish bakeries. I have added an egg to the mix, since my friend Shirley tells me that cholla is often referred to as 'egg-loaf'.

■ 14 g / ½ oz fresh yeast ■ ½ teaspoon sugar ■ 680 g / 1½ lb strong white flour ■ 1 teaspoon salt
■ about 341 ml / 12 fl oz warm water ■ 1 egg, beaten ■ about 2 teaspoons poppy seeds

Combine the yeast with the sugar and mix to a paste with a little of the water. Leave to stand for 5 minutes.

Combine the flour and salt in a bowl, then make a well in the centre. Add the yeast mixture to the flour, along with most of the beaten egg (reserve about 2 teaspoons to glaze the loaf). Stir in just enough warm water to combine to a firm dough.

Turn on to a floured board and knead for about 10 minutes, or until smooth. Set in a lightly oiled bowl, cover with clingfilm and leave to rise in a warm place for 1½–2 hours, or until well-risen.

Knock back with your fists, then shape into a round. Set on a lightly oiled baking sheet, brush with the reserved beaten egg and sprinkle with poppy seeds. Leave to prove in a warm place for 50–60 minutes, or until well-risen. Pre-heat the oven to 220°C/425°F/Gas mark 7.

Bake in the pre-heated oven for 15 minutes, then reduce the heat to 190°C/375°F/Gas mark 5 and continue cooking for a further 15 minutes, or until the loaf sounds hollow when tapped underneath.

Transfer to a wire rack to cool completely before slicing. ❈

SODA BREAD

Makes 1 loaf

The most common type of soda bread in Ireland is made from plain wholemeal flour, although some are mixed with white flour, and some are flavoured with raisins, caraway seeds or treacle. In Scotland, bicarbonate of soda is included in some breads and griddle cakes instead of yeast. Soda bread is quick to make because, unlike yeast-based breads which are left to rise before baking, soda bread is baked immediately. The baking powder or soda is mixed with the water or milk and then added to the flour. The alkali (bicarbonate of soda) combined with the acid (buttermilk or sour milk) produces an immediate reaction. Scones, too, work under the same principle.

The most common liquid to be used for soda bread in Ireland is buttermilk. Sour milk is a good substitute, as the essential sourness serves a definite purpose which sweet milk cannot replace. The acid content in buttermilk or sour milk helps aeration – the resulting texture is therefore light and the taste rich and lingering. If you cannot find buttermilk and do not have any sour milk, then add 2 teaspoons of lemon juice to 426 ml / ¾ pint milk and allow to stand for at least 6 hours at room temperature. Sour cream plus water is another good substitute.

It is not necessary to use strong flour for soda breads, nor is there any need for prolonged kneading, since the gluten in the flour does not need to be developed. Instead of the table-bashing, aggressive action required for good yeast-raised breads, you need a light, rapid touch. My recipe is based on one from an Irish friend, who says you should knead the dough very briefly, just until the side next to the board is smooth. My method – although by no means authentic – works well for those unaccustomed to applying a deft touch. I simply beat the dough with a wooden spoon to combine the ingredients. Once the dough is loose and sticky, I turn it on to a well-floured baking tray, shape quickly and bake at once. I find this easier, since the dough is too soft to work with unless you flour your hands constantly.

This bread is baked in the oven, but some Irish soda breads are still baked in a cast-iron pot over an open fire, or in a heavy cast-iron frying pan with a lid to ensure a soft crust. My recipe incorporates wheatgerm in the dough, which gives the bread a lovely gold-flecked colour. Any unused soda bread can be kept until the following day and toasted – it should be sliced thickly and toasted slowly until just golden brown.

■ 312 g / 11 oz plain wholemeal flour ■ 28 g / 1 oz wheatgerm ■ 170 g / 6 oz plain flour, sifted
■ 1 teaspoon salt ■ 1 rounded teaspoon bicarbonate of soda ■ 1 teaspoon sugar
■ 426 ml / ¾ pint sour milk

Pre-heat the oven to 220°C/425°F/Gas mark 7. Combine the flours, salt, soda and sugar in a large mixing bowl, then make a well in the centre of the dry ingredients.

Stir in sufficient sour milk (or equivalent) to combine to a loose, slightly moist dough, beating well with a wooden spoon between each addition. (It should take no longer than 2 minutes to combine the ingredients from the moment you add the liquid.)

Turn on to a floured baking tray and shape into a 23 cm/9 in round. Using a floured knife, mark a shallow cross in the top of the loaf.

Bake in the pre-heated oven for 15 minutes, then reduce the heat to 200°C/400°F/Gas mark 6 and bake for a further 20 minutes, or until the crust is brown and the loaf sounds hollow when tapped underneath. Transfer to a wire rack to cool completely before cutting.

❊ This is best toasted after freezing.

FOUGASSE

Makes 2 loaves

Although there are many recipes for sweet fougasses, it is not the most typical fougasses to be found in Provence. The sweet type, which is almost a brioche dough – although enriched with olive oil instead of butter – is usually flavoured with dried fruit such as candied orange peel. This is traditionally one of the 13 desserts (representing the 12 disciples and Christ) to be served on Christmas Eve in Provence. The concept of this special bread came from the Middle Ages, when ordinary bread was enriched with olive oil and served at Christmas.

It is, however, the plain fougasses – far more common in Provence – that you will find here. It is a fairly standard bread dough that is flavoured with olive oil. I divide the dough into 2, leaving one half plain and adding 'herbes de provence' to the other half to emulate the 'Fougasse de St Saturnin': a small, individual fougasse flavoured with herbs. St Saturnin is a small town in the Lubéron region of Provence. You can add a handful of sliced, pitted black olives to the following recipe if you like.

It is their characteristic shape that makes fougasses special. To achieve this, you simply form the dough into an oval shape, slit it diagonally as if you were drawing the veins of a leaf, then, just before baking, pull it apart slightly with your fingers to form holes.

■ 680 g / 1½ lb strong white flour ■ 2 teaspoons salt ■ 1 sachet easy-blend dried yeast
■ 2 tablespoons extra-virgin olive oil ■ 369–398 ml / 13–14 fl oz warm water
■ 1 heaped teaspoon herbes de provence – thyme, rosemary, savoury, marjoram and basil

Place the flour, salt and yeast in a bowl and stir well to combine. Make a well in the centre and pour in the oil, along with just enough warm water to form a stiff dough.

Turn on to a floured board and knead for about 10 minutes, or until smooth.

Place in a lightly oiled bowl, cover with cling-film and set in a warm place for about 1½–2 hours, or until well-risen.

Knock back with your fists, then divide into 2. Knead the herbs into one piece.

Shape into two ovals, then, using a blunt knife, make a series of diagonal slits along the length of each piece, as if you were drawing veins on a leaf. Set on lightly oiled baking trays and cover loosely with clingfilm.

Leave to prove at room temperature for 1–1½ hours. Pre-heat the oven to 220°C/425°F/Gas mark 7. Once the rolls have puffed up slightly, pull the slits apart gently with your fingers to create holes.

Bake in the pre-heated oven for about 15 minutes, or until golden brown. Transfer to a wire rack to cool. ❋

The ideal temperature for leaving bread dough to rise is 25–30°C/77–86°F. If it is cooler, it will take longer. Never try to rush the rising process by putting the dough on top of a radiator. An airing cupboard is ideal. Ensure the place is draught-free.

FRESH TOMATO BREAD

Makes 1 loaf

This is the simplest of breads and not unlike a rectangular pizza to look at. The flavours on top, however, are far less punchy than the anchovy/black olive/oregano blast on the average pizza. The idea for the topping on this bread came from a pasta dish made for my family by an Italian guest. He combined tomatoes, mozzarella, basil and garlic – all finely chopped – with salt, pepper, sugar and olive oil. This was left to stand for 30–45 minutes and then tossed into a bowl of freshly cooked pasta. The dish was so simple, yet the flavours were exquisite. The freshness of the tomatoes was the one striking taste, and this is what I wanted to reproduce in a bread recipe.

It is important to use ripe tomatoes with flavour – try to buy some which are actually ripened on the vine. If they are very juicy, pat them dry with kitchen paper before using them, or the bread dough may become soggy. If you can find buffalo mozzarella, try it; its flavour is less delicate than cow's milk mozzarella, making it the perfect partner to the fresh, sweet tomatoes on this delicious bread.

BREAD

■ 14 g / ½ oz fresh yeast ■ a pinch of sugar ■ 227 ml / 8 fl oz warm water
■ 340 g / 12 oz strong white flour ■ 1 teaspoon salt ■ 1 tablespoon olive oil

TOPPING

■ 2 large tomatoes (about 340 g / 12 oz in total) ■ 1 round mozzarella (113 g / 4 oz)
■ 4–6 basil leaves ■ ½ tablespoon olive oil ■ ½ teaspoon salt
■ 2 cloves garlic, peeled and finely chopped ■ pepper, to season ■ ½ teaspoon sugar

For the bread, dissolve the yeast and sugar in the warm water, then leave to stand for 2–3 minutes.

Mix the flour and salt in a bowl, make a well in the centre and pour in the oil and yeast liquid. Stir well to combine.

Using floured hands, turn on to a floured board and knead for about 10 minutes, or until smooth. Then place in a lightly oiled bowl, cover with clingfilm and leave to rise in a warm place for about 1 hour.

Knock back the dough with your fists, then shape into a swiss-roll tin, 23 × 30 cm/9 × 13 in. Press the dough gently up the sides to form a rim. Cover loosely and leave somewhere warm for 30 minutes.

Meanwhile, make the topping. Remove the seeds from the tomatoes, using a small teaspoon, then pat dry. Very finely chop the tomatoes, mozzarella and basil, then combine with the salt, garlic, pepper and sugar. Leave to stand for 20 minutes. Pre-heat the oven to 220°C/425°F/ Gas mark 7.

Pile the tomato mixture on top of the bread and spread evenly out to the edges. Bake in the oven for about 25 minutes, or until golden brown round the edges. Serve warm.

STOTTIE CAKE

Makes 2 cakes

Stottie cake – a white bread traditionally baked
on the bottom of a coal-fired oven – is
little known outside the north-east of England.
Newcastle-based food writer Joan Bunting
tells me that it should be baked on a flat baking
tray, never in a metal loaf tin, and
stipulates only one rising. I like to give it a brief
second proving, however, to lighten the
texture, which is rather soft, with a denser
crumb than regular batch bread. Bread
guru Silvija Davidson says the word 'stottie'
originates from the practice of bouncing –
or 'stotting' – the freshly baked bread to
check its texture!
With the increasing popularity of Italian
'focaccia' in Britain, it is worth pondering why
Brits grasp at every 'foreign' food with
such alacrity – to the detriment of our own, fine
regional (if old-fashioned) products.
Stottie cake and focaccia are similar – both are
'hearth' breads, and are ideal to fill with
all sorts of interesting ingredients. Although
sun-dried tomatoes, pesto and mozzarella
seem more appropriate with an olive-oil laced
focaccia, they also work perfectly with
stottie cake. Stottie cakes are traditionally split
open (to make 2 disc-shaped halves), then
buttered on one side and topped with ham and
pease pudding on the other. Both sides
are then re-assembled. Delicious as this is, it is
winter fare. In warmer weather, try stottie
cake with a thick spread of cream cheese topped
with salami, anchovies, salad leaves or
fresh tomatoes. In fact, any sandwich filling at
all. You do not need to be a Geordie to
become a Stottie addict.

STOTTIE CAKE

■ 567 g / 1¼ lb strong white flour ■ 1½ teaspoons salt ■ 14 g / ½ oz caster sugar
■ 1 sachet easy-blend dried yeast ■ 28 g / 1 oz lard or white fat ■ 341–369 ml / 12–13 fl oz warm water

Mix the flour, salt, sugar and yeast together in a bowl. Rub in the fat with your fingertips, then combine to a stiff dough with the warm water.

Turn on to a floured board and knead for about 10 minutes, or until smooth.

Place in an oiled bowl, cover with clingfilm and leave to rise in a warm place for about 1 hour, or until well-risen. Then knock back the dough with your fists, and divide into 2.

Form each piece into a disc shape, about 20 cm/8 in in diameter, and place on an oiled baking sheet. Cover loosely and leave to rise in a warm place for about 15–20 minutes. Pre-heat the oven to 220°C/425°F/Gas mark 7.

Create a series of 'dimples' in the top of each cake by pressing with your fingers. Bake in the oven for 12–15 minutes, or until golden brown. Cool on a wire rack for at least 15 minutes. ❄

BUTTERIES

Makes 12 rolls

These little buttery bread rolls are a speciality of the north-east of Scotland, particularly Aberdeen. Here, they are known as 'rowies', but in some towns outside the authentic butteries are termed 'Aberdeenies'. To my mind, they are every bit as good as the glamorous French croissant and, sadly, every bit as fattening for their name does not lie – they are full of butter.
Some recipes stipulate 340 g/12 oz fat to 454 g/1 lb flour. I have drastically reduced the amount – not only for health reasons, but also to make the buttery dough easier to handle.
The resulting taste is just as good. The principle of folding in the fat is similar to that used to make puff pastry; just spread softened fat over the dough, fold, then repeat and repeat.
The end product should be a light, buttery, vaguely flaky textured roll that is perfect for breakfast with marmalade or for lunch with soup – and far too easy to consume.

■ 14 g / ½ oz fresh yeast ■ a pinch of sugar ■ 284 ml / 10 fl oz warm water ■ 454 g / 1 lb strong white flour
■ 1 teaspoon salt ■ 2 teaspoons sugar ■ 113 g / 4 oz unsalted butter, softened ■ 57 g / 2 oz white fat, softened

Place the yeast in a small bowl and mix to a paste with a pinch of sugar and a little of the warm water. Leave to stand for 5 minutes.

Combine the flour, salt and sugar in a bowl. Pour in the yeast mixture, adding just enough warm water to combine to a fairly soft – but not

sticky – dough. Knead for 10 minutes, or until smooth, then place in a lightly oiled bowl. Cover with clingfilm and leave to rise in a warm place for about 1½ hours, or until well-risen.

Knock back with your fists, then turn on to a floured board and roll out to a rectangle, roughly

$25 \times 30\,cm/10 \times 12\,in$. Cream the fats together, then spread one third of the fat mixture over the top two-thirds of the rectangle. Fold up the unbuttered third over the fat, then fold down the top third to give 3 layers. Repeat several times until the fat is used up. By the end, your hands – and the board – will be very buttery, and the dough will probably look incredibly messy.

Roll into a rough rectangle and cut into 12 pieces, using a large biscuit cutter. Place on a baking tray, then cover and leave to prove in a warm place for about 45 minutes. Pre-heat the oven to $220°C/425°F/Gas$ mark 7.

Bake in the oven for about 15–20 minutes, or until well-risen and golden brown. Transfer to a wire rack to cool. Serve warm, without butter. ❊

DAMPERS

Makes 8–10 dampers

The original damper bread came from Australia, where stockmen on large cattle ranches would mix up flour with water or beer, to form a dough. This was then packed into a 'camp stove' – that is, a solid pot with a lid. Once cooked in the embers, the dampers were eaten dripping with syrup. Camp-fire damper bread tastes wonderful. But then, doesn't all food cooked outdoors? My version is easy – you make up the basic dough at home on the morning of the picnic, then, at the camp-fire, wrap pieces around sturdy twigs. Choose green sticks which are not likely to burn and strip off the bark from the top part. Although my son likes to dip his dampers into jam or honey, the rest of the family prefers eating them plain, straight from the fire. Do allow a couple of minutes for cooling down, however!

■ 454 g / 1 lb self-raising flour, sifted ■ 1 heaped teaspoon salt ■ 1 heaped teaspoon caster sugar
■ 8–10 tablespoons water and milk, mixed

Mix the flour, salt and sugar together. Now add enough water and milk to combine to a fairly stiff dough. This should be soft enough to mould around your sticks, yet not so sticky that it is impossible to manage.

Using a spoon or the back of a knife, mix everything together, but do not knead. Place the dough in a container with a lid, ready for your camp-fire.

Once the flames have died down, to reveal nicely glowing embers, start preparing your dampers. Take off a piece of dough and wrap it around your stick, moulding it around the end so

the dough is about $1\,cm/½\,in$ all round. Alternatively, roll it out to form a long rope, then wrap this around the stick to give a 'twister'.

Cook over the embers for about 5 minutes, turning gently to bake on all sides. Twisters will probably take less time to cook.

Once it is dark brown all over, remove it from the stick. The damper will be long and narrow, with a hole all the way through (twisters will resemble long coils). If you like, fill the hole with butter, jam, cheese, ham or even a camp-fire banger. But I like it plain.

CAKES
TO EAT FRESH

Here are cakes and muffins, large and small, which
should be eaten fresh. Although most will last for a
couple of days, they are best devoured on Baking Day.
Besides, there is little chance of them sitting in the tin
much longer – they simply taste too good.

GATEAU BASQUE

Makes 1 cake

Gâteau Basque is a speciality of the French Basque region. It is a very popular cake in the patisseries of Lourdes. During my year there, when I was not teaching in the Lycée, I enjoyed this delicious cake regularly. The usual size is a large round, but it is often sold as individual small cakes. It is essentially a lemon-flavoured cake-cum-pastry encasing a vanilla-flavoured crème patissière. Although it is best eaten fresh – still slightly warm, if possible – it will keep for a few days in the refrigerator. When I left my post in the Pyrenees, I was given some home-made gifts by friends and fellow-teachers to sustain me on the long drive north to Scotland. Two cherry clafoutis and three gâteaux Basques certainly helped pass the time.

When making this cake, bear in mind a couple of important points. First, since the dough is fairly soft, even when chilled, it helps to lift it into the cake tin using a large, round cake-slice. (I use a German 'Kuchenlöser', a little larger than the cake tin.) Secondly, make sure you cook the filling for at least 3 minutes to ensure there is no taste of raw flour, whisking constantly to avoid lumps.

PASTRY

■ 340 g / 12 oz self-raising flour ■ 57 g / 2 oz cornflour ■ 170 g / 6 oz unsalted butter, softened
■ 170 g / 6 oz caster sugar ■ 2 eggs, beaten ■ 1 large egg yolk (size 1) ■ the juice and zest of 1 lemon

FILLING

■ 1 large egg (size 1) ■ 57 g / 2 oz caster sugar ■ 2 tablespoons cornflour
■ 227 ml / 8 fl oz plus 2 tablespoons milk ■ 1 large egg white (size 1) ■ 2 teaspoons vanilla essence

First make the pastry dough. Sift together the flour and cornflour. In a separate bowl, cream the butter and sugar until light and fluffy, then beat in the eggs and egg yolk a little at a time, followed by the lemon zest.

Fold in the flour, then the lemon juice and combine gently but thoroughly to a soft dough. Wrap in clingfilm and chill in the refrigerator for about 45 minutes.

Meanwhile, make the custard filling. Place the egg and sugar in a heavy-based saucepan and whisk together over a very low heat for a couple of minutes. You must whisk constantly, to avoid burning (and lumps). Once the mixture is pale yellow, remove from the heat. Place the cornflour and 2 tablespoons of milk in a small bowl. Blend to a paste, then set aside.

Heat 227 ml/8 fl oz milk with 1 teaspoon vanilla. Just before it reaches boiling point, pour over the egg and sugar mixture, then add the cornflour liquid. Set the pan over a low heat and, whisking constantly to avoid lumps, cook for about 3 minutes, or until the mixture thickens. (I use a balloon whisk for this.)

Remove from the heat and cool for about 5 minutes. Whisk the large egg white until stiff, then fold into the custard with the remaining teaspoon of vanilla. Using a balloon whisk,

whisk until smooth. Allow the custard to cool, stirring occasionally to prevent a skin forming.

Grease a 24 cm/9½ in loose-bottomed cake tin. Pre-heat the oven to 180°C/350°F/Gas mark 4. Remove the pastry from the refrigerator, cut in half and roll one half into a fairly thick round, more or less the same diameter as your cake tin. Using a large cake slice, slide the pastry into the tin so it covers the bottom entirely.

Spread the custard filling over the pastry in the base of the tin, leaving a 1 cm/½ in border all round. Roll out the remaining pastry and lay carefully on top. Gently press the edges together with your fingers to seal them, making sure the custard filling does not spill out.

Bake in the oven for about 45 minutes, or until well-risen and golden brown.

Allow to cool in the tin for about 15 minutes, then release the sides. Very carefully slide on to a wire rack. Cool for at least an hour before cutting. Serve warm as a pudding, with whipped cream, or cold for tea. ✳

CRUSTY LEMON CAKE

Makes about 24 squares

I used to adore this cake when I was younger. Somehow it seemed so decadent not only to beat rather a lot of sugar into the cake mixture, but also to soak the baked sponge in even more sugar. Admittedly, the topping is mixed with plenty of tangy juice to balance the sweetness. I also enjoyed the contrasting texture of the soft buttery sponge (use butter for this, never margarine) and the crusty top, which is formed by pouring the lemon/sugar mixture over the cake while it is still hot.

CAKE

■ 170 g / 6 oz unsalted butter, softened ■ 170 g / 6 oz caster sugar ■ the grated zest of 1 large lemon
■ 2 eggs ■ 170 g / 6 oz self-raising flour, sifted ■ a pinch of salt

TOPPING

■ the juice of 2 large lemons ■ 99 g / 3½ oz golden granulated sugar

Pre-heat the oven to 180°C/350°F/Gas mark 4. Cream together the butter, sugar and grated lemon zest, until pale and fluffy.

Beat in the eggs, one at a time, alternately with the flour. Stir in the salt.

Pour into a buttered 18 × 25 cm/7 × 10 in cake tin and smooth the top. (I prefer to use a rectangular tin so it can be cut into squares.)

Bake in the oven for about 25 minutes, or until golden brown and cooked through. To make the topping, mix the lemon juice and sugar and pour over the cake immediately you take it out.

Allow to cool in the tin for at least 30 minutes, then cut into squares and transfer to a wire rack to cool completely before serving. ✳

Use unwaxed lemons, if possible. If using waxed lemons, always scrub well before use.

MACADAMIA, COCONUT AND PINEAPPLE CAKE

Makes 1 cake

The very title gives an inkling as to the origins of this cake. In Australia, I enjoyed many cakes, puddings and tarts made with macadamia nuts, coconut or pineapple. Since these are all grown in Australia, the locals can afford to experiment with them – not an option for us, who have the expense of importing them. Macadamia nuts – also known as Queensland nuts – were first discovered by European settlers in the 1820's. Some 30 years later, they were named macadamia nuts, after an Australian philosopher, Dr John Macadam. But this was by no means a new nut in Australia – the Aborigines had been collecting them as food for thousands of years. Their rich, creamy taste and velvety, almost waxy texture still makes them one of the world's gourmet nuts. Their contribution to this cake is a nice crunch and a good buttery flavour – since the cake is made without any butter or oil. The coconut and pineapple add even more tropical tang to this unusual but delicious cake. The texture is fairly rough, because of the desiccated coconut and the crushed pineapple. The filling and top are smooth and creamy, with a hint of pineapple flavouring from the juice. Top the cake with either coconut chips or large shreds of coconut, toasted first under the grill. Do watch them as they grill – they will burn the minute you turn your back on them.

MACADAMIA, COCONUT
AND PINEAPPLE CAKE

CAKE

- 142 g / 5 oz golden caster sugar ▪ 3 eggs ▪ 85 g / 3 oz raw macadamia nuts, roughly chopped
- 1 × 400 g / 14 oz tin of crushed pineapple (in natural juice) ▪ 142 g / 5 oz self-raising flour, sifted
- 85 g / 3 oz desiccated coconut

FILLING AND TOPPING

- 227 g / 8 oz mascarpone cream cheese ▪ about 2 tablespoons of pineapple juice, from the tin
- 28 g / 1 oz shredded coconut or coconut chips

Pre-heat the oven to 180°C/350°F/Gas mark 4. Using a balloon whisk, beat together the sugar and eggs until thick and creamy. Then stir in the chopped nuts.

Strain the pineapple, reserving the juice. Add to the bowl, stirring well to combine.

Fold in the flour and coconut and gently mix together. Spoon into 2 × 20 cm/8 in sandwich tins and smooth the tops.

Bake in the oven for about 20 minutes, or until golden brown on top and springy to the touch in the centre.

Leave to cool in the tins for 5 minutes before transferring to a wire rack to cool completely.

Meanwhile, toast the shredded coconut or coconut chips. Spread on a baking tray and set under a pre-heated grill for 2–3 minutes, or until golden brown. Watch them carefully and remove immediately they start to colour.

To make the filling, beat the mascarpone cheese until smooth, then mix with a little of the reserved pineapple juice – the consistency should be neither too thick, nor too runny.

Make sure the 2 cakes are completely cold before using half the mixture to sandwich them together. Spread the rest over the top. Decorate with the toasted coconut. To serve, cut into thin slices.

GINGERTORTE

Makes 1 torte

This is one of my mother's tea-time favourites. My recipe has plenty of ginger syrup, and I often add some finely chopped ginger too. For a treat, fill the two 'tortes' with ginger ice-cream instead. Or make them with ground cinnamon instead of ginger and fill with cinnamon-flavoured butter cream.

TORTE

- 113 g / 4 oz unsalted butter, cut into cubes ▪ 1 heaped teaspoon ground ginger
- 170 g / 6 oz self-raising flour ▪ a pinch of salt ▪ 57 g / 2 oz caster sugar ▪ 4 digestive biscuits ▪ 1 egg

FILLING

- 57 g / 2 oz unsalted butter ▪ 113 g / 4 oz icing sugar, sifted
- ½–1 tablespoon ginger syrup (from a jar of stem ginger) ▪ icing sugar, to dust

Pre-heat the oven to 180°C/350°F/Gas mark 4. Place the butter, ginger, flour, salt and sugar in a food processor. Break up the digestives and add them to the food processor, then process until the mixture resembles breadcrumbs. Add the egg and process briefly until just combined.

Divide the mixture into 2 and press into 2 buttered, base-lined 18 cm/7 in sandwich tins. Using floured hands, press the mixture into the base of the tins to give a flat, even surface.

Prick all over with a fork and bake in the oven for about 15–20 minutes, or until light golden brown and firm. Turn on to a wire rack (the mixture will be soft, so handle it carefully) and allow to cool.

To make the filling, cream the butter until soft, then sift in the icing sugar. Beat well, then add enough ginger syrup to give a good gingery flavour. (I add a good spoonful.)

Place one of the cool, hardened 'tortes' on a serving plate and spread evenly with butter cream. Place the other 'torte' on top and dust lightly with icing sugar. Allow the butter cream to harden a little before serving.

MARMALADE BREAKFAST MUFFINS

Makes 12 muffins

These are simplicity itself. So simple, in fact, that they really are worth getting up 30 minutes early for. They take only 10 minutes to prepare, so while you are mixing, the oven is heating up. Then, while they bake, you can have that much-needed early morning cup of tea. The muffins can be spread with a little butter, if you wish, but I prefer them plain. Use either thick-cut orange or lime marmalade. A good home-made strawberry or raspberry jam will also go well, although the overall taste will be much sweeter. Serve them warm with plenty of fresh coffee or tea.

■ 2 eggs, beaten ■ 85 ml / 3 fl oz vegetable oil (I use sunflower oil) ■ 142 ml / ¼ pint milk
■ 227 g / 8 oz plain flour, sifted ■ 1 tablespoon baking powder ■ ½ teaspoon salt
■ 57 g / 2 oz caster sugar ■ 12 heaped teaspoons marmalade

Pre-heat the oven to 200°C/400°F/Gas mark 6. Place the eggs, oil and milk in a mixing bowl and whisk together.

In a separate bowl, sift together the flour, baking powder and salt. Then, stir in the sugar. Using a wooden spoon, make a well in the centre, then pour in the whisked liquid.

Combine everything together with a large spoon – this must be done gently, but quite thoroughly. Do not panic if you see a few little lumps – these do not affect the light fluffy texture of the muffins. The main point to remember here is not to beat the mixture too vigorously.

Spoon half the mixture into muffin cases, set in a bun or muffin baking tray. Then spoon a heaped teaspoon of marmalade on top of each. Top with the remaining mixture, taking care you cover up the blobs of marmalade.

Bake in the oven for 20 minutes, or until well-risen and golden brown. Allow to cool for at least 10 minutes before serving.
❋ Warm through before serving.

ROSEMARY AND APRICOT MUFFINS

Makes 16 muffins

These little muffins are light in texture and have a combination of wonderfully interesting flavours.
The dried apricots add a good chewy texture and colour and the rosemary enhances
everything by its warm, resinous flavour. Make sure you use young, soft rosemary leaves
– older ones will be too tough.

Although you can buy rosemary oils, it is very easy to make your own. Place 5–6 thick sprigs of
rosemary in a jar and cover with extra-virgin olive oil. Add 1 teaspoon white wine vinegar
and seal tightly. Leave to stand for 2–3 weeks, shaking daily, then strain into a clean bottle and pop
in a clean sprig of rosemary. Store, sealed, in a cool place. Use the oil not only for these
muffins, but also to throw into salad dressings, to toss into pasta and to baste roast garlic lamb.

■ 142g / 5oz unsalted butter, softened ■ 142g / 5oz golden caster sugar ■ 2 eggs
■ 227g / 8oz self-raising flour, sifted ■ a pinch of salt ■ 99ml / 3½ floz milk
■ 57g / 2oz (no-soak) dried apricots, roughly chopped
■ 1 tablespoon young (tender) rosemary leaves, finely chopped ■ 2 teaspoons rosemary oil

Pre-heat the oven to 180°C/350°F/Gas mark 4.
Cream together the butter and sugar until pale,
then add the eggs and flour alternately. Use a
folding action, rather than a vigourous beating
action. Add the salt and milk, then stir well. Do
not overbeat.

Gently fold in the apricots and rosemary.

Spoon into 16 paper muffin (bun) cases, set in
a bun tray. (You will probably need 2 bun trays.)

Bake in the oven for about 20–25 minutes,
then transfer to a wire tray. While they are still
hot, brush the tops with rosemary oil.

Allow to cool for at least 10 minutes before
serving. ❋

BULGING CHOCOLATE MUFFINS

Makes 12 muffins

The title says it all. You could hardly include more chocolate if you tried. They are, indeed, bulging with chocolate. Not tiny, dainty chocolate drops – but great chunks of thick chocolate, which, I am sorry to say, you must chop by hand. Use only the best chocolate – I like to use a combination of milk and plain, but you could use one type, if you prefer. It is easiest to chop chocolate if it is first popped in the refrigerator for an hour or so, to become really hard.
The texture of the muffins is slightly unusual, because of the addition of semolina, that most versatile of flours. Semolina is ground from durum wheat and although usually associated with milk puddings in this country, it has far more uses. It is used in Italy to make pasta and gnocchi, or it can be added to biscuits, cakes and pastry to give a short, almost grainy texture.
Eat these muffins warm – after cooling them for about 15 minutes – while the chocolate is still melted and gooey. They are also delicious when cold, but the chocolate is slightly less soft.

■ 170 ml / 6 fl oz milk ■ 2 eggs ■ 85 ml / 3 fl oz sunflower oil ■ 142 g / 5 oz plain flour
■ 2 tablespoons cocoa powder ■ a pinch of salt ■ 1 tablespoon baking powder ■ 85 g / 3 oz semolina
■ 57 g / 2 oz caster sugar ■ 142 g / 5 oz plain or milk chocolate, cut into large chunks

Pre-heat the oven to 200°C/400°F/Gas mark 6. Place the milk, eggs and oil in a mixing bowl and whisk together.

Sift the flour, cocoa, salt and baking powder into a separate bowl, then stir in the semolina, sugar and chocolate. Combine thoroughly, then make a well in the centre.

Pour in the liquid, a little at a time, stirring gently between each addition until well-mixed. Do not beat.

Set 12 paper cases in a deep bun/muffin tin and, using 2 teaspoons, divide the mixture between the cases.

Bake in the oven for about 20 minutes, or until well-risen.

Transfer to a wire rack and allow to cool for 10–15 minutes. Serve warm.

Only cook or bake with a plain chocolate which has a minimum of 50 per cent cocoa solids; some recipes even require one with as much as 70 per cent cocoa solids.

For milk chocolate, use one with a minimum of 30 per cent.

CRUNCHY-TOPPED RASPBERRY AND CINNAMON MUFFINS

Makes 12 muffins

These muffins are unbelievably quick to make. You simply mix together everything except the berries in a bowl, then carefully stir in the raspberries. You must take care that you do not break up the berries as you stir, otherwise you will have pink muffins, instead of golden ones with flecks of whole red raspberries. Cinnamon complements raspberries very well, although it would work equally well with either blueberries or blackcurrants. The crunchy topping is formed by sprinkling the muffins with demerara sugar before baking. I feel I should advise you to eat them while still warm, but there is really no need. The minute they emerge from the oven they smell – and look – unbearably irresistible. There is the temptation of giving in too soon and devouring several of them while they are too hot. Eat them for breakfast with a thin smear of unsalted butter, or serve them for pudding with a dollop of ice-cream.

■ 142 g / 5 oz self-raising flour, sifted ■ 1 heaped teaspoon ground cinnamon ■ 57 g / 2 oz caster sugar
■ 1 egg, beaten ■ 3 tablespoons sunflower oil ■ 3 tablespoons milk
■ 113 g / 4 oz raspberries ■ 3 teaspoons demerara sugar

Pre-heat the oven to 180°C/350°F/Gas mark 4. Place the flour, cinnamon and caster sugar in a large bowl and stir to combine. Make a well in the centre and pour in the beaten egg, oil and milk. Combine, stirring gently but thoroughly.

Very gently stir in the raspberries, making sure they remain whole.

Spoon the mixture into paper cases, set in a muffin or bun tray, and sprinkle the tops with demerara sugar.

Bake in the oven for 20–25 minutes, or until well-risen and golden brown on top.

Transfer to a wire rack to cool.

❄ If freezing, use fresh (not frozen) raspberries.

CRUNCHY-TOPPED RASPBERRY AND CINNAMON MUFFINS
BULGING CHOCOLATE MUFFINS (page 65)

RHUBARB CLAFOUTIS CAKE

Makes 1 cake

Try to use young pink rhubarb for this – preferably 'champagne' variety. Although the slightly older or green variety will taste almost as good, it will certainly not look as stunning. With the vivid pink rhubarb, the finished dish looks very attractive, studded with the exquisitely coloured fruit. Since rhubarb freezes very well, chop young stalks of rhubarb and freeze them in bags. Drain them thoroughly before using in a recipe. Otherwise the result will be soggy.

This dish is essentially a batter pudding which is best served warm. It is reminiscent of a clafoutis, the famous French sweet batter pudding usually made with cherries. If you have buttered your cake tin well, you can turn the cake upside-down just before serving. However, if it has stuck around the sides, you may find it easier to serve it in wedges, straight from the dish. An elderflower cream goes well with this: simply mix 2 tablespoons of good elderflower cordial into a 200 g / 7 oz tub of crème fraîche or Greek yoghurt.

- 567 g / 1¼ lb young rhubarb, washed and chopped into small pieces ■ 142 g / 5 oz caster sugar
- 2 eggs ■ 99 ml / 3½ fl oz double cream ■ 99 ml / 3½ fl oz milk
- 1 teaspoon vanilla essence ■ 57 g / 2 oz plain flour ■ 28 g / 1 oz butter, melted

Pre-heat the oven to 200°C/400°F/Gas mark 6. Place the rhubarb in a saucepan with 3–4 table-spoons water and bring to the boil. Simmer gently for 10 minutes, then drain at once. The rhubarb should be tender, but not mushy.

Place the sugar and eggs in a bowl and whisk together, using a balloon whisk. Stir in the cream, milk and vanilla, then add the flour and melted butter.

Whisk well to form a smooth, thick batter. Then gently fold in the rhubarb – do not be too rough or the rhubarb will break up.

Butter a deep 20 cm/8 in cake tin or oven-proof dish. (Do not use a loose-bottomed tin or the batter might ooze out.) Pour in the batter.

Place the dish on a metal oven tray and bake in the oven for 35 minutes, or until puffed up and golden brown. Serve warm.

CHESTNUT AND PINE-NUT CAKE

Makes 1 cake

This cake is made from chestnut flour, which is available from good Italian delicatessens and is sometimes used instead of maize to make polenta. The strong, earthy flavour of chestnut flour is definitely an acquired taste. So if you are serving this cake to the uninitiated, serve in small slices. Its texture is fairly dense and moist.

Similar in taste to 'Castagnaccio', an unleavened chestnut cake particularly popular in Tuscany and Liguria, it can be served with chestnut purée and a spoonful of thick cream for dessert, or – my favourite – with a wedge of ewe's milk blue cheese, such as Roquefort or Lanark Blue. Do serve it in small slices, however, as it is very rich.

■ 170g / 6oz chestnut flour ■ 85g / 3oz self-raising flour ■ 1 teaspoon baking powder
■ a pinch of salt ■ 2 eggs (size 2) ■ 57g / 2oz caster sugar
■ 3 tablespoons extra-virgin olive oil ■ 57g / 2oz raisins
■ 1 tablespoon young (tender) rosemary, finely chopped ■ 28g / 1oz pine-nuts

Pre-heat the oven to 220°C/425°F/Gas mark 7. Place the flours, baking powder and salt in a mixing bowl.

In a separate bowl, beat together the eggs and sugar using a balloon whisk, then whisk in the olive oil.

Add the liquid ingredients to the dry ingredients a little at a time, stirring thoroughly with a wooden spoon between each addition. Now add the raisins and rosemary.

Spoon the mixture into a deep, oiled 18 cm/7 in cake tin, level off the surface and sprinkle with pine-nuts.

Bake in the oven for 25–30 minutes, or until a skewer comes out clean when inserted into the centre of the cake. If necessary, cover with foil towards the end of cooking to prevent the crust from burning.

Leave to cool in the tin for 10 minutes, then transfer to a wire rack to cool completely.

Chestnut flour does not keep well at room temperature. If you are not using a whole bag, store surplus in the freezer for up to 6 months.

PASSION CAKE

Makes 1 cake

Passion cake is nothing to do with passion fruit, nor does it seem to have much to do with passion. Unless, of course, you feel the same way about this wonderfully nutty, moist cake as I do. It is really a variation on that old favourite, carrot cake, with the inclusion of a little honey: either in the cake as a substitute for sugar or – as in my recipe – in the cream cheese topping.
It is not too heavy, so it makes a good dessert, perhaps with a little extra yoghurt and honey poured over the top. Or serve it with a cup of morning coffee or afternoon tea. Although it is best served fresh, it will keep for 2–3 days in the refrigerator, covered with clingfilm.

CAKE

■ 170 g / 6 oz butter, softened ■ 170 g / 6 oz soft light brown sugar ■ 3 eggs
■ 198 g / 7 oz self-raising wholemeal flour ■ ½ teaspoon baking powder ■ 1 teaspoon ground cinnamon
■ 28 g / 1 oz desiccated coconut ■ 57 g / 2 oz raisins ■ 170 g / 6 oz carrots (peeled weight), finely grated
■ 57 g / 2 oz chopped walnuts

TOPPING

■ 2 tablespoons mascarpone cheese ■ 2 tablespoons natural yoghurt
■ 2 teaspoons runny honey ■ 1 tablespoon chopped walnuts

Pre-heat the oven to 180°C/350°F/Gas mark 4. Using an electric beater (on low speed), cream together the butter and sugar until light and fluffy. Then beat in the eggs, one at a time, until well-mixed.

Sift the flour, baking powder and cinnamon into a bowl. Using a metal spoon, gently fold into the creamed mixture, followed by the coconut, raisins, carrots and walnuts. Mix gently but thoroughly.

Turn into an 18 cm/7 in loose-bottomed, base-lined cake tin. Level the top, then bake in the oven for about 1 hour, or until a fine skewer comes out clean when inserted into the centre of the cake.

Remove from the oven and allow to cool in the tin for at least 5 minutes. Transfer to a wire rack to cool completely.

To make the topping, beat together the mascarpone cheese, yoghurt and honey until smooth. Spread over the top of the cold cake and sprinkle with chopped nuts.

✳ This can be frozen completely iced. Store in the refrigerator after defrosting.

POPPY SEED AND ALMOND CAKE

Makes 1 cake

There are 2 types of poppy seed – creamy yellow ones, often used in Indian cooking, and blue-grey ones, common to Eastern European and Jewish cooking. It is the dark seeds which should be used in this moist cake. The texture of the finished cake is slightly nutty and the orange lends a sharp citrus tang. Although I prefer to eat it plain – perhaps with a little crème fraîche or almond or honey ice-cream on the side – I have given the recipe for an optional cream cheese topping (similar to that found on carrot cake), which is equally delicious, if just a hint more fattening!

CAKE

■ 113g / 4oz ground almonds ■ 170g / 6oz caster sugar ■ 57g / 2oz self-raising flour, sifted
■ the grated zest of 1 orange ■ 85g / 3oz poppy seeds ■ 113g / 4oz butter, melted
■ 4 large egg whites (size 1)

TOPPING (OPTIONAL)

■ 198g / 7oz cream cheese ■ the juice of 1 small orange ■ 2–3 teaspoons caster sugar
■ 1 tablespoon poppy seeds

Pre-heat the oven to 190°C / 375°F / Gas mark 5. Place the almonds, sugar, flour, orange zest and poppy seeds in a food processor and process briefly until just mixed.

With the blade running, pour the melted butter through the feeder tube and process until combined. Do not overprocess. Turn into a mixing bowl.

Whisk the egg whites until they form soft peaks. Fold into the mixture, one spoonful at a time, until fully incorporated.

Spoon the mixture into a greased 18 cm / 7 in cake tin and level the surface with the back of a knife. Bake in the oven for about 40 minutes, or until a skewer comes out clean when inserted into the centre of the cake.

Leave to cool in the tin for about 5 minutes, then loosen the edges with a knife and transfer to a wire rack to cool completely.

To make the topping, beat together the cheese, orange juice and sugar until light and fluffy. Spread over the top of the cake and sprinkle with poppy seeds.

Freeze left-over egg whites, remembering to mark the exact number on the freezer sticker.

BANANA UPSIDE-DOWN CAKE

Makes 1 cake

This is a marvellous pudding which everyone in my family loves. All the ingredients are the children's favourites – and yet it is sophisticated enough to serve adults for dinner. The bananas are placed on the base with a mixture of butter and brown sugar, then a banana sponge mix is poured on top. After cooking, the cake is turned upside-down so that the bananas sit amid a toffee sauce, on top of a light, banana-flavoured sponge. Do not be afraid when it comes to turning the cake out. Just use one bold, deft movement. If you cannot feel it dropping on to the plate, then one good sharp shake should do the trick. Serve warm with clotted cream or crème fraîche.

CAKE

■ 170g / 6oz self-raising flour, sifted ■ a pinch of salt ■ 1 medium banana, mashed
■ 2 tablespoons crème fraîche ■ 1 teaspoon vanilla essence ■ 170g / 6oz caster sugar
■ 85g / 3oz unsalted butter, softened ■ 2 eggs, beaten

BASE/TOPPING

■ 85g / 3oz soft light brown sugar ■ 85g / 3oz unsalted butter, softened ■ 2–3 bananas

Pre-heat the oven to 180°C/350°F/Gas mark 4. Sift the flour and salt into a bowl.

In a separate bowl, mix the mashed banana with the crème fraîche and vanilla.

Cream the sugar and butter until light and fluffy, then beat in the eggs a little at a time.

Now fold in the flour and banana mixture alternately, stirring until thoroughly combined.

To make the base/topping, cream the sugar and butter until light and fluffy and smear over the base and a little way up the sides of a heavy-based ovenproof pan, about 25 cm/10 in in diameter and 5 cm/2 in deep. Slice the bananas and arrange over the base.

Spoon over the sponge mixture, smoothing the top.

Bake in the oven for about 45–50 minutes, or until the sponge is golden brown on top and feels slightly springy to the touch.

Leave to cool in the dish for about 5–10 minutes, then turn upside-down on to a large serving dish. Serve warm.

ROASTED HAZELNUT CAKE

Makes about 12 squares

This very simple cake is one of my favourites. But that is possibly because I love nuts of all sorts. Roast the hazelnuts first to bring out the flavour. If you do not have sufficient time to roast them as suggested below, simply place them on a sheet of foil under a medium-hot grill. Watch them carefully, though, or they are liable to burn.

■ 113 g / 4 oz blanched hazelnuts ■ 85 g / 3 oz unsalted butter, softened ■ 170 g / 6 oz caster sugar
■ 3 eggs ■ 170 g / 6 oz self-raising flour ■ ½ teaspoon baking powder
■ 2 tablespoons hazelnut oil

Pre-heat the oven to 190°C/375°F/Gas mark 5. First roast the nuts: spread on a baking tray and place in the oven for 10 minutes, or until golden brown. Shake after 5 minutes to give an even colour. Then remove and allow to cool. Turn the oven down to 180°C/350°F/Gas mark 4.

Once cold, tip the nuts into a food processor and process until roughly ground – not finely ground, or they will turn into a paste.

Cream together the butter and sugar, then beat in the eggs one at a time.

Sift in the flour and baking powder, then add the ground nuts. Stir well to combine, then add the oil and stir again.

Spoon into a buttered 18 cm/7 in square cake tin and bake for about 35–40 minutes, or until cooked through. If necessary, cover loosely with foil for the last 10 minutes to prevent the crust from burning.

Allow to cool in the tin for at least 30 minutes, then cut into squares and transfer to a wire rack to cool completely.

RICE CAKE

Makes 1 cake

This cake is really a type of baked rice pudding, flavoured with raisins, lemon and vanilla. It has a good crunchy topping and sides, achieved by coating the cake tin with sugar. I prefer it to plain rice pudding, as it is richer and has a better contrast of textures: a soft, moist inside and a crusty, crisp outside.

■ 710 ml / 1¼ pints milk ■ 198 g / 7 oz short-grain (pudding) rice ■ 1 vanilla pod ■ a pinch of salt
■ 57 g / 2 oz raisins ■ 85 g / 3 oz caster sugar ■ 57 g / 2 oz butter, melted
■ the grated zest of 1 large lemon ■ 2–3 teaspoons demerara sugar ■ 2 eggs, beaten

Place the milk and rice in a saucepan with the vanilla pod and salt. Bring slowly to the boil, then cover and simmer over a very low heat for about 30 minutes, or until the rice is soft. Remove the vanilla pod, scrape out the sticky black seeds and add to the rice.

Add the raisins, sugar, melted butter and lemon zest, and stir well to combine. Leave to cool. Pre-heat the oven to 180°C/350°F/ Gas mark 4.

Meanwhile, prepare the baking tin. Generously butter the base and sides of a 18 cm/7 in loose-bottomed cake tin. Then coat the sides with half the demerara sugar.

Once the rice mixture is completely cold, add the eggs and stir well to thoroughly combine. Spoon into the prepared tin and sprinkle with the remaining demerara sugar.

Bake in the oven for about 40 minutes, or until crusty and golden brown on top.

Transfer to a wire rack and allow to cool for at least 30 minutes.

Serve warm – in slices – as a dessert, accompanied by pouring cream.

POLENTA CHOCOLATE CAKE

Makes 1 cake

This cake is very light, deeply chocolatey and unusually crunchy – almost grainy – in texture, from the polenta. I love to serve it for dessert, in small slices while it is still just warm, with either a tangy fruit purée, such as raspberry, or a dollop of thick clotted cream. A combination of both is best of all.

■ 142 g / 5 oz caster sugar ■ 142 g / 5 oz unsalted butter, softened
■ 113 g / 4 oz dark chocolate (look for one with at least 55 per cent cocoa solids) ■ 1 tablespoon brandy
■ 3 eggs, separated ■ 113 g / 4 oz fine polenta ■ 28 g / 1 oz cocoa powder, sifted

Pre-heat the oven to 180°C/350°F/Gas mark 4. Cream together the sugar and butter until light and fluffy.

Place the chocolate and brandy in a small mixing bowl and set over a pan of simmering water until melted.

Beat the egg yolks into the butter mixture, then stir in the polenta with the cocoa and melted chocolate.

Whisk the egg whites until stiff. Fold 1 tablespoon into the chocolate mixture, then add the rest. Use as light a touch as possible, but ensure it is completely mixed.

Spoon into a buttered 24 cm/9½ in loose-bottomed cake tin. Bake in the oven for about 30–35 minutes, or until springy to the touch.

Transfer to a wire rack to cool. Serve barely warm or just cold. ✳

CHOCOLATE MUD CAKE

Makes 1 cake

The reason for the marvellous title of this chocolate cake is its thick, dense and fudgey texture. My
daughter Jessica also thinks the raw cake mixture is reminiscent of mud – both in colour and
texture. And who would dare argue with a child over the qualities of mud?
I like to use a dark chocolate with 55–60 per cent cocoa solids – not too bitter – for the cake mixture.
It is a very versatile cake, which can be served for dessert or tea. For dessert, serve it
barely warm with some tangy crème fraîche and either raspberry purée or a dollop of fresh lemon
curd (see page 88). To serve as a cake, ice with fudge icing and either leave as it is,
or drizzle with white chocolate.

CAKE

■ 142g / 5oz unsalted butter ■ 142g / 5oz plain chocolate ■ 142g / 5oz caster sugar
■ 99ml / 3½ floz very hot (but not boiling) water ■ 142g / 5oz self-raising flour
■ 28g / 1oz cocoa powder ■ 2 eggs

FUDGE ICING

■ 57g / 2oz unsalted butter ■ 3 tablespoons milk ■ 198g / 7oz icing sugar, sifted
■ 28g / 1oz cocoa powder, sifted

Pre-heat the oven to 180°C/350°F/Gas mark 4.
For the cake, place the butter and chocolate in a
large bowl. Set over a pan of simmering water
and stir well, until melted completely. Remove
from the heat and stir in the sugar and hot water.

Sift together the flour and cocoa, then stir
into the mixture. Beat in the eggs, one at a time,
and mix well.

Pour into a buttered and floured 24cm/9½ in
loose-bottomed cake tin and level off the top.

Bake in the oven for 35 minutes, or until a
skewer inserted in the middle of the cake comes
out clean.

Leave in the tin for 10–15 minutes, then
transfer to a wire rack to cool before icing. (Or
serve warm, as a dessert.)

To make the icing, place the butter, milk,
sugar and cocoa in a bowl and set over a
saucepan of gently simmering water. Stir until
the mixture is glossy and smooth.

Remove from the heat and allow the icing to
cool completely.

Beat well until the cold icing becomes thick,
then spread over the cooled cake.

✳ Chocolate mud cake should only be frozen
un-iced.

CHOCOLATE CHEESE-SWIRLED SQUARES

Makes about 12 little square cakes

These are a mixture of light, creamy cheesecake and dark, rich chocolate brownies. The 2 mixtures are swirled together to give a marbled look. Do not overmix, however, or you will end up with a solid block of colour rather than a swirled, marbled effect. Serve the cakes barely warm.

BROWNIE MIX

■ 113g / 4oz quality milk chocolate ■ 71g / 2½oz unsalted butter ■ 57g / 2oz caster sugar ■ 1 egg ■ 85g / 3oz plain flour, sifted ■ 1 heaped teaspoon baking powder ■ a pinch of salt

CHEESECAKE MIX

■ 113g / 4oz cream cheese ■ 1 teaspoon vanilla extract ■ 28g / 1oz caster sugar

Pre-heat the oven to 190°C/375°F/Gas mark 5. To make the brownie mix, place the chocolate and butter in a bowl. Set over a pan of simmering water and stir well, until melted completely. Cool for 5 minutes.

In a separate bowl, beat together the sugar and the egg until pale and creamy, then stir into the cooled chocolate mixture.

Now stir in the flour, baking powder and salt. To make the cheesecake mix, thoroughly beat together the cream cheese, vanilla and sugar until light and smooth.

Pour the chocolate mixture into a buttered 18 cm/7 in square cake tin. Spoon the cheese mixture on top and, using the tip of a knife, gently swirl the 2 mixtures together to create a marbled effect.

Bake in the oven for about 25 minutes, or until crusty around the edges.

Cool in the tin, then cut into squares.

CAKES WHICH KEEP

These are 'cake-tin cakes' – ones which will happily wait, wrapped in foil in a tin for several days until required. Some taste even better after a couple of weeks' maturing. You'll find old favourites such as Madeira or Dundee cake here, as well as the less conventional ice-cream meringue cake, lemon curd polenta cake or pain d'épice topped with white chocolate basil sauce.

DUNDEE CAKE

Makes 1 cake

Confession: I am from Dundee and I have never seen a Dundonian eating Dundee Cake! But do not let that put you off this truly delicious cake. It is rich, fruity and wonderfully moist. It also keeps very well and is therefore the most ideal cake to have sitting in your cake tin, ready for unexpected guests. It is also excellent as a wedding or christening cake. I like to make this, without the whole almonds on top, as a light Christmas cake.

■ 170g/6oz unsalted butter, softened ■ 170g/6oz caster sugar ■ the grated zest of 1 orange
■ 4 eggs ■ 57g/2oz ground almonds ■ 170g/6oz plain flour ■ 1 teaspoon baking powder
■ ½ teaspoon mixed spice ■ 113g/4oz sultanas ■ 113g/4oz raisins ■ 113g/4oz currants
■ 57g/2oz mixed peel ■ 1 tablespoon brandy ■ 16–20 whole blanched almonds

Pre-heat the oven to 150°C/300°F/Gas mark 2. Cream together the butter, sugar and orange zest until light and fluffy, then beat in the eggs, one at a time. Add a little of the flour if the mixture starts to curdle.

Sift in the flour, baking powder and spice, then add the ground almonds. Fold gently but thoroughly. Once everything is incorporated, stir in the dried fruits and mixed peel, together with enough brandy to form a soft consistency.

Spoon into a buttered, lined 18 cm/7 in cake tin and smooth the top. Bake in the oven for about 2½–3 hours, or until cooked through. Halfway through baking, arrange the almonds on top and return to the oven.

Cool completely in the tin before serving. ❋

FOCHABERS GINGERBREAD

Makes 1 loaf

This is one of the many regional British gingerbreads. Its origins are Scottish – from the area around Fochabers in the very north of Scotland, roughly between Inverness and Peterhead. Its characteristic ingredients – apart from the usual black treacle and ground ginger – are dried fruits and beer. Most recipes also insist on the addition of mixed peel, but since peel is not one of my favourite ingredients, I have omitted it. Should you wish to keep to the authentic recipe, however, add 57g/2oz chopped mixed peel. The flavour of this cake is dark, rich and strong, from the mixture of beer and treacle – just the thing for a cold, damp winter's day.

This cake will keep very well for some time, wrapped in foil and tightly sealed in a tin.

■ 170g / 6oz unsalted butter, softened ■ 170g / 6oz light muscovado sugar
■ 4 rounded tablespoons black treacle ■ 1 egg ■ 340g / 12oz plain flour, sifted
■ 57g / 2oz sultanas ■ 57g / 2oz currants ■ 57g / 2oz ground almonds ■ 1 teaspoon ground ginger
■ 1 teaspoon mixed spice ■ a generous pinch of ground cloves ■ 1 teaspoon bicarbonate of soda
■ 142 ml / ¼ pint beer

Pre-heat the oven to 150°C / 300°F / Gas mark 2. Beat together the butter and sugar until creamy. Heat the treacle very gently (I do this in a microwave), then add to the butter. Stir in the egg and combine well.

Stir in the flour, sultanas, currants, ground almonds and spices and beat well.

Dissolve the bicarbonate of soda in the beer, then add to the mixture, beating well.

Pour into a buttered, base-lined tin. A 20 cm / 8 in square tin is traditionally used, but you could use a wide-lipped 907 g / 2 lb loaf tin. (If you use a narrow one, make sure you place it on a baking sheet in case it overflows.)

Bake in the oven for 1 hour 15 minutes to 1 hour 30 minutes, or until a skewer inserted into the middle comes out clean. (If you use a loaf tin, the cake will take longer to cook since it is deeper.)

Place the tin on a wire rack and allow the cake to cool completely before removing it from the tin. ✳

HOT GINGERBREAD PUDDING

Serves 4

Ever wondered what to do with that left-over gingerbread lurking in the bottom of your cake tin? This pudding is flavoured with brandy and speckled with chocolate. Try it with Orkney Broonie (page 82), Apple Gingerbread (page 83) or Fochabers Gingerbread. Choose a chocolate with at least 55 per cent cocoa solids.

■ 57g / 2oz butter, softened ■ 2 eggs, separated ■ 57g / 2oz dark chocolate, roughly chopped
■ 85g / 3oz gingerbread, cut into cubes ■ 3 tablespoons brandy ■ 28g / 1oz caster sugar

Pre-heat the oven to 180°C / 350°F / Gas mark 4. Beat together the butter and egg yolks until creamy. Then stir in the chopped chocolate.

Soak the gingerbread in the brandy for about 5 minutes. Meanwhile, whisk the egg whites until stiff, then slowly fold in the sugar and beat until glossy.

Stir the gingerbread (and any remaining brandy) into the butter mixture, then spoon in a little of the whisked egg whites. Mix thoroughly, then gradually incorporate the rest, folding gently. Pour the mixture into a buttered 852 ml / 1½ pint soufflé-style oven dish.

Place in a bain-marie (a roasting tin filled with boiling water is ideal) and bake in the oven for 35 minutes, or until well-risen and springy to the touch. Cool for 5–10 minutes – it will sink a little. Serve warm with clotted cream.

PARKIN

Makes 1 parkin

I hesitate to write the word Yorkshire or Lancashire before parkin, for both counties lay claim to this deliciously oaty gingerbread. The only difference I can find is that most recipes for Lancashire Parkin add chunky marmalade. To avoid potential confrontation, let me simply call this cake – traditionally made for Guy Fawkes' night – Parkin. Its texture is decidedly oaty, slightly nutty and crumbly. Denser than the broonie, but not as sticky as the Fochabers Gingerbread, it is the type of loaf which not only tastes good, but also makes you feel it is doing you good!

■ 142g / 5oz plain flour ■ a pinch of salt ■ 1 rounded teaspoon ground ginger
■ ¼ teaspoon ground nutmeg ■ 1 teaspoon baking powder ■ 85g / 3oz soft light brown sugar
■ 284g / 10oz medium oatmeal ■ 113g / 4oz unsalted butter ■ 3 rounded tablespoons black treacle
■ ½ teaspoon white distilled malt vinegar

Pre-heat the oven to 160°C/325°F/Gas mark 3. Sift the flour, salt, ginger, nutmeg and baking powder into a mixing bowl, then stir in the sugar and oatmeal.

Gently heat together the butter and treacle, then pour into the bowl.

Stir well to combine, then add the vinegar and stir again.

Spoon into a buttered base-lined 907 g/2 lb loaf tin and smooth the top.

Bake in the oven for 60–65 minutes, or until a skewer inserted into the middle comes out clean.

Cool in the tin, then remove. Allow to become completely cold before wrapping in foil. ❄

To measure out black treacle or golden syrup, either flour the scales, or dip your metal measuring spoon in boiling water.

ORKNEY BROONIE

Makes 1 broonie

This is one of my favourite gingerbreads. The texture and colour are fairly light, but it is not as crumbly as the parkin and still nicely moist inside and full of flavour. Broonie comes from the Norse *bruni*, which is the word in both Orkney and Shetland for a thick bannock. The ingredients are almost identical to the parkin, but the quantities differ. The method is also different – the broonie is made using the rubbing-in method, whereas for the parkin the fat and treacle are warmed, then poured into the dry ingredients. This keeps well and is good both plain and buttered.

■ 170 g / 6 oz medium oatmeal ■ 170 g / 6 oz self-raising flour, sifted ■ a pinch of salt
■ 85 g / 3 oz unsalted butter, cut into cubes ■ 1 rounded teaspoon ground ginger
■ 85 g / 3 oz soft light brown sugar ■ 2 rounded tablespoons black treacle ■ 1 egg
■ 142 ml / ¼ pint buttermilk (or fresh milk with ½ teaspoon lemon juice)

Pre-heat the oven to 160°C/325°F/Gas mark 3. Combine the oatmeal, flour and salt in a bowl.

Rub in the cubes of butter, then stir in the ginger and sugar.

Place the treacle in a small pan and heat very slowly over a low heat, then stir in the egg. Pour into the dry ingredients, with the buttermilk.

Stir well until thoroughly combined, then pour into a buttered, base-lined 907 g/2 lb loaf tin. Bake in the oven for 60–70 minutes, or until a skewer inserted into the middle comes out clean.

Set on a wire rack to cool completely before removing from the tin. Store, wrapped in foil. ❄

APPLE GINGERBREAD

Makes 1 cake

This gingerbread is even more moist and soft than usual. The apples add not only a lovely flavour but also a good texture. Make sure you drain the cooked apples really well, or the mixture will be too wet. The cake tastes best after a couple of days' maturing. It will keep well, wrapped in foil, for over a week. If you plan to eat the cake while still fairly fresh, top with a ginger-flavoured icing. This is made by mixing ground ginger with a little boiling water, then beating it into icing sugar as if you are making regular glacé icing.

■ 227 g / 8 oz cooking apples ■ 28 g / 1 oz caster sugar ■ 1 tablespoon water
■ 1 rounded tablespoon golden syrup ■ 1 rounded tablespoon black treacle ■ 85 g / 3 oz butter
■ 57 g / 2 oz light soft brown sugar ■ 1 egg ■ 227 g / 8 oz self-raising flour, sifted
■ 1 teaspoon ground ginger ■ ½ teaspoon cinnamon

First prepare the apples: peel, cut into chunks and cook with the caster sugar and water until just tender. Drain really well and mash to a purée. Allow to cool. Pre-heat the oven to 180°C/350°F/Gas mark 4.

Melt the syrup, treacle, butter and brown sugar in a heavy-based pan. Beat in the egg, followed by the apple purée. Finally, slowly fold in the flour and spices with a wooden spoon.

Spoon the mixture into a base-lined, buttered 454 g/1 lb loaf tin and smooth the top. Place on a baking tray – just in case the mixture spills over the top as it rises.

Bake in the oven for about 45 minutes, or until a skewer inserted into the middle comes out clean. Remove from the oven and place the tin on a wire rack to cool completely. Only ice when completely cold. ❄

BOILED FRUIT CAKE

Makes 1 loaf

This is a moist fruit cake which is very quick indeed to make. Although it is good freshly-baked (cold, not warm), served in thick slices, it is also excellent if kept for several days and served in thinner slices, thickly buttered.

- 284 g / 10 oz mixed dried fruit (e.g. sultanas, raisins and currants) ■ 142 g / 5 oz soft light brown sugar
- 113 g / 4 oz butter ■ 227 ml / 8 fl oz cold water ■ 2 teaspoons mixed spice
- 227 g / 8 oz self-raising flour, sifted

Combine the fruit, sugar, butter, water and spice in a saucepan. Warm over a low heat until the butter has melted, then bring to the boil. The moment the bubbles appear, remove from the heat and allow to cool.

Now pre-heat the oven to 180°C/350°F/Gas mark 4.

Once the mixture is completely cold, carefully fold in the sifted flour. Pour into a buttered, base-lined 907 g / 2 lb loaf tin.

Bake in the oven for about 1 hour, or until a skewer inserted into the middle comes out clean.

Leave the cake to cool completely in the tin, before turning out on to a wire rack.

BLACK BUN

Makes 1 bun

Traditionally served at Hogmanay – New Year's Eve – in Scotland, this is the cake which fortified revellers as they went 'first-footing' from one house to the next. Alongside a plate of shortbread, a cherry cake and wedges of Cheddar cheese, black bun served to soak up the drams of whisky proffered at each household. It is a rich, dense cake enclosed in a pastry case, although in former times it was wrapped in a thin casing of bread dough rather than shortcrust pastry. An indication of how wickedly rich it is is suggested by this evocative quotation from Scottish writer F. Marion McNeill's book *The Scots Kitchen*, first published in 1929:

'Fierce raisin-devils and gay currant-sprites
Hold lightsome leap-frog in a pastry hell.'
(Augustus Bejant, *Invocation to Black Bun*)

I prefer to think the last word should be 'shell' – rather than hell – but I suppose it depends how well you make your pastry!

I have altered the traditional recipe a little. First of all, the 'hellish' pastry is lightened by the addition of grated lemon zest and juice. Also, I have added more nuts – simply because I love nuts! Finally, although blanched almonds are found in most recipes, I use whole (unblanched) almonds which retain their white colour better during baking. Once you have rolled out the pastry case and fitted it snugly into the baking tin, make sure you dampen the edges well so that the lid sticks fast. Otherwise, it might separate from the base and expose the dark, fruity innards.

It is often recommended that black bun be made several months in advance, to allow it to mature, but I prefer to eat it about 2 weeks after baking. Unlike rich fruit or Christmas cake, which can be generously doused with brandy or rum to keep the texture moist, this cannot be done with black bun because of its pastry casing. I find that it dries up somewhat after a couple of months, and requires more than just one wee dram to help it down! So, to enjoy it at its rich, succulent best, I advise waiting for no longer than 2 weeks. Once cut into, however, it will keep well for several weeks.

PASTRY

- 284g / 10oz plain flour, sifted ■ ½ teaspoon baking powder ■ 142g / 5oz unsalted butter, cut into cubes
- the grated zest and juice of 1 lemon ■ 3–4 tablespoons cold water ■ beaten egg, to glaze

FILLING

- 454g / 1lb raisins ■ 567g / 1¼ lb currants ■ 113g / 4oz whole almonds, roughly chopped
- 57g / 2oz walnuts, roughly chopped ■ 142g / 5oz plain flour, sifted ■ 85g / 3oz caster sugar
- 1 teaspoon ground allspice ■ 1 teaspoon ground ginger ■ 1 teaspoon ground cinnamon
- ½ teaspoon cream of tartar ■ ½ teaspoon baking powder ■ 2 tablespoons whisky ■ 4 tablespoons milk

First make the pastry. Sift the flour and baking powder into a bowl, rub in the butter, then stir in the grated lemon zest. Add the lemon juice and enough cold water to combine to a stiff dough. Turn on to a lightly floured board and roll out thinly. Use two-thirds of the pastry to line a 23 cm/9 in square buttered cake tin. Roll out the remaining pastry for the lid and set aside. Pre-heat the oven to 140°C/275°F/Gas mark 1.

For the filling, mix everything – except the whisky and milk – in a large bowl. (I find it easiest to do this with my hands.) Once it is really well combined, stir in the whisky and sufficient milk to moisten the mixture. Turn into the pastry case, pressing down well.

Dampen the edges of the pastry all round and place the rolled-out pastry lid on top. Press the edges together to seal, then cut off any remaining pastry. Prick all over with a fork. Then, using a very thin skewer, prick right through to the bottom of the tin – about 6–8 pricks altogether. Finally, brush all over with beaten egg. (If the egg blocks the fork marks, re-prick a little.)

Bake in the oven for 2–2¼ hours, or until golden brown on top. Re-glaze after 1 hour of baking with any remaining egg.

Allow to cool in the tin for at least 2 hours before transferring to a wire rack to cool completely. Wrap in foil and store for 2–3 months, or eat after a few days' maturing. ❊

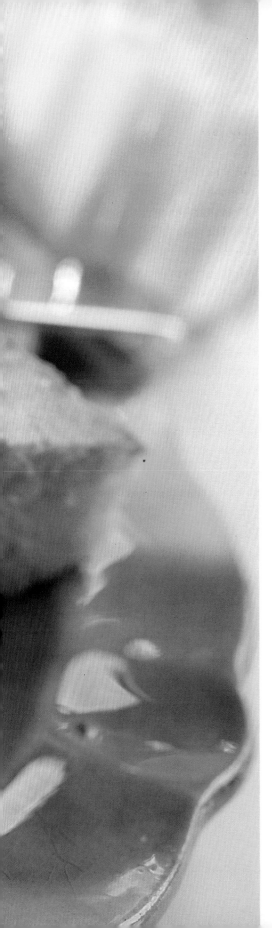

LEMON CURD POLENTA CAKE

Makes 16 small squares

The texture of this lovely yellow cake is
slightly rough, from the polenta, and
the flavour is tangy, from the lemon curd. There
is also a good background hint of olive
oil. Use a fruity oil, not a peppery one, and
make sure it is extra-virgin.
This cake is good served cold with a cup of tea,
or still barely warm, as dessert, with
some whipped cream flavoured with a spoonful
of the fresh lemon curd (see page 88).

- 85 g / 3 oz fine polenta
- 142 g / 5 oz self-raising flour, sifted
- ¼ teaspoon baking powder ■ a pinch of salt
- 113 g / 4 oz caster sugar ■ 3 eggs
- 3 tablespoons extra-virgin olive oil
- 3 tablespoons fresh lemon curd

Pre-heat the oven to 200°C/400°F/Gas mark 6.
Place the polenta, flour and baking powder in
a bowl with the salt and sugar. Stir well to
combine.

Whisk together the eggs and oil until thick,
then add to the bowl with the lemon curd. Fold
everything together using a gentle stirring
action, until thoroughly combined. Spoon into a
buttered 18 cm/7 in square tin.

Bake in the pre-heated oven for 10 minutes,
then lower the heat to 180°C/350°F/Gas mark
4 and cook for a further 15 minutes. Transfer to a
wire rack to cool, before cutting into squares. ❄

LEMON CURD POLENTA CAKE

LEMON CURD

Makes approximately 4 × 454g/1lb jars

Lemon curd is one of those things I feel passionately about, yet I only really enjoy eating it thinly smeared on bread. As a cooking medium, however, I find it useful and versatile.

There is quite simply no alternative to home-made lemon curd. Most commercial brands seem to contain additives and emulsifiers, to give them a longer shelf-life. The result is a texture that is thicker and more cloying and a taste that is far less tangy and buttery.

You can use this basic recipe with lime – to make lime curd, which is even more tangy and sharp – but you will need an extra couple of limes, as they are much smaller than lemons.

Once you have made the curd, it should keep in your refrigerator, tightly sealed, for at least 6 weeks. Use on hot toast, muffins or crumpets; dollop on to hot, sweet pancakes or waffles; spread on to slices of brioche or panettone to make a rich, lemony bread and butter pudding; or whisk into whipped cream or thick yoghurt as a delicious filler for meringues or sponge cakes. Or try the most simple lemon tart of all, by spreading lemon curd on to a part-baked sweet shortcrust pastry base and finishing in the oven.

The following method is for the microwave, but if you prefer to do this in the old-fashioned (albeit more time-consuming) way, then simply place everything in a double boiler and cook until thick, stirring constantly.

Always make sure you scrub your lemons really well before using: even if you use unwaxed lemons (which I recommend), you should wash them first.

■ 227 g / 8 oz unsalted butter ■ 454 g / 1 lb granulated sugar ■ 341 ml / 12 fl oz freshly squeezed lemon juice ■ the grated zest of 6 large lemons ■ 6 eggs, beaten

Place the butter, sugar, lemon juice and zest in a large microwave bowl. Cook, uncovered, on High, for about 4–5 minutes, stirring every minute. When the butter has melted completely, remove from the microwave and allow to cool for about 2 minutes.

Now strain the eggs into the bowl using a fine plastic sieve, whisking all the time.

Return the bowl to the microwave and cook on High for a further 6–8 minutes, whisking vigorously every minute. When the curd has thickened, remove from the microwave. (The curd should be the consistency of lightly whipped cream – it will thicken up further on cooling.)

Pour at once into warmed, sterilised jars. Tap the base of the jars to level the surface and remove any air bubbles. Then wipe the tops of the jars and allow to cool. Cover when completely cold and store in the refrigerator.

Only seal jars of lemon curd when the contents are completely cold.

MADEIRA CAKE

Makes 1 cake

During the 19th century, this cake was served with a glass of Madeira or another of the sweet wines that were popular in those days. Although now it is more likely to be eaten with a cup of tea, it really is to be recommended with a glass of Madeira.

This is one of the simplest of cakes to make. Like all simple foods, it should be made with the best ingredients – only good unsalted butter will do. I suggest you use unwaxed lemons for any recipe requiring grated lemon zest. Madeira cake is very similar to popular cakes in America and France. Although the French 'quatre-quarts' and American pound cake each require a pound of sugar, butter, flour and eggs, the resulting tastes are reminiscent of our Madeira cake. Personally, I prefer the light citrus tang given by the addition of lemon in Madeira cake. Another traditional feature of Madeira cake is the thin slices of candied lemon peel that are placed on top of the cake about 20 minutes before it is removed from the oven.

■ 113 g / 4 oz unsalted butter, softened ■ 113 g / 4 oz caster sugar ■ the grated zest of 1 lemon
■ 198 g / 7 oz self-raising flour, sifted ■ 2 eggs, beaten ■ thinly sliced candied lemon peel

Pre-heat the oven to 160°C/325°F/Gas mark 3. Cream the butter and sugar together until light and fluffy, then beat in the lemon zest.

Stir in the flour and eggs, alternately, a little at a time. Beat thoroughly to ensure everything is well-mixed.

Spoon into a buttered, base-lined 454 g/1 lb loaf tin.

Bake in the oven for 40 minutes, then place 2 thin strips of lemon peel on top (avoid removing the cake from the oven – watch you don't burn your hands) and bake in the oven for a further 20 minutes.

Transfer to a wire rack and allow to cool in the tin for at least 20 minutes before turning out. Slice only when completely cold. ❄

Test if a cake is ready by inserting a wooden skewer (or cocktail stick) into the centre. If any of the soft cake mixture adheres, it is not yet ready.

SEED CAKE

Makes 1 cake

Seed cake is an old-fashioned English cake that has been around for quite some time. It was traditionally flavoured with caraway seeds. Jill Norman, in her excellent *The Complete Book of Spices*, quotes 17th-century herbalist John Parkinson as writing about caraway: 'the seed is much used to be put . . . into bread, cakes etc. to give them a relish.'

Caraway was also widely used to make 'comfits' – caraway seeds coated in sugar and served as an aid to digestion. But I confess I am not a great fan of the aromatic, yet faintly bitter taste of caraway, so I prefer to use fennel seeds, which, with their warm, slightly aniseed flavour, make for an altogether more fragrant cake flavouring. The Italians use fennel seeds as a flavouring in a range of foods from wild boar sausages to heady alcoholic drinks. Fennel seeds were used in Roman times, too, both medicinally and in the kitchen.

My recipe has the basic flavour of a typical Tuscan 'Torta al Finocchio', but the basic idea is pure English. I have added ground almonds to the recipe to make it moist, so do not be afraid that it will taste dry and sandy, as some seed cakes do.

Although this cake works very well with afternoon tea, it can also be served at the end of dinner with a sliver of strong blue cheese, such as Blue Wensleydale or Cashel Blue.

■ 170 g / 6 oz unsalted butter, softened ■ 170 g / 6 oz caster sugar ■ 1 tablespoon fennel seeds
■ 2 large eggs (size 1), separated ■ 170 g / 6 oz self-raising flour, sifted ■ 57 g / 2 oz ground almonds

Pre-heat the oven to 180°C/350°F/Gas mark 4.

Place the butter and sugar in a mixing bowl, and beat together until the mixture is light and creamy. Add the fennel seeds and stir well.

Beat in the egg yolks, one at a time, then fold in the flour and almonds. Whisk the egg whites until stiff, then fold into the mixture: start by folding in one spoonful, then add the rest.

Pour into a buttered 907 g/2 lb loaf tin and bake in the oven for about 50 minutes, or until a skewer inserted into the middle comes out clean. Transfer to a wire rack to cool.

CARDAMOM CHOCOLATE CAKE (page 92)
SEED CAKE

CARDAMOM CHOCOLATE CAKE

Makes 1 cake

Cardamom is often used in spice cake in Scandinavia. Although I have tasted cardamom cake in Denmark, it is in Finland where I have enjoyed it most often. The combination of the fragrant spice with chocolate is a great favourite of mine. As long as you use a good-quality dark chocolate (at least 55 per cent cocoa solids) you will see how beautifully the 2 flavours combine. The chocolate should be cut into chunks – not too large, but certainly far bigger than the tiny commercial chocolate chips found in supermarket packets. This cake tastes good freshly made, but it will keep very well for up to 10 days, if wrapped in foil. Try it with a cup of Arab-style coffee, made by popping a few cardamom pods in the spout of your coffee pot. Make sure you use green cardamom pods for this – they are far superior to white or brown.

■ 142 g / 5 oz unsalted butter ■ 142 g / 5 oz soft light brown sugar ■ 2 eggs, beaten
■ 284 g / 10 oz self-raising flour, sifted ■ 2 tablespoons milk ■ 12 large green cardamom pods
■ 85 g / 3 oz dark chocolate, cut into large chunks

Pre-heat the oven to 180°C / 350°F / Gas mark 4. Cream together the butter and sugar until light and fluffy.

Beat in the eggs, a little at a time, until thoroughly mixed.

Then stir in the flour and milk and beat well – the mixture will be soft, but not too liquid.

Snip open the cardamom pods with a pair of scissors. Tip the seeds into a pestle and mortar and crush. Add the crushed seeds and chocolate chunks to the cake mixture and stir to combine.

Spoon into a buttered 907 g / 2 lb loaf tin and smooth the top.

Bake in the oven for about 1 hour, or until a skewer inserted into the middle of the cake comes out clean.

Leave to cool in the tin for about 15 minutes, then transfer to a wire rack to cool completely.

CHOCOLATE BANANA CAKE

Makes 1 cake

This cake is best eaten freshly baked, but it will keep well for at least a week in an air-tight tin. The addition of bananas ensures that it does not dry out. The crumbly topping – made from oatflakes, flour, sugar and butter – is an unusual addition that not only looks good, but also adds an interesting crunch. Depending on the size of your bananas, some of the cake mixture might spill over the edge of the loaf tin. This is not a problem – the cake will still look wonderful – but make sure you place the tin on another baking tray for easy cleaning! Any spilled bits are, of course, the cook's perks!

CAKE

■ 170 g / 6 oz butter, softened ■ 170 g / 6 oz soft light brown sugar
■ 85 g / 3 oz dark chocolate (look for one with 50–60 per cent cocoa solids)
■ 284 g / 10 oz self-raising flour ■ a pinch of salt ■ ½ teaspoon bicarbonate of soda
■ 2 large eggs, beaten ■ 2 small bananas, mashed

TOPPING

■ 28 g / 1 oz plain flour ■ 28 g / 1 oz oatflakes ■ 28 g / 1 oz demerara sugar
■ 1½ tablespoons sunflower oil

Pre-heat the oven to 160°C/325°F/Gas mark 3. Place the butter and sugar in a saucepan and set over a low heat until the butter has melted. Then add the chocolate and melt that too. Remove from the heat and sift in the flour, salt and bicarbonate of soda. Mix well together.

Beat in the eggs and fold in the mashed bananas. Turn into a buttered 1 kg/2 lb loaf tin. For the topping, mix together the flour, oats and sugar, then stir in the oil. Spoon gently over the cake.

Bake in the oven for about 1 hour 10 minutes, or until a skewer inserted into the middle comes out clean. Allow to cool in the tin for 30–45 minutes, then loosen the edges and transfer to a wire rack to cool. If some of the topping falls off, simply press it back on top. Allow to cool completely before cutting.

PAIN D'ÉPICE

Makes 1 loaf

Like gingerbreads in Britain, there are a multitude of different recipes throughout France for this spiced bread. Honey is an integral part of this bread, so it is generally found in areas that produce lots of honey. I have tried it in Provence and also in Normandy.

The texture of pain d'épice comes as rather a shock to those brought up on sticky, moist gingerbreads. The texture tends to be drier – in fact too dry in some cases – and altogether much lighter, as there is no fat in it at all. Although it keeps well, I like to serve it freshly-baked and warm with the most exotic of sauces – White Chocolate and Basil Sauce (see next recipe).

For the flavouring, the French use anise, a ground spice available only from chemists. Anise is not only the main flavouring in popular French drinks such as Pernod and Ricard (both types of 'pastis'), it was also one of the prime constituents in that muse of Parisian poets and artists at the turn of the century, absinthe. The favourite drink of such poets as Baudelaire, Verlaine and Rimbaud, and artists such as Van Gogh, Manet and Toulouse-Lautrec, anise reached its heyday in 1905 when the French consumed more than 2 million litres of absinthe a year! It was banned by the French government in 1915 – after being lobbied by temperance groups and wine makers – because it caused madness and death.

French recipes for pain d'épice usually call for a teaspoon of anise and sometimes orange or lemon zest for flavouring. I prefer to use a tablespoon of Pernod and warm spices such as cinnamon and ginger. A couple of pinches of ground caraway and fennel seeds reinforce the aniseed taste.

■ 113 g / 4 oz thick honey ■ 142 g / 5 oz soft dark brown sugar ■ 1 teaspoon ground cinnamon
■ 1 teaspoon ground ginger ■ 99 ml / 3½ fl oz boiling water ■ 1 tablespoon Pernod
■ 255 g / 9 oz plain flour ■ 1 rounded teaspoon bicarbonate of soda ■ 1 egg

Pre-heat the oven to 150°C/300°F/Gas mark 2. Place the honey, sugar, cinnamon and ginger in a bowl. Pour over the boiling water and Pernod and, using a wooden spoon, beat until the honey has melted.

Sift in the flour and bicarbonate of soda, then add the egg. Beat again until the ingredients are thoroughly combined.

Pour into a well-buttered 907 g / 2 lb loaf tin.

Bake in the oven for 60–75 minutes, or until a skewer inserted into the middle comes out clean. If necessary, cover with foil towards the ends of cooking to prevent the top from burning.

Set on a wire rack and allow to cool in the tin for at least 30 minutes before turning out.

Either eat cold, in slices, accompanied by a glass of cider, or serve warm with a drizzle of White Chocolate and Basil Sauce (page 96). ❋

PAIN D'ÉPICE WITH WHITE CHOCOLATE AND BASIL

WHITE CHOCOLATE AND BASIL SAUCE

This sauce is very versatile, and is especially good with any bitter chocolate recipe. Primarily it is to be served with the previous recipe – Pain d'Épice. The sweetness of the white chocolate and the exotic, aromatic, yet undeniably sweet flavour of the basil enhance the sweet aniseed flavour of the bread. Served for dessert, this sauce will certainly get you marks for originality.

I first saw this unusual sauce in a menu at The Herbfarm restaurant in Fall City, Washington. This much-acclaimed restaurant, with a well-stocked herb garden, specialises in herb cookery.

■ 142 ml / ¼ pint double cream ■ 14 g / ½ oz fresh basil leaves ■ 113 g / 4 oz best white chocolate

In a small heavy-based saucepan, bring the cream slowly to the boil. Add the basil leaves, stir well and cover tightly. Remove from the heat and allow the basil to infuse for 10 minutes. (Do not leave it for more than 15 minutes or the flavour will be too strong.)

Strain the cream through a sieve into another, clean saucepan. Using the back of a spoon, press down on the basil in the sieve to release all the flavour. Discard the leaves.

Roughly chop the chocolate and add to the pan. Return to a very low heat and cook slowly for 2 minutes, or until the chocolate is melted. Remove from the heat, cover and allow to stand for about 10 minutes.

Whisk the sauce, then serve warm.

To recognise quality white chocolate, scrutinise the label. Cocoa butter should be high on the list. (Some inferior brands use vegetable oil instead of cocoa butter.) Also look at the colour: it should be ivory, not white.

CIDER CAKE

Makes 1 cake

This cake is based on an old English recipe. The characteristic flavourings are grated nutmeg and cider. Jane Grigson, in her book *English Food*, also adds Calvados (apple brandy) to her cider cake.

I prefer a delicate hint of cider, without the reinforcement of a stronger alcohol. You should use one with a good strong flavour – I prefer to use medium-sweet for cooking. Try a natural cider, made without any yeast, for really good results.

■ 113 g / 4 oz unsalted butter, softened ■ 113 g / 4 oz caster sugar ■ 2 eggs
■ 227 g / 8 oz self-raising flour ■ ½ teaspoon grated nutmeg ■ 114 ml / 4 fl oz cider

Pre-heat the oven to 180°C/350°F/Gas mark 4. Beat together the softened butter and sugar until light and fluffy, then gradually beat in the eggs, one at a time.

Now sift in the flour and nutmeg and fold gently together.

Add the cider and stir gently to combine.

Spoon into a buttered 18 cm/7 in square cake tin and bake in the oven for 30–35 minutes, or until well-risen and springy to the touch.

Transfer to a wire rack to cool, then cut into squares. ❄

SOMERSET APPLE CAKE

Makes 1 cake

Somerset, Dorset and Kent all have traditional apple cake recipes. This one is more or less a combination of all 3, but is most like the one found in Somerset. Only the addition of black treacle makes it different – this imparts not only a rich caramel taste, but also a good dark colour. I like to serve the cake warm with Greek yoghurt or thick cream.

■ 170 g / 6 oz unsalted butter, softened ■ 170 g / 6 oz soft light brown sugar ■ 3 eggs, beaten
■ 1 tablespoon black treacle ■ 227 g / 8 oz self-raising wholemeal flour ■ 113 g / 4 oz self-raising flour
■ 1 teaspoon mixed spice ■ 1 teaspoon ground cinnamon ■ 680 g / 1½ lb cooking apples, peeled
■ about 3 tablespoons milk ■ caster sugar, to dust

Pre-heat the oven to 160°C/325°F/Gas mark 3. Cream the butter and sugar together until light and fluffy. Beat in the eggs, a little at a time, with the black treacle.

Sift the flours and spices into a bowl and stir well. Cut the apples into chunks and add to the mixture, with just enough milk to combine

to a soft, dropping consistency. Turn into a base-lined, greased, loose-bottomed 24 cm/9½ in cake tin.

Bake in the oven for about 1¼ hours, or until a skewer inserted into the middle comes out clean.

Sprinkle with caster sugar, then set on a wire rack. Allow to cool in the tin. Serve warm. ❄

ICE-CREAM MERINGUE CAKE

Makes 1 cake
Serves up to 10 people for dessert

This is not really a cake, but a dessert which can be made well in advance and kept in the freezer until required. The base is made from chocolate digestive biscuits and the filling is vanilla ice-cream. This is topped with meringue, baked briefly in a very hot oven, then placed in the freezer until about 30 minutes before it is ready to be eaten. It is important to cool down the meringue very quickly after baking or the ice-cream is liable to melt completely. I usually put the dish in the coldest place in the house until barely warm, then transfer it to the refrigerator to cool. Only when it is completely cold, can it go into the freezer.

Serve this cake in slices, accompanied by Hot Chocolate Fudge Sauce.

BASE
■ 170 g / 6 oz milk chocolate digestive biscuits ■ 57 g / 2 oz butter, melted

FILLING AND TOPPING
■ 994 ml / 1¾ pints quality vanilla ice-cream ■ 2 egg whites ■ 71 g / 2½ oz caster sugar

HOT CHOCOLATE FUDGE SAUCE
■ 99 g / 3½ oz dark chocolate ■ 85 g / 3 oz unsalted butter ■ 85 g / 3 oz soft light brown sugar
■ 1 tablespoon cocoa powder ■ 142 ml / ¼ pint double cream

To make the base, crush the biscuits into crumbs, then stir into the melted butter and combine well.

Press into a 20 cm / 8 in buttered flan tin. Chill for at least 1 hour. Pre-heat the oven to 230°C / 450°F / Gas mark 8.

Soften the ice-cream very slightly, then spoon into the biscuit base: using 2 spoons dipped in hot water, first cover the base, then pile it up high. Leave a biscuit border around the edge. Set in the freezer to firm up again.

To make the meringue topping, whisk the egg whites until stiff, then gradually whisk in the sugar until thick and glossy. Now spoon the meringue over the ice-cream, taking care to cover the edges completely.

Bake on a low shelf in the oven for 4 minutes, or until golden brown. Watch very carefully, as the topping might burn.

Set in a cold room to cool. Once cold, place in the freezer.

Remove from the freezer well before serving – allow 15 minutes at room temperature or 30–40 minutes in the refrigerator.

To make the sauce, melt the chocolate and butter in a double boiler – that is, in a bowl over a pan of simmering water. Add the sugar and cocoa, then whisk in the cream. Continue cooking over a low heat for about 20 minutes, or until thick and piping hot.

To serve, cut the meringue cake into wedges and pour over the hot chocolate sauce. ✳

GINGERBREAD ICE-CREAM

Serves 6

Like the Hot Gingerbread Pudding (page 81), this is a recipe that uses up left-over gingerbread. For the Hot Pudding you can use really stale gingerbread, but for this one I recommend you use one that is no more than 1 week old. Use a nice moist one, though, with bags of dark flavour and colour. Although I always use an ice-cream machine, it is easy to make it without one. Simply pour the cooled custard into a freezer container with a lid. Freeze for 2 hours, then whisk. Repeat every hour, or until frozen.
This ice-cream is delicious served on its own – or with crunchy lemon-spiked shortbread. It is also very good served with the White Chocolate and Basil Sauce on page 96, or scooped alongside a plate of poached pears.

■ 284 ml / ½ pint full milk ■ 142 ml / ¼ pint double cream ■ 4 egg yolks ■ 113 g / 4 oz caster sugar
■ 113 g / 4 oz gingerbread, cut into cubes

Place the milk and cream in a heavy-based saucepan and bring to the boil over a gentle heat. Remove from the heat immediately the bubbles appear.

Meanwhile, whisk together the egg yolks and sugar until pale and creamy.

Add the cubed gingerbread to the saucepan and stir to combine. The gingerbread will almost dissolve in the cream.

Once the gingerbread has soaked up all the liquid, slowly pour into the yolk and sugar mixture. Whisk well until thoroughly combined.

Return to the pan and cook over a low heat for about 5 minutes, or until it thickens slightly. Stir often.

Pour into a jug and cover tightly with clingfilm. Allow to cool completely.

Remove the clingfilm and pour into an ice-cream machine. Churn until frozen. Remove ice-cream from the freezer at least 30 minutes before serving.

Another excellent – and delicious – way to use up stale gingerbread is to cut into thick slices and place on an oven tray. Pour over just enough ginger syrup – from a jar of stem ginger – to lightly soak, then reheat in a medium oven until hot. Serve for pudding with clotted cream.

SCONES

We all know that fresh scones with clotted cream and home-made strawberry jam make for a splendidly wicked cream tea. And how very British it sounds. But scones should not merely sit imperiously on the cake stand. Why not serve cheese scones with soup, salami scones with salad or olive oil scones with a glass or two of red wine? Read on, and feast your eyes.

CRANBERRY SCONE ROUND

Makes 1 round or 8 wedges

This is a light-textured large scone round with an extremely pleasant tart cranberry flavour. You can add a handful of dried fruit – raisins, sultanas or currants – if you wish, to provide a contrasting sweet flavour. It is important when making the scones not to crush the cranberries; they should be left intact, rather like the currants or sultanas in fruit scones. Do not cook them for more than about 2 minutes and be very gentle when you mix them into the scone dough. I usually mix everything together with the back of a knife, then knead the dough lightly with my hands for a minute or so before placing it on the baking sheet. You can then gently flatten the top to form the round shape.

■ 113 g / 4 oz cranberries ■ 85 g / 3 oz caster sugar ■ 1 tablespoon water
■ 227 g / 8 oz self-raising flour ■ 1 teaspoon cream of tartar ■ ½ teaspoon bicarbonate of soda
■ 57 g / 2 oz butter, cut into cubes ■ 4 tablespoons milk

Pre-heat the oven to 200°C/400°F/Gas mark 6. Place the cranberries and 57 g/2 oz of the sugar in a small saucepan with the water. Bring very slowly to the boil, uncovered, stirring occasionally. Once they start to boil, lower the heat and cook for about 2 minutes, or until the skins start to split. Remove from the heat immediately and drain through a sieve, discarding the liquid.

Sift the flour, cream of tartar and bicarbonate of soda into a bowl. Then rub in the butter, until the mixture resembles breadcrumbs. Stir in the remaining sugar.

Gently stir in the cranberries with the back of a knife. Add the milk and carefully mix to a dough, ensuring the cranberries remain whole.

Bring everything together with your hands and turn on to a lightly floured board. Knead very lightly for a minute or so, just to smooth away any cracks.

Place on a buttered baking sheet and press into a round shape, about 20 cm/8 in in diameter. With the tip of a sharp knife, score the scone round into 8, then lightly dust with flour.

Bake in the oven for about 20 minutes, or until well-risen and golden brown.

Transfer to a wire rack to cool for at least 20 minutes before splitting into wedges and spreading with butter.

❊ Warm through before serving.

When making scones, use the lightest touch possible; if you're in a bad mood, make bread instead!

TREACLE SCONES

Makes 6–8 scones

I am aware this is a personal foible, but I have always loved anything to do with treacle – real black treacle, that is – not golden syrup, which is so often confused with treacle. Treacle tart or treacle sponge are made from golden syrup – not rich, dark, glossy, black treacle. In Scotland, we are well acquainted with real treacle. This is used at Hallowe'en for 'treacle scones'. Large, plain scones are hung by string to a clothes line (preferably over sheets of newspaper, as you will see). Just before the start of the game, each scone is daubed with black treacle. A line of children approaches, hands tied behind their backs, and each one stands under a scone so it is just at chin level. The aim is for the child to eat as much of the scone as possible, without it breaking. The result – you will have guessed – is the most enormous black sticky mess. But luckily the next game is always 'dooking for apples' in a bowl of water, which washes off the treacle from their faces. Apart from these, we always had treacle scones – the real things, not Hallowe'en impersonators – throughout the year. These are scones flavoured with a little treacle, which imparts a dark rich flavour and colour. This is the recipe here. Although most recipes require a mixture of plain flour, bicarbonate of soda and cream of tartar, I have adapted mine to suit modern tastes by substituting self-raising flour. The secret of good scone-making is to handle the dough very lightly and for a minimum of time. Ignore those scone recipes which call for 2 minute kneading. The result will be tough and leathery, not light and airy.

■ 57 g / 2 oz unsalted butter ■ 1 heaped tablespoon black treacle ■ 227 g / 8 oz self-raising flour
■ a pinch of salt ■ ½ teaspoon ground ginger ■ ½ teaspoon mixed spice
■ approximately 57–71 ml / 2–2½ fl oz milk

Pre-heat the oven to 220°C/425°F/Gas mark 7. Warm the butter and treacle in a small pan over a low heat until just melted. Remove from the heat and allow to cool for about 5 minutes.

Sift the flour, salt and spices into a mixing bowl. Make a well in the centre, then pour in the treacle and butter mixture, together with just enough milk to combine to a softish dough. (Start with about 3 tablespoons.)

Bring the dough together with your hands, handling it gently with a very light touch. Roll out (with your hands, not a rolling pin) to a thickness of about 2 cm/¾ in, kneading it very gently if there are any cracks.

Using a round scone or pastry cutter, cut out 6–8 scones and place them on a lightly greased baking tray.

Bake in the middle of the oven for 9–10 minutes, or until well-risen.

Transfer at once to a wire rack and allow to cool for at least 15 minutes before splitting. Serve with a little butter. ❋

RUM, RAISIN AND RYE SCONE RING

Makes 1 scone ring or 8–9 scones

This might sound rather an incongruous combination for a scone, but the raisins soaked in rum add a real depth of flavour to these light rye scones. I like to form them into a ring by placing the 8–9 scones side by side on the baking tray. They are nicely spiced with cinnamon and slightly sweet, so I like to serve them not only with butter, but also with a little honey.

The idea for rye scones comes from a Russian recipe for 'Rye Bulochki', which are yeast-raised rolls with a texture somewhere between bread and scone. I have also enjoyed savoury rye buns and scones in Finland. I like to add sugar and spice to my recipe, since they lighten the earthy flavour of the rye flour.

■ 57 g / 2 oz raisins ■ 1 tablespoon dark rum ■ 85 g / 3 oz rye flour
■ 142 g / 5 oz self-raising flour, sifted ■ ½ teaspoon salt ■ ½ teaspoon baking powder
■ 28 g / 1 oz caster sugar ■ ½ teaspoon ground cinnamon ■ 43 g / 1½ oz butter, cut into cubes
■ 1 egg, beaten ■ 3 tablespoons milk ■ beaten egg white, to glaze

First soak the raisins in the rum for at least 2 hours. Pre-heat the oven to 220°C/425°F/Gas mark 7.

Combine the flours, salt, baking powder, sugar and cinnamon in a bowl. Rub in the butter, then stir in the raisins and the rum. Now stir in the egg and enough milk to combine to a fairly stiff dough.

Press out to a thickness of about 2.5 cm/1 in, then cut out 8–9 scones with a fluted cutter. Set on a baking tray in a ring so that they are just touching. Brush with beaten egg white. Bake in the oven for about 15 minutes, or until golden brown on top.

Serve warm with butter, honey or jam. ❋

HOT COBBLED FRUIT

Serves 5–6

I developed this unbelievably moreish pudding from another of my recipes – Blackcurrant and Mint Slump. This is an American idea whereby the fruit – usually blueberries – sits under blobs of light scone dough. As the dough cooks, it gradually slumps into the fruit.

This Hot Cobbled Fruit recipe is a mixture of the American slump and the good old-fashioned English cobbler. The latter is usually decidedly regimented – in true English fashion – with the scones for the topping positioned neatly in a circle. As the cobbles cook, they join together, but by no means slump – that would be most undignified!

The topping for my Hot Cobbled Fruit recipe spreads slightly, but rather than slumping into the fruit, it manages to amalgamate with the other scones to form a cobbled topping. Under this is a layer of creamy mascarpone cream cheese. As the pudding cooks, the mascarpone also spreads out to form a complete layer on top of the fruit. The result: layers of fruit, then a luscious layer of mascarpone, then a crusty, light, scone-like topping.

For the fruit, I like to combine gooseberries and rhubarb. These are enhanced by orange, which also flavours the scone. Not only do the colours look superb, but the sharp flavours of both fruits work beautifully with the rich mascarpone cheese and sweet scone cobbles.

Do not invite too many guests to join you for lunch when you cook this pudding – you will want seconds yourself, believe me.

FILLING

■ 454 g / 1 lb gooseberries, topped and tailed ■ 113 g / 4 oz granulated sugar ■ 2 oranges
■ 454 g / 1 lb rhubarb, trimmed and chopped ■ 2 teaspoons cornflour
■ 227 g / 8 oz mascarpone cheese ■ 14 g / ½ oz caster sugar

SCONE MIXTURE

■ 170 g / 6 oz self-raising flour ■ 1 teaspoon baking powder ■ 57 g / 2 oz caster sugar
■ the grated zest and juice of 1 large orange ■ 57 g / 2 oz unsalted butter

First cook the fruit: place the gooseberries in a saucepan with half the sugar and the grated zest and juice of 1 orange. Bring to the boil and simmer gently for about 10 minutes, or until just tender. Combine 1 teaspoon cornflour with 2 teaspoons cold water and mix to a paste. Add to the fruit and, stirring all the time, cook for a further 2–3 minutes, or until slightly thickened. Repeat this process with the rhubarb. Pre-heat the oven to 200°C/400°F/Gas mark 6.

Place the gooseberry mixture in a deep, round 20 cm/8 in ovenproof dish. Carefully spoon the rhubarb mixture over the top.

Beat the mascarpone cheese and caster sugar until smooth. Using 2 dessertspoons, spoon 6 blobs of the cream cheese mixture around the outside of the dish to form a circle.

To make the scone mixture, sift the flour and baking powder into a bowl. Stir in the sugar and the zest and juice of the orange. Melt the butter and pour into the centre while still hot. Using a wooden spoon, gently stir everything together quickly and thoroughly. Do not beat.

Using 2 dessertspoons, spoon 6 blobs of the scone mixture on top of the mascarpone blobs. Try to cover them completely, but do not worry if the dough falls down on to the fruit.

Place immediately in the oven and bake for at least 25 minutes, or until the fruit is bubbling around the sides and the mascarpone is oozing out from beneath the well-risen, golden-crusted cobbles. Remove from the oven and allow to cool for 4–5 minutes before serving. No pouring cream is required, since the luscious mascarpone is already there.

If possible, cook this pudding in an ovenproof glass dish, to show the colourful layers of pink and green.

SOUR SKONS

Makes 6 scones

These are a variation on an Orcadian recipe for sour-skons, which are made with a mixture of oatmeal, flour, baking soda, caraway seeds and buttermilk. I have substituted sour cream for the buttermilk to add the essential sourness. I have added only the merest suggestion of sweetness for I think they go well with savoury accompaniments such as a sliver of mature Cheddar or a young, tangy goat's cheese.

■ 170g / 6oz self-raising flour, sifted ■ 57g / 2oz medium oatmeal ■ ½ teaspoon baking powder
■ ½ teaspoon caraway seeds ■ 14g / ½oz caster sugar ■ a pinch of salt
■ 114ml / 4fl oz sour cream ■ 1–2 tablespoons milk

Pre-heat the oven to 220°C/425°F/Gas mark 7. Place the flour, oatmeal, baking powder, caraway seeds, sugar and salt in a large mixing bowl and combine thoroughly.

Make a well in the centre. Gradually pour in the sour cream and milk and combine to a soft – but not sticky – dough.

Turn on to a greased baking tray and shape into a round, about 1 cm / ½ in thick. Mark into 6 pieces, using a knife.

Bake in the oven for about 15 minutes, or until golden brown on top and cooked through.

Cool on a wire rack for at least 10 minutes before serving warm. ❄

OLIVE OIL SCONES

Makes 10 scones

The method of making these scones is certainly not taken from a text book on scone cookery. The dough is mixed together with a wooden spoon and then scooped, by the spoonful, on to the baking tray. The shape, therefore, is not as perfect as for most cut scones, but they have a certain character of their own – haphazard and unrestrained. It is essential to use extra-virgin olive oil – the fruitier the better – so that the olive flavour comes through. The result is a lightly-textured scone which has a marvellous, rich taste of olive oil. Serve these warm with or without butter. I actually like them dunked in olive oil, with a well-dressed tomato and basil salad.

■ 227g / 8oz plain flour ■ 2 teaspoons baking powder ■ ¼ teaspoon salt ■ 4 tablespoons olive oil
■ 1 egg, beaten ■ 114ml / 4floz milk

Pre-heat the oven to 230°C/450°F/Gas mark 8. Sift the flour, baking powder and salt into a mixing bowl.

Make a well in the centre and pour in the olive oil. Using a wooden spoon, mix to a soft dough with the egg and milk. Do not beat.

Using 2 dessertspoons, spoon small amounts of the mixture on to a lightly oiled baking tray.

Bake in the oven for 10–12 minutes, or until golden brown and cooked through.

Cool on a wire rack for at least 5 minutes before serving. ❄

FAT RASCALS

Makes 7–8 scones

Many recipes for these Yorkshire delicacies exist, as do explanations for their name. One can only assume that 'fat' refers to the relatively high fat content, and 'rascal' derives from 'rusk', a little round cake. Here is one example of regional baking that is very much alive and well – and no more so than at Betty's tea-room in Harrogate. Here, fat rascals are 13 cm/5 in across (much larger than average) and decorated with cherry 'eyes' and almond 'teeth' to make a devilish face that suits the name perfectly!

Fat rascals originate from the moorland areas near Whitby, where locals cooked them on griddles over open turf fires and called them 'turf cakes'. Rough and open-textured, they were made at the end of the baking day from left-over bits and pieces, then sprinkled with sugar and dried fruit. Although currants are usually used nowadays, dried bilberries were often used in the past, as bilberries grew in abundance on the moors. I have added dried cherries for this recipe, since I like their flavour. Although lard was traditionally used, I prefer the taste of butter. If you have never eaten a fat rascal, you will find its texture is halfway between a scone and a rock bun. That is why I like to serve them straight from the oven, without butter – rock bun style. If allowed to go cold, I split them and serve with plenty of butter – scone-style.

■ 227 g / 8 oz plain flour ■ 1 heaped teaspoon baking powder ■ a pinch of salt
■ 85 g / 3 oz butter, cut into cubes ■ 28 g / 1 oz caster sugar
■ 57 g / 2 oz dried cherries (or currants) ■ 114–128 ml / 4–4½ fl oz milk

Pre-heat the oven to 200°C/400°F/Gas mark 6. Sift the flour, baking powder and salt into a bowl. Rub in the butter.

Stir in the sugar and dried fruit.

Add enough milk to combine to a soft dough. Then, using floured hands, bring the dough together and turn on to a floured board. Roll out to a thickness of about 1 cm/½ in – I prefer to simply press the dough flat with my hands. Using a large cutter, cut out the scones into rounds 6–8 cm/2½–3 in across.

Set on a buttered baking sheet and bake in the oven for 12–15 minutes, or until well-risen and golden brown. ❄

SQUASH SCONES

Makes 8 large scones

No, these are not squashed scones, but scones flavoured with a member of the squash family. In this recipe I stipulate butternut squash, now available for most of the year, but you can use acorn squash, or even pumpkin during its short autumn season. The many Australian recipes for squash scones and breads advocate grating the raw flesh into the dough. When I make bread, I like to use it raw because the grated flecks of orange look so attractive. For these scones, however, I cook the squash first, then mash it. It is very important to drain it well. The other flavouring is ginger, which works well with all close relatives of the squash family. Indeed, the spices in that American classic, pumpkin pie, usually include ginger and cinnamon.

The easiest way to peel butternut squash is to stand it on its wide end, then cut across the middle. Use the seedless top (narrow) end; after peeling, it should yield a little over 227 g/8 oz flesh – just sufficient for this recipe. Use the bottom end in soup, made with chicken stock, onions, potatoes and a hint of either ground coriander, ginger or cumin.

You will find the dough for this recipe is very soft indeed, so do not even attempt to knead it. Simply press gently into the thickness you require and cut with a scone cutter. Once baked, the scones should have a glorious orange colour, a subtle ginger flavour and a soft, light texture.

■ 227 g / 8 oz peeled butternut squash, cut into cubes ■ 227 g / 8 oz self-raising flour
■ 2 teaspoons baking powder ■ 1 heaped teaspoon ground ginger
■ 57 g / 2 oz unsalted butter, cut into cubes ■ 57 g / 2 oz caster sugar ■ 2–3 tablespoons milk

Pre-heat the oven to 220°C/425°F/Gas mark 7. Place the squash in cold water, bring to the boil and simmer for about 10 minutes, or until tender. Drain, then mash with a potato masher. Drain again, so the mash is not at all soggy.

Sift the flour, baking powder and ginger into a bowl. Rub in the butter until the mixture resembles breadcrumbs.

Stir in the sugar, then the mashed squash. Stir in sufficient milk to make a softish dough. Combine well, but gently, with a wooden spoon.

Turn on to a floured board and press down lightly to a thickness of about 2.5 cm/1 in. Using a large scone cutter (mine is 6 cm/2½ in in diameter), cut out the scones and place on a lightly greased baking tray. (It helps if you flour the scone cutter each time.)

Using a flour shaker, dust with flour, then set in the oven. Bake for about 12–15 minutes, or until well-risen and golden brown.

Transfer at once to a wire tray. Serve warm, with a smear of butter.

YOGHURT AND BRAMBLE SCONES (page 110)
SQUASH SCONES

YOGHURT AND BRAMBLE SCONES

Makes 10–12 scones

These are tangy, crumbly scones that look marvellous speckled with flecks of berries. It is important not to squash the berries into the dough, if at all possible, otherwise you will end up with purple-pink scones, rather than golden scones bulging with whole berries. Known as blackberries in England, brambles have the most intense, fruity taste when collected from the wild. Those which are cultivated and sold at fruit farms are very acceptable substitutes. Cultivated brambles are always larger than wild ones, so if you use them in these scones, you should take even more care not to crush them. Brambles – like raspberries – freeze very well. If you use frozen brambles, make sure you thaw and drain them really well.

When adding the yoghurt to the scone dough, make sure it is at room temperature, and stir it very gently into the flour and butter mixture. The addition of yoghurt produces a similar flavour to traditional scones, when either buttermilk or sour milk was used. The lactic acid from the sour milk combines with the raising agent (baking powder, or bicarbonate of soda and cream of tartar) to make it more effective. There is absolutely no sour flavour from the use of sour milk, buttermilk or yoghurt. It all cooks out to produce a light, airy texture.

■ 227 g / 8 oz plain flour ■ 2½ teaspoons baking powder ■ a pinch of salt ■ 28 g / 1 oz caster sugar
■ 85 g / 3 oz unsalted butter, cut into cubes ■ 85 g / 3 oz brambles (blackberries)
■ 3–4 tablespoons natural yoghurt ■ milk, to glaze

Pre-heat the oven to 220°C/425°F/Gas mark 7. Sift the flour, baking powder and salt into a bowl, then stir in the sugar.

Rub in the butter until the mixture resembles breadcrumbs. Carefully stir in the brambles, taking care not to break or bruise them.

Add the yoghurt, one tablespoon at a time, mixing it in gently with the back of a knife. Once the mixture starts to come together, transfer to a lightly floured board and knead gently for a few seconds to eliminate cracks. Flatten the dough lightly with your hand, then cut into 10–12 rounds.

Set on a buttered baking sheet and brush lightly with milk.

Bake in the oven for 12–15 minutes, or until golden brown. Do not expect these to rise as high as regular scones, for they are different in texture and appearance.

Transfer the scones to a wire rack and allow to cool slightly before splitting open. Serve with unsalted butter.

CHEESE SAUCE SCONES

Makes 8 large scones

The idea for these scones came from Australian food writer Maureen Simpson, whose Cheese Sauce Scones are topped with a thick mixture of butter, cheese and mustard. I developed the concept further by topping regular cheese scones with actual cheese sauce. The result is a nicely flavoured scone coated with a gooey cheese topping which becomes golden brown and crusty on cooling.

When you are making cauliflower cheese or macaroni cheese, make a little extra sauce (you need less than 142 ml/¼ pint for this recipe). Store it in the refrigerator for up to 3 days, then give it a quick stir before using. It should be a thick sauce, not one of pouring consistency.

The scones are delicious freshly-baked, spread with a little butter, served with hot soup in winter or a tossed salad in summer.

SCONES

■ 227 g / 8 oz self-raising flour ■ 1 teaspoon cream of tartar ■ ½ teaspoon bicarbonate of soda
■ ¼ teaspoon mustard powder ■ a pinch of cayenne (optional) ■ ¼ teaspoon salt
■ 57 g / 2 oz unsalted butter, cut into cubes ■ 85 g / 3 oz mature cheddar, grated
■ 142 ml / 5 fl oz milk (sour milk is best)

TOPPING

■ a scant 142 ml / ¼ pint thick cheese sauce

Pre-heat the oven to 220°C/425°F/Gas mark 7. Sift the flour, cream of tartar, bicarbonate of soda, mustard, (cayenne, if using) and salt into a bowl. Rub in the butter, then stir in the grated cheese. Using a knife, stir in the milk, then combine to a soft dough with your hands. Handle the mixture gently – do not knead.

With a light touch, form the dough into a ball, then flatten out to a thickness of about 2.5 cm/1 in. Cut out, using a fairly large scone cutter, and place on a lightly buttered baking tray. Spread a level dessertspoonful of cheese sauce on top of each scone, taking care not to press down too much. Bake in the oven for about 15 minutes, or until the top is golden brown and crusty. Remove the scones to a wire rack and allow to cool for about 5 minutes before splitting and spreading with butter.

When buying Cheddar cheese, always opt for a cloth-bound farmhouse cheese, if possible. Store in the refrigerator, wrapping only the cut edges with clingfilm to allow the cheese to breathe through the rind. Bring to room temperature before eating.

SALAMI AND SAGE SCONES

Makes 8–10 scones

Strange as it might seem to incorporate salami into scones, believe me, it works really well. That is, providing you have good salami. I would suggest one of the Milano salamis or a peppery German one. Try to avoid the bright pink, artificial-looking ones, which are far too greasy. I like the combination of sage with salami, but if you prefer to use another herb, try some finely chopped thyme, oregano or rosemary. Serve these scones warm, with a little butter or a drizzle of olive oil and some sun-dried tomatoes. If you do not have any sour milk, then sour regular milk by adding ½ teaspoon lemon juice to 142 ml / ¼ pint fresh milk. Then leave to stand at room temperature for a couple of hours.

- 170 g / 6 oz self-raising flour ▪ 57 g / 2 oz wholemeal self-raising flour
- ¼ teaspoon salt ▪ 57 g / 2 oz butter, cut into cubes
- approximately 6 large sage leaves (or 1 tablespoon fresh herbs of your choice)
- 28 g / 1 oz salami, thinly sliced then chopped ▪ about 142 ml / ¼ pint sour milk

Pre-heat the oven to 220°C/425°F/Gas mark 7. Sift the flours into a large bowl and stir in the salt. Rub in the butter.

Finely chop the herbs and add to the mixture with the salami.

Pour in enough sour milk to combine to a softish dough.

Handling the mixture very gently, gather together with your hands and turn on to a lightly floured board. Press out gently to a thickness of about 2.5 cm / 1 in, using the palm of your hand – not a rolling pin. Cut into 8–10 rounds with a scone or pastry cutter, then place on a lightly greased baking tray.

Bake in the oven for 12–15 minutes, or until well-risen and lightly brown on top.

Cool for 5–10 minutes on a wire rack before splitting and eating. ❋

All scones taste better warm, but should never be served hot. If allowed to cool, reheat in a loose foil parcel in a low oven.

SALAMI AND SAGE SCONES
LEEK GRANARY SCONES (page 114)

LEEK GRANARY SCONES

Makes 10 scones

Leeks form the rather unusual flavouring of these very tasty savoury scones. I like to combine a little granary flour with regular wheat flour, but you could use half granary to half self-raising flour for a coarser texture. Make sure you cook the leeks really well – until the butter has soaked into the leeks and they are completely soft.
In this recipe, two-thirds of the leeks are worked into the scone mixture and the rest is used as a topping. The topping becomes wonderfully crunchy and golden brown as the scones bake. Serve the scones warm and lightly buttered, with a bowl of soup or salad.

■ 142 g / 5 oz leeks, cleaned and finely sliced ■ 85 g / 3 oz butter
■ 85 g / 3 oz granary flour ■ 142 g / 5 oz self-raising flour, sifted ■ ¾ teaspoon salt
■ 1 teaspoon baking powder ■ 114–142 ml / 4–5 fl oz milk

First cook the leeks in 28 g / 1 oz of the butter: place in a saucepan and set over a low heat for about 15 minutes, or until soft. Allow to cool in the pan. Pre-heat the oven to 220°C / 425°F / Gas mark 7.

Place the flours, salt and baking powder in a bowl and rub in the remaining butter. Add two-thirds of the leek mixture and stir well. Then add just enough milk to combine to a fairly soft – but not sticky – dough.

Gently bring the mixture together with your hands, then place on a floured board. Lightly flatten to a thickness of about 4 cm / 1½ in using the palm of your hand – not a rolling pin. Cut into 10 rounds and place on a lightly buttered baking tray.

Top with the remaining leek mixture, dividing it evenly over all the scones.

Bake in the oven for about 15 minutes, or until well-risen and golden brown.

POTATO SCONE ROUND

Makes 1 scone round or 8–10 wedges

This is a sweet, thick potato scone that is baked in the oven, unlike the thinner griddle potato scones. It is crusty on the outside and nicely soft inside. It is important to mix everything together while the potatoes are still hot. Be sure to weigh your potatoes *after* peeling, not before. You can always add mixed spice instead of the cinnamon if you prefer. Eat warm, either plain, or buttered and topped with a drizzle of golden syrup.

■ 454g / 1 lb peeled potatoes (this is the peeled weight) ■ 57g / 2oz butter, melted
■ 57g / 2oz caster sugar ■ 57g / 2oz raisins ■ a pinch of salt ■ ½ teaspoon ground cinnamon
■ 170g / 6oz self-raising flour, sifted ■ caster sugar, to dust

Pre-heat the oven to 220°C/425°F/Gas mark 7. Cut the potatoes into chunks and boil in unsalted water until tender. Drain well.

Mash with the melted butter, then stir in the sugar, raisins, salt and cinnamon while the potatoes are still hot.

Using a wooden spoon, incorporate the flour a little at a time until you have a stiff dough.

Shape into a round, about 5 cm/2 in thick, with your hands and set on a lightly buttered baking tray. Mark into 8–10 segments and bake in the oven for about 30 minutes, or until golden brown and crusty on top.

Transfer to a wire rack and sprinkle with caster sugar while still hot. Cool for about 10 minutes before eating.

APPLE SCONES

Makes 8 scones

These light-textured, delicately flavoured scones are 'free-form', not neatly cut with a scone cutter.
This is because the mixture is fairly moist, so it is dolloped haphazardly on to the baking
tray just before baking. I like to spread them with a little unsalted butter and the thinnest smear
of fresh lemon or lime curd (see page 88) – not too much or it will overwhelm
the apple and clove taste.

■ 227g / 8oz self-raising flour ■ 1 teaspoon baking powder ■ a pinch of salt ■ a pinch of ground cloves
■ 57g / 2oz unsalted butter, cut into cubes ■ 28g / 1oz caster sugar
■ 113g / 4oz grated dessert apples (peeled, prepared weight) ■ 114ml / 4 floz milk

Pre-heat the oven to 220°C/425°F/Gas mark 7. Sift the flour, baking powder, salt and cloves into a bowl. Rub in the butter until the mixture resembles breadcrumbs.

Stir in the sugar, followed by the grated apple.

Add the milk and stir briefly to combine. Do not overwork.

Using 2 spoons, spoon the mixture on to a buttered baking tray. Bake in the oven for 12–15 minutes, or until well-risen and golden brown.

GRIDDLE COOKERY

This is fast food. If you have no griddle, a heavy-based frying pan will usually do. Simply make up a batter or a dough, slap it on the griddle and hey presto – flat breads, cakes, scones or pancakes ready in a flash. Serve them warm, straight from the griddle, and all you will need is a spread of butter – for the royal slice of bread . . . or muffin, crumpet, crepe or pikelet.

SCOTCH PANCAKES OR DROP SCONES
Makes 20–24 small pancakes

As a child, I took 'pancakes' to mean drop scones. They were small – 'two-bite' size – and served warm with butter and home-made raspberry jam, or with blackcurrant or apple jelly. It is only in Scotland that they are called pancakes. Elsewhere they are called drop scones: which is probably a more apt term, since the batter is dropped from a spoon on to a hot griddle. There is further confusion about vocabulary, however: in Scotland, crumpets are very similar to these drop scones, but the batter is thinned down with extra milk to give a thinner pancake that is soft enough to roll up. Scottish crumpets are rolled around the butter and jam filling just before serving.
Many recipes for drop scones now include self-raising flour, but I find that the old-fashioned method, using plain flour and a mixture of cream of tartar and bicarbonate of soda, is best.
I also add a teaspoon of sugar to the batter, to give a hint of sweetness, although my mother never did.
The trick with griddle pancakes is to make sure the griddle is hot enough before you start cooking. Test by dropping a teaspoon of the batter on to the very lightly buttered surface. It should 'set' almost at once; if it begins to bubble within 1 minute, the griddle is ready.
Once you begin to cook the entire batch, do not attempt to do more than 5 at one go. Otherwise you will be too late turning some and they will become hard and over-browned. Equally, if you have not got the griddle hot enough, the pancakes will be leathery and pale in colour.
Once fairly large bubbles appear on the surface, it is time to turn them over; do this with either a spatula or a palette knife. You can tell when they are cooked because no batter oozes out when you press them gently. Allow 1–2 minutes for each side. Once cooked, wrap the pancakes in a clean tea-towel and keep them warm, before serving.

■ 113g / 4oz plain flour ■ ½ teaspoon cream of tartar ■ ¼ teaspoon bicarbonate of soda
■ a pinch of salt ■ 1 teaspoon caster sugar ■ 1 egg, beaten ■ 142 ml / ¼ pint milk

Sift the first 4 ingredients into a large bowl, then stir in the sugar. Make a well in the middle.

Add the egg and, using a balloon whisk, start beating it in. Gradually pour in the milk, whisking everything together as you do so. Continue whisking until you have a smooth batter. Start heating the griddle (mine takes 3–4 minutes to reach the correct heat).

Using a piece of kitchen paper smeared with butter, very lightly grease the griddle. When it has reached the correct temperature, drop spoonfuls of the batter on to the griddle, spacing them well apart. Use a dessertspoon for 'two-bite' pancakes.

When you see the large bubbles forming, flip them over and cook on the other side for another minute or so, or until just done. Remove and keep warm. Depending on how reliable your griddle is, you might have to grease it in between each batch of pancakes. ✳

FATTY CUTTIES

Makes 8 wedges

These wonderfully named griddle cakes are from Orkney. They are very similar to Northumberland's Singin' Hinnies, which are in turn not dissimilar to Welsh cakes. Fatty Cutties are slightly thinner than the other 2, and are traditionally cut into wedges before cooking. They are the quickest to prepare since, instead of rubbing the fat into the flour, the butter is melted, then poured into the mixture and combined to a stiff dough with your hands.

The origin of the term 'Fatty Cutties' was related to me by Mrs Scott, who now lives in Kirkwall, the capital of Orkney. She says the recipe came from the northerly island of Westray, where she used to live. Many years ago, when people were poorer and there was not much in the way of ingredients to work with, the daily 'bread' was a griddle bannock, made from beremeal (barley flour) and little else. As people became better off, they used plain flour instead of barley and added fat – usually butter – to their griddle cakes. Eventually, they came to be known as Fatty Cutties – because of the fat-enriched content of the cakes and the fact that they were cut into wedges before baking – unlike the beremeal bannock, which was cooked as a large round. Mrs Scott insists they should be as flat as possible, and spread with butter – although I find that when they are freshly made and eaten warm, they need no butter at all. These are still regarded on Orkney as a treat, because of their high fat content.

■ 170 g / 6 oz plain flour ■ ¼ teaspoon bicarbonate of soda ■ 85 g / 3 oz caster sugar
■ 85 g / 3 oz currants ■ 85 g / 3 oz butter, melted ■ approximately 1 tablespoon milk

Sift the flour and bicarbonate of soda into a mixing bowl. Stir in the sugar and currants.

Make a well in the centre and pour in the melted butter with just enough milk to combine to a stiff dough. Add only 1 tablespoon at first and try to bring the mixture together with your hands. If it is still 'bitty', add an extra ½ tablespoon milk.

Knead very lightly and divide into 2. Roll each half into a round, about 5 mm / ¼ in thick. Cut each into 4 wedges.

Pre-heat the griddle to medium-hot. Grease very lightly, then cook the fatty cutties for 3–4 minutes on each side, or until golden brown. Serve warm. ❊

A heavy-based frying pan can be used instead of a griddle for most recipes, although the heat distribution is not as even. You will find it is easier to flip the goods over on a griddle, because it has no sides.

SINGIN' HINNIES

Makes 8–10 wedges

These Northumberland griddle cakes are very tasty indeed. Since most recipes for these cakes contain no sugar at all, they have the added advantage (certainly for me with far too sweet a tooth!) of being less compulsive eating! Quite delicious and wonderfully short in texture, they are, like all griddle cakes, at their best eaten freshly-cooked and still warm. For my recipe, I have suggested cooking the cake whole, as a large round (which just fits snugly on to my griddle). When it comes to turning it, I use a large metal cake slice, then flip the cake over carefully. If you prefer, you can cut it in half or quarters, for more convenient turning.

Some recipes add some ground rice to the basic flour mix, and some require sour milk or cream instead of milk. The end product might vary slightly, but the origin of the recipe remains the same: Singin' Hinnies are so called because as they cook, they sizzle; and as the butter and milk melt, it sounds as if they are singing. 'Hinny' is an affectionate north-eastern name for a woman – used like 'luv', 'hen' or 'duck' in other parts of the country.

Jane Grigson, in her book *English Food*, writes that she remembers eating hot Singin' Hinnies at childhood birthday parties, occasionally with silver sixpenny and threepenny pieces – wrapped in greaseproof paper – tucked inside. Singin' Hinnies were sometimes actual substitutes for birthday cakes: the birthday child was always carefully 'guided' to select the Singin' Hinny that contained the money. Serve these split in half and spread with butter.

■ 227 g / 8 oz plain flour ■ 1 heaped teaspoon baking powder ■ a pinch of salt
■ 57 g / 2 oz butter, cut into cubes ■ 57 g / 2 oz white vegetable fat, cut into cubes
■ 85 g / 3 oz currants ■ approximately 85 ml / 3 fl oz milk

Sift the flour and baking powder into a mixing bowl with the salt.

Rub in the butter and white fat, until the mixture resembles breadcrumbs. Stir in the currants, then add just enough milk to form a stiff dough.

Mix well together, then roll out to a round with a thickness of about 1 cm / ½ in.

Heat the griddle and grease lightly. Cook for 8–10 minutes on each side, or until the cake is a golden brown. Cut into wedges and serve warm, split in half and spread with butter. Keep warm by wrapping loosely in a clean tea-towel. ❋

A well-used griddle should need very little greasing. Use the minimum fat possible with either a new griddle or a heavy frying pan.

POTATO SCONES

Makes 6–8 wedges

Known in Scotland as tattie scones, these are often eaten for breakfast, topped with some crispy fried bacon or even a fried egg. There are many varieties of potato scone. The following recipe is for a thinnish, soft griddle scone, which is quite delicious spread with a little butter and eaten while still warm. They are also excellent toasted on the following day or served with a little mature Cheddar. To make cheesy potato scones, add a little grated cheese to the mix – about 28 g / 1 oz for this amount.

Although they can be cooked in a heavy frying pan, potato scones are best made on a griddle. If you use a frying pan, you have to fry them in about 28 g / 1 oz butter, which makes the resulting flavour far more greasy than it should be. If you do have to resort to a frying pan, I suggest drying them off a little on kitchen paper, then toasting before eating.

It is important that you use freshly cooked potato for this, which must be mixed with the flour while still warm. Try to use a floury potato, such as Maris Piper or King Edward.

■ 1 large potato (about 227 g / 8 oz) ■ 28 g / 1 oz unsalted butter ■ 57 g / 2 oz plain flour
■ ½ teaspoon salt ■ ¼ teaspoon baking powder

Peel the potato and cut into chunks. Cook in boiling water until tender, then drain well. Using a potato masher, mash with the butter. Now weigh it – you should have about 198 g/ 7 oz mashed potato.

Sift the flour, salt and baking powder into a bowl. While the mashed potato is still warm, stir into the flour and combine thoroughly.

Then, using your hands, gently shape into a ball and turn on to a lightly floured board. Roll out with a rolling pin to form a circle, about 5 mm / ¼ in thick.

Cut into wedges – either 6 or 8 – and prick all over with a fork.

Heat a griddle to medium-hot. Using a butter wrapper (or buttered paper towel) grease the surface of the griddle very lightly. Transfer half the potato scones to the griddle with a fish slice.

Cook for 3–4 minutes on each side, or until golden brown and firm. When they are ready, transfer to a wire rack and cool for about 5 minutes. Serve warm, spread with a little butter. (If there are any left, toast on the following day.)

Keep griddle goods and scones warm by wrapping loosely in a clean tea-towel.

OATCAKES

Makes 8 wedges

These are very quick to make – and absolutely delicious spread with a thin smear of butter and some cheese or honey. They can also be served with soused herrings or other oily fish. In Scotland, they used to be served for breakfast with marmalade, and also at tea-time with either milk or tea. The customary shape was a round bannock (the size depending on the size of the griddle), which was marked with a cross before baking. Once these were cut into wedges – either before or after baking – they were called 'farls'.

There are many variations on both the ingredients for oatcakes and the method. Catherine Brown, in her book *Scottish Cookery*, tells how Highlanders prefer a thin, crisp cake made primarily from medium oatmeal, while Lowlanders often add wheat flour and rough pinhead oatmeal to give a good bite. I like to make oatcakes with mostly medium oatmeal, for a fairly rough texture, but I also like to include a little fine oatmeal, for easier handling. The resulting oatcakes are crisp and crumbly. In fact, you must be careful when you transfer them to the pan, or they will crumble. Once they are 'dried out', they are less fragile. My recipe only cooks them on one side, then dries them in the oven, but traditionally the drying process was always carried out in a special toasting rack, or on a toasting stone in front of the fire. I use melted butter for the fat, but if you can obtain either beef dripping or bacon fat – which was traditionally used – the flavour will be even better.

■ 57 g / 2 oz fine oatmeal ■ 170 g / 6 oz medium oatmeal ■ ½ teaspoon salt
■ ¼ teaspoon baking powder ■ 28 g / 1 oz butter, melted ■ 57 ml / 2 fl oz boiling water

Place the first 4 ingredients in a mixing bowl and stir to combine.

Pour in the butter and sufficient boiling water to form a fairly stiff paste (you might need a little more than 57 ml/2 fl oz). Sprinkle some fine oatmeal over a table or board and gently roll out the mixture until it is as thin as possible, without cracking. Dust your hands with the fine oatmeal and shape into a circle with your hands.

Cut into 8 wedges. Pre-heat the oven to 140°C/275°F/Gas mark 1.

Heat the griddle so that it is moderately hot. Using either a butter wrapper or a greased paper towel, rub a thin smear of butter all over the griddle.

Using a large fish slice, carefully transfer 4 of the oatcakes to the griddle and cook for 4–5 minutes on one side only. Once they are a light golden brown underneath, carefully transfer them to a wire rack. Place the rack on a baking tray and set in the oven for about 25 minutes, or until completely dried out.

Serve straight from the oven, or allow to cool and store in a large container filled with oatmeal. (I bury mine in a large box of porridge oats.) Reheat very slightly just before serving.

CRUMPETS

Makes 10–12 crumpets

Butter running down your chin, a roaring fire and a pot of fresh tea . . . the only missing items are the crumpets. The holes in a crumpet mean that once they are buttered (never margarined), the butter sinks into the holes, then gradually all over your plate, fingers and chin. You can either eat them at once, straight from the griddle, or allow them to cool and toast them. Serve plain with butter, or with jam, syrup or anchovy paste (*patum peperium* – the quintessential English gentleman's relish.) The crumpet rings used for shaping the crumpets on the griddle are available from old-fashioned ironmongers or from specialist kitchen shops.

■ 170g / 6oz plain flour ■ 170g / 6oz strong white flour ■ 1 teaspoon salt
■ 14g / ½oz fresh yeast ■ 1 teaspoon caster sugar ■ 341ml / 12floz warm milk
■ ½ teaspoon bicarbonate of soda ■ 3 tablespoons warm water

Sift the flours into a bowl. Add the salt and mix well together, then form a well in the centre.

In a separate bowl, blend the yeast and the sugar with the warm milk. Stir until the yeast dissolves, then pour into the well. Mix everything together, then beat vigorously with a wooden spoon for about 3–4 minutes, or until the batter is smooth. This is really hard work, but it is essential if you want to achieve a light, holey crumpet. Cover and leave to rise somewhere warm for 1 hour.

After an hour, the batter will have risen and then fallen slightly (you should be able to see the sticky marks on the sides of the bowl where it reached before it dropped slightly).

Mix the bicarbonate of soda with the water and beat into the batter. Beat well for 2–3 minutes, then cover and leave to rest at room temperature for 20–25 minutes. The consistency will be fairly sticky and 'globby' – neither too runny nor too thick. If the batter is too thick, no holes will form; if it is too thin, it will ooze out from underneath the crumpet rings.

Meanwhile prepare your crumpet rings: butter the insides, top and bottom really well. Very lightly butter your griddle, set the crumpet rings on top and heat over a medium heat.

Using a dessertspoon, drop 2 spoonfuls of the crumpet mixture into each ring. Cook for about 3 minutes, or until you see bubbles on the surface, then, wearing thin ovengloves, carefully remove the crumpet rings. (If no holes have formed after 3–4 minutes, add a spoonful or 2 of warm water to the remaining batter mixture, which is obviously too thick.) Using a spatula or fish slice, flip the crumpets over and cook the other side for about 3 minutes, or until cooked through. Once cooked, the crumpets should look lightly browned and feel firm to the touch, with no batter oozing from the sides.

Serve immediately, generously buttered, or cool on a wire rack and toast to reheat. ❋

WELSH CAKES

Makes about 12 griddle cakes

Welsh cakes are traditionally cooked on a bakestone. This was originally a large slab of stone, heated up on a peat fire or a log. Today, however, bakestones are usually made of iron or some other heavy metal. The cakes are no longer placed on the fire, but on a gas or electric hotplate. As with all griddle cookery, a large heavy frying pan will do instead, although it is less easy to maintain an even temperature.

Like Singin' Hinnies (see page 120), there are many variations of this recipe: some include ground spices such as ground nutmeg, mace, cinnamon or mixed spice; some contain currants; and some have a mixture of currants and sultanas, or even lemon peel. Their texture is short and soft, and their exterior almost crumbly. The cakes are often sprinkled with caster sugar immediately after cooking. They need no butter if eaten hot; once they are cold, however, a little butter or even jam would not go amiss. Another popular cake in Wales, 'Teisan Lap' (see page 192), uses almost the same ingredients as the Welsh cake, but this is a flat cake which is baked in the oven, not on the bakestone.

The original recipe for Welsh cakes was given to me by Mrs Barbara Saunders, from Gwent. I have added some ground mace, for extra spiciness. Also, she recommends using 1–2 eggs, to bind. I prefer to use 1 egg and 1 tablespoon milk, to achieve just the right consistency – the mixture should be fairly light, but firmer and less soft than a scone dough.

■ 227 g / 8 oz self-raising flour ■ a pinch of salt ■ ½ teaspoon mixed spice ■ ¼ teaspoon ground mace
■ 57 g / 2 oz butter, cut into cubes ■ 57 g / 2 oz white vegetable fat, in cubes ■ 85 g / 3 oz caster sugar
■ 85 g / 3 oz dried fruit ■ 1 egg, beaten ■ approximately 1 tablespoon milk
■ caster sugar, to sprinkle (optional)

Sift the flour, salt and spices together into a mixing bowl.

Rub in the fats until the mixture resembles breadcrumbs.

Stir in the sugar and dried fruit.

Add the beaten egg and just enough milk to form a soft dough. The result should be firmer than a scone dough. Roll this out on a floured board to a thickness of about 5 mm / ¼ in. Using an 8 cm / 3 in pastry cutter, cut into rounds.

Lightly grease a bakestone or griddle and heat to medium-hot. Cook the Welsh cakes (in 2 batches) for 4–5 minutes on each side, or until golden brown on both sides, but still soft in the middle. For a crunchy exterior, sprinkle with caster sugar. Eat warm. ❊

STAFFORDSHIRE OATCAKES

Makes 8 oatcakes

These oatcakes are light-years away from the crisp, dry oatcakes of Scotland. Although both are traditionally made on a griddle, these Staffordshire ones are more akin to a pikelet, pancake or even French crepe than a biscuit. They are made with half oatmeal (make sure you use fine oatmeal for a fine texture) and half wheat flour. Yeast-based, they are light, airy and soft. I like to make them for breakfast – Sunday morning is the best (laziest!) morning since you can make up the batter and leave it to rise while you have that first cup of tea and (hopefully) the first browse at the Sunday papers. One hour later, when you are feeling more wide-awake, you can start cooking the oatcakes. Serve them with butter and either jam, honey or crispy-fried bacon. I also like them with butter and cheese for lunch.

■ 113 g / 4 oz fine oatmeal ■ 113 g / 4 oz plain flour, sifted ■ 1 teaspoon salt
■ 1 teaspoon sugar ■ 1 rounded teaspoon easy-blend dried yeast
■ 426 ml / ¾ pint milk and water (mixed), warmed ■ 14 g / ½ oz butter, melted ■ butter, to cook

Combine the first 5 ingredients in a bowl, then add the warm liquid. Using a balloon whisk, beat until smooth.

Cover and leave to stand in a warm place for about 1 hour.

After the hour (by which time the mixture will be frothy), beat in the melted butter.

Heat a griddle (or heavy-based frying pan) to medium-hot with a little butter. Drop 2 table-spoons of batter on to the surface, smooth over slightly and fry for about 2 minutes on each side (turn over once you see the bubbles appear).

Either eat at once, or stack on a plate to keep warm in a low oven.

MUFFINS

Makes 8 muffins

I suppose I should prefix this muffin recipe with the word 'English', for the fairly recent invasion of these shores by the delicious – but totally different – American muffin has, sadly, created a form of culinary amnesia. Today, the word muffin is associated solely with those large, puffed-up fairy cakes bulging with fruit, nuts and all manner of wicked things.

The English muffin is very different and has been around for a very long time. Elizabeth David cites examples of muffin recipes from the mid-18th century.

The well-known nursery rhyme 'Do you know the Muffin-man . . . who lived in Drury Lane' is possibly our children's only acquaintance with muffins today. The muffin-man used to sell warm, freshly-made muffins in the streets. The ringing of a hand-bell announced the arrival of the muffin-man, cap padded to support his tray of well-swaddled muffins. Since his disappearance, some time after the First World War, it has become difficult to source real muffins. Supermarkets thankfully have begun recently to produce very acceptable muffins, but once you have made your own, you will see how easy it is and how satisfying the results.

Muffins can be cooked in a heavy-based frying pan, but it is difficult to regulate the heat. Therefore, unless you have had a lot of practice, it is easy to burn the outsides before the insides are properly cooked. Using a griddle, the results are – even for the first timer – very good.

The dough is usually made from either strong flour or a mixture of strong and plain, but I like to add just a little wholemeal flour (fine flour, not strong bread flour) to impart a slightly rough texture and colour. Rice flour or ground rice is also used to give the muffins their classic dry surface, which prevents them becoming sticky or patchy.

■ 397 g / 14 oz strong white flour ■ 57 g / 2 oz plain wholemeal flour ■ 1 teaspoon salt
■ 1 sachet easy-blend dried yeast ■ 142 ml / 5 fl oz warm water ■ 170 ml / 6 fl oz warm milk
■ ground rice, to dust ■ a little butter, to cook

Place the 2 flours in a china or glass mixing bowl. Warm the flour either by placing the bowl in the microwave on High for 15–20 seconds, or by setting in a low oven (150°C/300°F/Gas mark 2) for about 5 minutes. This helps to give the muffins a light texture and to activate the yeast in cold weather.

Stir in the salt and yeast, then make a well in the centre.

Add the warm water and milk and combine with a spoon. Then, dipping your hands in some of the ground rice, bring the mixture together with your hands. Turn on to a board, lightly dusted with ground rice, and knead for about 10 minutes, or until the dough no longer feels sticky, but is soft and smooth. Place in an oiled bowl, cover with clingfilm and leave to rise in a warm place for about 1 hour, or until well-risen.

Turn out the dough, knock it back with your fists and divide into 8. Flour your hands and the board with ground rice, then shape the pieces into fairly thick rounds with your hands. Flatten the tops slightly to give a good 'muffin' shape and sprinkle with a little ground rice. Cover loosely with clingfilm and leave to prove somewhere warm for about 20 minutes.

Then heat your griddle (or heavy frying pan) with a very little butter. The heat should be moderately hot – no more – or the muffins will burn before they are cooked. Place 4 of the muffins on top, spacing them around the edges – not near the centre, which will be the hottest part. Cook very slowly for about 8–10 minutes on each side. By this time the top and bottom will be nicely browned and the insides just cooked. To test, press a finger gently against the thick sides – the 'waist', as Elizabeth David calls them – they should spring back.

Remove and split open with your fingers, spread with butter and eat at once. Or allow to cool and toast either side, open with your fingers or a fork and spread copiously with butter. ✳

PIKELETS

Makes 10 pikelets

Pikelets are crumpets with a free spirit. They are really halfway between the English crumpet and the Scottish drop scone. Since they are not confined to crumpet rings when cooked, they are thinner, slightly crispier and decidedly free-form. The batter is thinner than a crumpet batter, and it is made with yeast, unlike the drop scone. Depending on the size of your griddle, you cannot make more than 2 at a time – only one if you use a frying pan. Australian pikelets are what we would call drop scones. They are sometimes flavoured – for example, with potato and horseradish, for savoury, or with mashed ripe bananas for sweet. Although our pikelets are not usually flavoured with anything, they can be served with things other than butter and jam. Try rolling a warm pikelet around some vanilla or nutty ice-cream and drizzling over some maple syrup, or spread with grated cheese (I suggest farmhouse Lancashire) and grill until bubbly and golden. If by any chance there are any left, you can toast them on the next day.

■ 227 g / 8 oz plain flour ■ a pinch of salt ■ 1 teaspoon caster sugar
■ 1 sachet easy-blend dried yeast ■ 284 ml / 10 fl oz warm milk ■ 1 egg

Sift the flour, salt and sugar into a mixing bowl. Stir in the dried yeast.

Make a well in the centre and pour in the warm milk and the egg. Using a balloon whisk, whisk for about 1 minute, or until lump-free.

Cover with a tea-towel and leave to stand in a warm place (such as an airing cupboard) for about 1 hour. After this time, the mixture should look frothy.

Heat the griddle to medium-hot and lightly grease. Drop about 2 tablespoons of the mixture on to one side of the griddle and another 2 tablespoons on to the other side. Spread the mixture out a little with a palette knife, to give 2 circles.

When the top of each pikelet shows little holes, like bubbles, in the surface, flip it over. (This should take about 2 minutes.) Then cook for a further 2–3 minutes on the other side.

Keep the pikelets warm in a folded cloth, or eat straight from the griddle. Serve with butter and jam, or honey. ❄

ITALIAN GRIDDLE CAKES

Makes 20 griddle cakes

These flat griddle cakes, known as 'Piadina Romagnola' in Italy, are really a type of thick pancake, made with bread dough. They are often sold at road-sides, anywhere from Rome north to Emilia Romagna. They are originally from Emilia Romagna, hence the name. They are usually served warm – freshly made – and split and filled with smoked ham, cured sausage or cheese.
My recipe is similar, but by no means identical to *piadine*. My griddle cakes are slightly thicker, so they are more like a cross between a thick pancake, a small pitta bread and a very thin muffin!
The dough is similar to muffin dough, apart from the addition of olive oil, which makes them nicely moist. This means that you do not need to spread them with oodles of butter. Once the cakes are rolled out, they are sprinkled with fine polenta, which gives the outsides not only a slightly golden yellow colour, but also a pleasantly rough texture. You might need to oil the griddle at first, but you should not need to do so for subsequent batches.

■ 454 g / 1 lb strong white flour ■ 1 teaspoon salt ■ 1 sachet easy-blend dried yeast
■ 3 tablespoons extra-virgin olive oil ■ 256 ml / 9 fl oz warm water ■ fine polenta, to dust

First combine the flour and salt in a bowl, then stir in the yeast.

Make a well in the centre and pour in the oil and the warm water, stirring well to combine.

Bring the dough together with your hands and shape into a ball. Turn on to a board, lightly dusted with the fine polenta. Knead for about 10 minutes, or until smooth.

Place in an oiled bowl, cover with clingfilm and leave to rise in a warm place for 2 hours. Once it has risen well, knock back with your fists and divide into 20 balls. Flatten the tops with your hand and sprinkle with fine polenta.

Using a very light touch, roll out with a rolling pin to a thickness of about 5 mm / ¼ in. Leave to rest, uncovered, for about 20 minutes.

Very lightly oil a griddle and heat to medium-hot. Cook the griddle cakes in batches for about 3 minutes on each side, or until they are flecked with golden brown on the outside and slightly soft and moist inside. Wrap in a tea-towel to keep warm.

BRETON CREPES

Makes 7 or 8 large crepes

These buckwheat pancakes are similar to the ones that are often sold at markets in Brittany, cooked on large open griddles. I have added cider to the batter, to add an air of Breton authenticity. They are sometimes known as 'galetous' or 'crêpes au blé noir' in Brittany. If the batter thickens up a little on resting, simply add a little more cider. It should be the consistency of pouring cream.
Eat these crepes warm, with a savoury or a sweet filling. My children like to have them for pudding with lemon juice and maple syrup; I like them folded round some coarsely grated mature Cheddar or a slice of Cumbrian air-dried ham.

■ 113g / 4oz plain flour, sifted ■ 113g / 4oz buckwheat flour ■ ½ teaspoon salt ■ 1 egg
■ 28g / 1oz butter, melted ■ 284ml / 10floz strong dry cider ■ butter, to cook

Place the plain and buckwheat flours and the salt in a food processor.

Add the egg and the melted butter.

With the machine running, pour in the cider and blend until smooth.

Pour the mixture into a bowl, cover with a damp tea-towel and leave to rest at room temperature for about 1 hour.

After an hour, check the consistency – it should have the consistency of pouring cream. You will probably need to add a little more cider: whisk vigorously, to incorporate.

Heat a crepe pan until medium-hot and smear with a tiny amount of butter. Once you see the butter bubbling slightly, pour in one ladleful of the batter. Swivel the pan around, until the base is covered with the batter.

Cook on one side until you see tiny bubbles, then flip over and cook on the other side for about 1 minute, or until just cooked through.

Either eat at once, or stack on a plate and keep warm in a medium-hot oven.

❈ To freeze, layer with greaseproof paper.

---

*To ensure pancakes or crepes do not stick, add 14g/
½oz melted butter to the batter.*

MEXICAN-STYLE TORTILLAS

Makes 6 tortillas

These wheat flour tortillas are titled 'Mexican-style' because they are not truly Mexican. The genuine wheat-flour tortillas ('Tortillas de Harina de Trigo'), which come from northern Mexico, are larger than the more common corn tortillas ('Tortillas de Maiz'). They are traditionally made from wheat (plain) flour, but I have added a little maizemeal, for a touch of colour. Make sure you use maizemeal for this – not polenta, which is too coarsely ground. I recommend cooking these on a griddle, but you can use a reliable, heavy-based frying pan – reliable, because you do not cook them in any fat, so you must make sure they do not stick. Once they are cooked, stack them inside a folded (clean!) tea-towel to keep them soft and pliable, then put this inside a large plastic bag (I use a bin-liner). This ensures they remain floppy and soft, since they almost steam inside the bag. These tortillas should always be eaten hot. If you want to make them in advance, the best method of reheating them I know is to pop them in the microwave, rather than in the oven where there is a danger of them drying out. In my family, we like to eat these tortillas with absolutely anything – buttered and rolled around spicy sausage, salami, ham or cheese; or with salad, avocado, sour cream and tomatoes. The authentic Mexican way would be to convert them into 'Burritos' – that is, to stuff them with refried beans, cheese, salad and tomatoes, and then fold them up. These are then heated and served with a spicy salsa or guacamole. Alternatively, you could make 'Enchiladas' by stuffing them with cheese and onions, rolling them up and deep-frying them.

■ 142 g / 5 oz plain flour ■ 28 g / 1 oz maizemeal ■ 1 heaped teaspoon baking powder
■ ½ teaspoon salt ■ approximately 114 ml / 4 fl oz warm water

Stir together the flours, baking powder and salt.

Pour in enough water to form a fairly stiff dough. Turn this on to a lightly floured board and knead for 2–3 minutes, or until smooth. Then divide into 6 pieces, shaping each piece into a ball.

Place the 6 balls on a board, cover with cling-film and leave to stand at room temperature for about 1 hour.

Then roll out each ball on a lightly floured board to a diameter of about 20 cm / 8 in. Mean-while, pre-heat a griddle (or heavy-based frying pan) to medium-hot.

Place a tortilla on the griddle – almost immediately, tiny blisters will appear. When they do, turn over, using a fish slice. Then cook for 2 minutes on the other side, or until the blisters turn golden brown.

Stack the cooked tortillas in a cloth, in a large plastic bag, to keep them warm and soft.

❊ To freeze, layer between greaseproof paper; defrost for 30 minutes before serving.

DOSA WITH BANANA SOUFFLÉ

Makes 6 filled pancakes

I first enjoyed dosas – fermented Indian pancakes, usually eaten for breakfast – in Delhi, although the recipe originates in the south of India. Usually served with spicy potato curry, chutneys, sambals and freshly grated coconut (yes, even for breakfast!), they are also excellent vehicles for sweet fillings. They are authentically made from a mixture of rice flour and 'urud dhal' (small pale-yellow split peas), which are soaked overnight then ground together with the rice flour. Although baking powder is often added as the leavening agent, I have used natural yoghurt, which is used in many dishes all over India. My recipe combines plain flour with rice flour. The dosas are cooked on the same type of griddle that is used for chapatis (see page 134). It is usually sprayed with vegetable oil once the dosas have been flipped over.

The following recipe is a dessert, rather than something to have in place of your cornflakes. The banana soufflé is very light, since it is made from only bananas, egg whites and the merest suggestion of sugar. Once you have tried the method – that is, popping a soufflé mixture into a pancake – and seen how the mixture rises up beautifully, you will want to experiment with different fillings. Try it as a starter, using a savoury filling – a simple cheese soufflé mixture, for example. When making any type of soufflé, make sure everyone is ready at the table, expectantly. A soufflé waits for no man!

DOSA

■ 85 g / 3 oz rice flour ■ 85 g / 3 oz plain flour ■ 2 tablespoons natural yoghurt
■ 14 g / ½ oz butter, melted ■ about 227 ml / 8 fl oz cold water

SOUFFLÉ

■ 3 very ripe bananas ■ 2 teaspoons lemon juice ■ 28 g / 1 oz caster sugar ■ 3 egg whites
■ a pinch of cream of tartar ■ caster sugar, to sprinkle

For the dosa, sift the flours into a bowl. Add the yoghurt, melted butter and sufficient water to make a pouring batter – about the consistency of double cream. Using a balloon whisk, whisk well until there are no lumps. Cover the bowl with a damp tea-towel and leave at room temperature for at least 6 hours (or overnight, if possible).

After this time, pre-heat the oven to 190°C/375°F/Gas mark 5. Lightly butter a pancake pan (the base of my pan measures 18 cm/7 in). While the pan is heating, check that the pancake batter is not too thick. If it is, beat in a little more water.

Then fry the pancakes – you should have enough for 6 large pancakes. Stack them on a plate to keep warm.

Now make the soufflé mixture. Peel the bananas and place in a food processor with the lemon juice and sugar. Process until really well-blended. Whisk the egg whites with the cream of tartar until stiff. 'Loosen' the banana mixture by folding in a spoonful of egg whites. Then carefully fold in the remaining whites, combining until well-blended.

Lay the pancakes on a greased baking tray. Drop one-sixth of the soufflé mixture (about 2 tablespoons) on to one half of every pancake. Fold over the other half. (Do not expect the pancake to enclose the mixture – it will bulge out slightly.) Bake in the oven for 12–15 minutes, or until puffed up and just beginning to brown. Serve at once.

JOHNNY BREAD

Makes one 'bread'

This is a type of bread or cake that I got to know about in Bermuda, where it is very popular. It is usually made with plain flour, vegetable oil, egg and milk, then rolled into a round and fried in a frying pan. There is also a Canadian 'Johnny Cake', which is similar, but made with a combination of wheat and maize flours, and baked in the oven, rather than in a frying pan. Both Canadian and Bermudian versions make ideal breakfast fare, served warm with plenty of butter.

My friend Peggy, who has lived on Bermuda for most of her life, told me that the original name 'Johnnie' is a corruption of 'Journey': the bread was taken on long sea journeys, because it kept better than regular bread on board ship. My recipe uses both maizemeal and wheat flour, and is cooked on a griddle. It is so very quick and easy, it can be rustled up while you put on the kettle in the morning. Eat within 10 minutes of cooking, if possible.

■ 85 g / 3 oz maizemeal ■ 85 g / 3 oz plain flour ■ 1 teaspoon baking powder ■ ½ teaspoon salt
■ 1 heaped tablespoon black treacle ■ 43 g / 1½ oz unsalted butter ■ 1 egg, beaten

Mix together the first 4 ingredients in a bowl.

Gently heat the treacle and butter together until the butter is melted.

Make a well in the centre of the dry ingredients and pour in the treacle mixture and the egg. Stir everything together, to combine.

Heat a buttered griddle to hot. Now drop the Johnny bread mixture into the centre. Then, using the back of a metal spoon or spatula, spread out the mixture to make a round, about 20 cm / 8 in in diameter.

Lower the heat to medium and cook for 7–8 minutes, or until the underside is golden brown. Using a large fish slice, carefully flip over the Johnny bread and cook the other side for 6–7 minutes more, or until both sides are golden brown. Check after 5 minutes, since after this time the Johnny bread tends to burn quickly.

Remove to a wire rack and serve as soon as possible. To serve, cut or tear into quarters and gently split open (horizontally). Open out the 2 sides and spread with butter.

CHAPATIS

Makes 4 chapatis

Chapatis are the daily bread of millions of Indians. They are cooked on a type of griddle or 'tava',
and are eaten with every meal. Delhi chef Gev Desai told me that the daily fare of
the very poor people in India often consists of nothing more than chapatis with some fiery chilli
on top. My recipe is for a basic chapati, but there are, of course, variations – some have
vegetables, such as peppers or onion, or herbs such as coriander chopped into the dough. You can also
add a little freshly chopped chilli to give a little heat.
The cooking method I advise is suited to most British cookers. The chapati starts cooking
on a very lightly greased griddle, then is finished over a naked flame. If you are wary of doing this,
simply place it under a hot grill until it puffs up. Serve warm.

■ 198 g / 7 oz plain (fine) wholemeal flour ■ a pinch of salt ■ ½ tablespoon vegetable oil
■ 142 ml / ¼ pint warm water ■ oil, to cook

Sift the flour and salt into a bowl, then stir in the oil. Add just enough water to form a firm dough, then gather together with your hands and knead for 8–10 minutes, or until smooth.

Place in a bowl, cover with a damp cloth and leave to stand at room temperature for at least 30 minutes.

Divide into 4, then roll out each piece – on a lightly floured surface – to a thin circle, about 15 cm / 6 in in diameter. Heat the griddle to hot, oil it very lightly, then slap on the chapati. Cook for about 1 minute on each side.

Then, using oven gloves and 2 pairs of tongs, hold the chapati over a direct flame for about 20 seconds on each side, or until it puffs up. (It will not puff up all over, but in irregular bulges!) If you do not have a gas cooker (or do not feel confident about dallying beside a direct flame), then place the chapati as near as you dare to a hot grill, until it puffs up. Watch very carefully, in case it burns.

Eat while still warm. To store the chapatis, stack them together under a large napkin or cloth until serving time.

BLINIS

Makes about 30 blinis

I visited Moscow in the mid-1970's, long before Glasnost. I was on a trip from Helsinki with a party of Finnish tourists. It was February and there was a thick blanket of snow on the ground. Cold conditions and snow were nothing new for the Finns (nor to me – I had already lived in Finland for 6 months), but the temperature inside the buildings in Russia was a revelation. As we sat in vast, grandiose hotel dining rooms, lit by fabulous, sparkling chandeliers, the icy Siberian wind swirled in from the top sections of the large windows, which were completely open to the elements. Obviously there had been a run on glass recently. The only thing we had to console ourselves in this chilly atmosphere was the champansky and the blinis. Bottles of champagne were unbelievably cheap; and the blinis were accompanied by equally cheap caviar. I remember spooning thick, creamy smetana on to blinis with indecent quantities of caviar. The remaining items of each meal faded into insignificance beside the memorable blinis and champagne.

The authentic Russian blini is made with fresh yeast and buckwheat flour. I usually make mine with a mixture of plain and buckwheat flour (I find 100 per cent buckwheat is too heavy); and I substitute a touch of baking powder for the yeast. The result is a light – yet not puffy – little pancake that is perfect to serve with such savoury toppings as smoked salmon or trout, caviar, smetana or sour cream, chopped onion, dill and hard-boiled egg.

As an alternative to the plain blini, try cooking some smoked salmon into the actual pancake. You will need a thick piece of smoked salmon fillet, which you can slice into fairly thick, but small slices – just a little smaller in diameter than the blini. Once one side of the blini is cooked, place a piece of salmon into the centre, flip over and cook the other side as normal. Serve while still warm, with a dollop of sour cream and some finely chopped chives or dill. The piece of salmon adheres to the blini, to form a crusty base. This is really worth trying, for special occasions.

Although I have a genuine cast-iron blini pan, I prefer to use a heavy-based (preferably non-stick) crepe pan, so I can cook more than one at a time. For tiny canapé-size blinis, use a teaspoon, instead of a dessertspoon, to drop the batter on to the pan.

■ 199 ml / 7 fl oz semi-skimmed milk ■ 14 g / ½ oz butter ■ 113 g / 4 oz plain flour, sifted
■ 57 g / 2 oz buckwheat flour ■ ½ teaspoon baking powder ■ ½ teaspoon caster sugar
■ ¼ teaspoon salt ■ 1 large egg (size 1), separated ■ butter, to cook

Heat the milk and butter together in a small saucepan until the butter is melted and the milk is lukewarm.

Place the flours, baking powder, sugar, salt and egg yolk in a food processor. Then pour in the liquids and process until blended and smooth.

Place the mixture in a bowl, cover with clingfilm and leave to rest at room temperature for about 1 hour.

Whisk the egg white until stiff, then gently fold 1 spoonful into the mixture. Once this is fully incorporated, fold in the rest, very gently.

Heat a heavy-based pan and lightly smear with butter. Drop a dessertspoon of batter (or a teaspoon, for canapés) into the pan and cook for 1 minute on each side, or until you see tiny bubbles. Keep warm, wrapped loosely in buttered foil, in a low oven. ❋

PANNUKAKKU (FINNISH OVEN PANCAKE)

Makes 1 large pancake

Serves 6

One of the traditional dishes throughout Finland is an oven pancake, which in certain areas is flavoured with ground cardamom. It billows from the oven like a huge Yorkshire pudding – and indeed it is very similar, but sweet. Served hot, straight from the oven, it is usually topped with sugar or jam. My favourite in Finland was lingonberry or blueberry jam. It is also excellent topped with vanilla ice-cream. There is a tradition in the north of Finland to serve lunch on Thursdays of thick, hearty pea soup (which the Finns always enhance by stirring in plenty of mustard at the end) and pancakes, usually these oven pancakes.

■ 511 ml / 18 fl oz full-fat milk ■ 57 ml / 2 fl oz water ■ 1 egg ■ 43 g / 1½ oz caster sugar
■ 142 g / 5 oz plain flour, sifted ■ 4–6 green cardamom pods, open, seeds crushed (optional)
■ 28 g / 1 oz butter

Place the milk, water, egg and sugar in a large bowl and, using a balloon whisk, beat well. Incorporate the flour (and cardamom pods, if using) a little at a time, until well-mixed. Beat really well, to ensure there are no lumps.

Leave the mixture to stand at room temperature for about ½ hour. Pre-heat the oven to 220°C/425°F/Gas mark 7.

Place the butter in a deep roasting tin (mine measures 33 cm/13 in by 23 cm/9 in – slightly smaller will do, but not bigger). Place the tin in the oven until the butter has melted and is piping hot. Whirl the pan around, so the butter coats the base and sides. Then whisk the mixture again and pour into the roasting tin while the butter is still piping hot.

Bake in the oven for 30–35 minutes, or until puffed up and golden brown – the centre should be cooked through and the sides crisp. Serve at once, cut into squares and topped with jam.

BISCUITS

'Who stole the cookie from the cookie jar? Not I stole the cookie from the cookie jar', goes the skipping-rhyme my daughters love to chant. Changed days – it was biscuits from the biscuit barrel in my youth. Whether American cookies, antipodean Anzacs, Dutch speculaas or good old-fashioned macaroons, they all taste wonderful when you make them yourself.

CHRISTMAS COOKIES

Makes about 30 cookies

The time to make these is the week before Christmas – unless you are terribly well-organised and plan to freeze them, along with everything else, in October! I have tasted many varieties of Christmas spice biscuits in different European countries. When I was living in Germany, we were served 'Pfeffernüsse' just before Christmas, instead of the 'Kuchen' that we normally ate with our coffee. These little biscuits, which were flavoured with cloves, cinnamon and cardamom, as well as lemon zest, were often cut into stars or other Christmas shapes. Sometimes a hole was pierced in the top so they could be hung with red ribbon from the Christmas tree.

Swedish 'Pepparkakor' are very similar, although they are usually flavoured with ginger as well as cinnamon and cloves. They are cut into angels, Santas, gingerbread-men and even formed into magnificent gingerbread houses with icing cement. These biscuits are also popular in Finland, where they are known as 'Piparkakut'. Here they are almost identical to the Swedish biscuits, but often with the addition of dried orange peel.

The taste of all these Christmas cookies, therefore, varies slightly from country to country, as does the texture – from crisp and brittle to slightly soft and almost chewy. I prefer the slightly chewy ones, which remind me of the treacly, spicy American cookie.

It is important with this recipe to roll out the dough while it is still warm. Do not panic that it will stick – a lightly floured board will prevent this happening. Choose whichever shape of cutter you like. If you have no bells or reindeer, use a plain round one.

An optional extra is to decorate the biscuits, once they are completely cold. My children love a spoonful of glacé icing and a shake of 'hundreds and thousands' – not exactly sophisticated, but Christmas is, after all, for kids!

■ 511 g / 1lb 2 oz plain flour ■ 1 teaspoon baking powder ■ 1 teaspoon bicarbonate of soda
■ 1 teaspoon ground ginger ■ 1 teaspoon ground cinnamon ■ ¼ teaspoon ground cloves
■ 142 g / 5 oz butter ■ 170 g / 6 oz soft light brown sugar ■ 3 tablespoons black treacle
■ 2 tablespoons golden syrup ■ 1 egg, beaten

Pre-heat the oven to 180°C/350°F/Gas mark 4. Sift the flour, baking powder, bicarbonate of soda and spices into a large bowl.

Melt the butter, sugar, treacle and syrup together – I do this on Medium-high in the microwave for 3–4 minutes, but you can do it in a saucepan over a gentle heat for 4–5 minutes.

Once the butter has melted, stir everything together to combine.

Make a well in the middle of the dry ingredients and pour in the liquids, then add the egg. Stir briskly together, before turning out on to a floured board. Do this while the dough is still warm.

Press out to a thickness of 1 cm/½ in – I do this with the palm of my hand, but you can use a rolling pin.

Then, working quickly, cut into shapes and place on a lightly greased baking tray. (Do not over-grease the tray, or the mixture will spread.)

Bake in the oven for about 10 minutes, or until they have risen a little, are still slightly soft in the middle and are a dark golden brown colour. (If you want to thread them on to ribbons to hang on the Christmas tree, now is the time to make a hole at the top of each. Do this very quickly, while the biscuits are still soft – they will harden a little as they cool.)

Transfer to a wire rack to cool, then either decorate garishly with 'hundreds and thousands' and glacé icing, or leave plain – understated, yet still decidedly Christmassy. ❄

ROCKY ROAD COOKIES

Makes 15–16 cookies

These marvellously garish cookies are every child's idea of heaven. They are thick and chocolatey, with a marshmallow and chocolate topping. Depending on the colour of your marshmallows, the tops can be pink or white. After a few minutes in the oven, the marshmallows melt together to form a golden-crusted coating. Try to find mini American marshmallows for this – otherwise, chop up large ones. As for the chocolate, chop it yourself into chunks, rather than using tiny commercial chips.

In the States, Rocky Road is very popular in cookies, in ice-creams, and in the most simple of forms – slabs of unadulterated chocolate, marshmallows and nuts. It is the bumpy, rocky surface which explains the rather appropriate name of these cookies.

COOKIES

■ 113 g / 4 oz butter, softened ■ 113 g / 4 oz soft light brown sugar ■ 2 eggs ■ 227 g / 8 oz plain flour
■ 1 heaped tablespoon cocoa powder ■ a pinch of salt ■ 57 g / 2 oz milk-chocolate chunks

TOPPING

■ 28 g / 1 oz mini marshmallows ■ 57 g / 2 oz milk-chocolate chunks

Pre-heat the oven to 180°C/350°F/Gas mark 4. Cream the softened butter and sugar together until light and fluffy, then add the eggs. Sift in the flour, cocoa and salt, and stir well to combine thoroughly.

Add the chocolate chunks and mix well, then drop spoonfuls of the mixture on to a very lightly greased baking sheet. Bake in the oven for 10–12 minutes, or until the centres are still soft, but the edges are beginning to firm up.

Remove from the oven and quickly sprinkle with marshmallows and chocolate chunks, pressing them down well into the cookies, then return to the oven for a further 5 minutes. Allow to cool in the tin for a couple of minutes before transferring to a wire rack to cool.

AZTEC COOKIES

Makes 20–22 cookies

This recipe is based on one from 2 talented American chefs, Mary Sue Milliken and Susan Feniger. Their Bordergrill restaurant, which specialises in Mexican and Latin-American food, is one of the most pleasant, relaxed places to eat in Los Angeles. The decor is bold and loud and the food simply sings out with wonderful, spicy flavours. They are also well-known for their desserts and cookies. They have a recipe for 'Pajas', chewy 'haystack' cookies that are reminiscent of those sticky coconut candies found in Mexico City's sweet shops. I have changed some of the ingredients. The resulting cookie is full of coconut and walnuts, with chopped dried apricots and dark-chocolate chunks. Do not chop the chocolate, nuts or fruit too finely – you want large chunks for this recipe. There ought to be a warning issued with these: one bite and you become an addict!

■ 170 g / 6 oz walnuts, roughly chopped ■ 284 g / 10 oz desiccated coconut
■ 113 g / 4 oz dried apricots (no-soak variety) ■ 113 g / 4 oz dark chocolate, roughly chopped
■ 1 × 397 g / 14 oz tin of sweetened condensed milk

Pre-heat the oven to 160°C/325°F/Gas mark 3. Roughly chop the apricots, chocolate and nuts. Place everything together in a large mixing bowl and, using a wooden spoon, beat together until thoroughly mixed. Using 2 tablespoons, drop about 20 blobs of the mixture on to a buttered baking tray and gently flatten down the tops.

Bake in the oven for about 20 minutes, or until golden brown.

Transfer at once to a wire rack to cool. ❋

AZTEC COOKIES
CHOCOLATE CHUNK COOKIES (page 144)
PEANUT BUTTER COOKIES (page 144)

PEANUT BUTTER COOKIES

Makes about 24 cookies

Although these are flavoured with peanut butter, the taste is not overpowering. In fact if you use smooth peanut butter, you can hardly detect the peanut flavour at all. For maximum peanut impact, however, choose a crunchy-textured peanut spread. These are true cookies – slightly dense and fudgey in the centre, with a crisp and light exterior. To achieve this effect, make sure you remove the biscuits from the oven while they are still slightly soft.

■ 113 g / 4 oz butter, softened ■ 113 g / 4 oz peanut butter ■ 85 g / 3 oz caster sugar
■ 85 g / 3 oz soft light brown sugar ■ 1 egg, beaten ■ 227 g / 8 oz plain flour
■ ¼ teaspoon baking powder ■ ¼ teaspoon bicarbonate of soda

Pre-heat the oven to 190°C/375°F/Gas mark 5. Cream the butter and peanut butter together, then beat in the caster and brown sugar. Beat well until smooth.

Add the egg, stir well, then sift in the flour, baking powder and bicarbonate of soda. If you have used a salt-free peanut butter, add a pinch of salt too. Using a wooden spoon, mix together thoroughly.

Spoon dessertspoonfuls of the mixture on to 2 lightly greased baking sheets and bake in the oven for 12–15 minutes, or until golden brown with firm edges and slightly soft centres. Remove at once to a wire rack and allow to cool. ✳

CHOCOLATE CHUNK COOKIES

Makes 20–24 cookies

For these cookies, make sure you use chocolate chunks, not the tiny commercial chocolate chips available from supermarkets. Buy the best milk chocolate you can find – I use one with 40 per cent cocoa solids – and cut it into large, mouth-size chunks yourself.
When spooning the biscuit mixture on to the baking tray, make sure you allow plenty of space between each spoonful, as they do tend to spread out during baking.

■ 170 g / 6 oz golden caster sugar ■ 170 g / 6 oz unsalted butter ■ 2 eggs
■ 1 teaspoon vanilla essence ■ 170 g / 6 oz plain flour, sifted ■ 57 g / 2 oz oatflakes
■ a pinch of salt ■ 170 g / 6 oz chocolate chunks

Pre-heat the oven to 180°C/350°F/Gas mark 4. Place the sugar, butter and eggs in a food processor and process until combined. Add the vanilla, flour and oats, with the pinch of salt. Process until well-combined.

Turn into a mixing bowl and stir in the chocolate chunks. Then, using 2 spoons, drop small amounts of the mixture on to a lightly greased baking tray, spacing them well apart. With floured fingers, flatten the tops slightly.

Bake in the oven for 15–20 minutes, or until slightly soft to the touch and just golden brown. Cool in the tin for about 2 minutes, then transfer to a wire rack to cool completely. ✻

PINE-NUT COOKIES

Makes 12 cookies

Pine-nut kernels are not only invaluable in pesto sauce and salads, they are also excellent in baked goods. You can make a pine-nut tart, as you would a pecan or walnut tart, or scatter them over a sponge cake about 10 minutes before it is ready. They take on a golden brown colour and make a lovely crunchy topping for your finished cake.
In this recipe, the nuts are ground up to form the basis of the cookie mix. Similar cookies can be made with ground almonds, hazelnuts or walnuts. The finished texture is light and crisp at the edges and slightly chewy in the middle, reminiscent of the best American cookies. Make sure you space them out really well on the baking tray, since they do spread.

■ 113 g / 4 oz pine-nut kernels ■ 113 g / 4 oz golden caster sugar ■ 113 g / 4 oz unsalted butter, softened
■ 113 g / 4 oz plain flour, sifted ■ a pinch of salt ■ ½ teaspoon baking powder ■ 1 egg

Pre-heat the oven to 180°C/350°F/Gas mark 4. Reserve 24 pine-nuts for the topping, and place the rest in a food processor. Process in short bursts: you want them to be finely ground, but not a paste.

Beat together the sugar and softened butter until light and creamy, then add the flour, salt and baking powder.

Stir well to combine. Beat in the egg.

Drop 12 spoonfuls of the mixture on to a lightly buttered baking tray, spacing them well apart. Top each mound with 2 pine-nuts.

Bake in the oven for about 20 minutes, or until golden brown around the edges and still slightly soft in the centre.

Carefully transfer to a wire rack, taking care not to break up the cookies. Allow to cool before eating. ✻

Always space apart 'drop cookies' – that is, biscuits made from a soft mixture and dropped on to the baking sheet. They invariably spread during baking.

SPECULAAS

Makes 24–28 biscuits

Christmas comes early in Holland. On the night of the 5th of December, Dutch children put out their shoes for St Nicholas, just as our children hang up their stockings on Christmas Eve. Instead of leaving a carrot for Rudolph, Dutch children leave hay and carrots for St Nicholas' white horse. In the morning, miraculously, the horse fodder is gone and the shoes are bulging with presents. On St Nicholas' Day, the tradition is to bake and eat special little spice biscuits, called 'Speculaas'. These are flavoured with spices – cinnamon, nutmeg and cloves – which are added in an exact ratio. Sometimes, nibbed almonds and grated orange or lemon zest are also added. The biscuits are rolled into shape using a special wooden speculaas board, which acts on the same principal as a shortbread board. The dough is rolled over the board and the shapes are made from this. Presuming you are not in possession of a speculaas board, roll out the dough (which I advise you to leave in the refrigerator overnight) and cut out with pastry or scone cutters.

■ 255 g / 9 oz plain flour ■ a pinch of bicarbonate of soda ■ a pinch of salt
■ 170 g / 6 oz unsalted butter, cut into cubes ■ 142 g / 5 oz soft light brown sugar
■ ½ teaspoon ground cinnamon ■ ¼ teaspoon grated nutmeg ■ ¼ teaspoon ground cloves
■ a little grated orange or lemon zest (optional) ■ 57 g / 2 oz nibbed almonds (optional)
■ about 3 tablespoons milk

Sift the flour and bicarbonate of soda into a bowl. Add the salt. Rub in the butter until the mixture resembles breadcrumbs.

Stir in the sugar, then add the spices and, if you are using them, the citrus zest and almonds.

Stir in just enough milk to combine to a stiff dough. Shape into a ball with your hands and wrap in clingfilm. Chill in the refrigerator overnight (or for at least 2 hours). Pre-heat the oven to 180°C/350°F/Gas mark 4.

Roll out the dough to a thickness of 1 cm/ ½ in, then cut into shapes using a pastry cutter. I use an 8 cm/3 in pastry cutter, which makes 24–28 biscuits.

Set on a very lightly buttered baking sheet and bake in the oven for about 20 minutes, or until they are still slightly soft to the touch. Transfer to a wire rack to cool completely, during which time the biscuits will become crisp and firm. Store in an air-tight container. ❄

PETTICOAT TAILS

Makes 12 biscuits

This is a type of shortbread that is very popular in Scotland. There are various explanations about its name. Some believe it to be a corruption of the French *petites galettes*, little cakes. This theory is certainly not impossible, since the Auld Alliance between France and Scotland was one of our strongest cultural ties. Indeed, many other Scottish words are corrupted from the French. Also, there are short, buttery 'galettes' in Brittany that bear a strong resemblance to these shortbread biscuits. There is another school of thought which is far simpler. This suggests they are the shape of the individual gores in the full, bell-hooped petticoats of long ago. Whichever derivation is true, there is no disputing the fact that they were a great favourite of Mary Queen of Scots, so these shortbread biscuits certainly date back as far as the 16th century.
The trick with any shortbread-baking is not to overhandle the dough or your biscuits will be tough. Bake the biscuits very slowly, to dry out the dough, rather than baking it to a brown crispness. You should only remove the shortbread from the oven when it looks a very pale golden colour. Sprinkle immediately with caster sugar so it sticks to the hot surface.
This is one of the few times I do not stipulate the use of unsalted butter. If you only have unsalted butter, however, you must add a generous pinch of salt.

■ 113 g / 4 oz slightly salted butter ■ 43 g / 1½ oz caster sugar
■ 113 g / 4 oz plain flour, sifted ■ 43 g / 1½ oz farola (fine semolina)

Pre-heat the oven to 150°C/300°F/Gas mark 2. Cream together the butter and sugar until light and fluffy.

Add the flour and farola, then, using the back of a wooden spoon, draw the mixture together. Using one hand, bring the mixture together to form a dough and eliminate cracks. Take care not to overwork.

Press into a lightly buttered 20 cm/8 in fluted sandwich tin and prick all over. (If you do not have a fluted tin, pinch around the edges with forefinger and thumb to form a scalloped edge.)

Bake in the bottom half of the oven for about 40–45 minutes, or until a very pale golden brown all over.

Remove from the oven, sprinkle with caster sugar and cut into 12 wedges. Allow to cool in the tin for at least 25–30 minutes, before transferring to a wire rack to crisp up. ❄

Never overwork or knead shortbread or biscuits, or they will become tough once baked.

CHOCOLATE SHORTBREAD

Makes 24 fingers

This recipe really ought to bear a health warning. There is no doubt about it, it is addictive. If you are able to stop after just one piece, then I admire your self-discipline. This is not true Scottish shortbread, which is simply a combination of butter, sugar and flour – although many recipes add either rice flour, cornflour or fine semolina to make the shortbread even more 'short'. I have also added milk chocolate chunks – I mean chunks, not those tiny little chocolate drops – to the basic mixture of butter, sugar, flour and semolina. If you mix them in very carefully, the chunks should remain more or less whole and only melt a little into the shortbread. The result is a crumbly, buttery biscuit bulging with chocolate. It is very important to use only best-quality milk chocolate. That means scrutinising the label. Try to find one with a minimum of 30 per cent cocoa solids – preferably 40 per cent, which is very high for milk chocolate. Serve the shortbread with a cup of tea or coffee, or for dessert, with some creamy vanilla or nutty ice-cream.

■ 284 g / 10 oz unsalted butter, softened ■ 170 g / 6 oz caster sugar
■ 170 g / 6 oz milk chocolate, cut into chunks ■ 227 g / 8 oz plain flour, sifted ■ 113 g / 4 oz semolina

Pre-heat the oven to 150°C/300°F/Gas mark 2. Place the softened butter and sugar in a bowl. Using an electric mixer (on the lowest speed), beat together until light and fluffy. This takes only a couple of minutes.

Add the chocolate chunks, then the flour and semolina. Using a wooden spoon, combine everything together. Do not over-beat or stir vigorously at this stage, or you will have tough shortbread.

You should end up with a slightly crumbly – but thoroughly combined – mixture.

Turn into a lightly buttered swiss-roll tin, 23 × 33 cm / 9 × 13 in. Using the palms of your hands, press the mixture down well into the tin. You may need to lightly flour your hands, depending on how warm they are.

Bake in the oven for about 40 minutes, or until golden brown around the edges.

Cut into squares or fingers while still hot and leave to cool in the tin for 30–40 minutes. Using a large fish slice, transfer to a wire rack to cool completely before eating. ❄

Most biscuits and shortbread cook more evenly if pricked with a fork all over.

CHICKPEA AND CARDAMOM SHORTBREAD

Makes 16 wedges

In Margaret Shaida's marvellous book, *The Legendary Cuisine of Persia*, there is a recipe for chickpea shortbread. Traditionally made in the shape of a four-leafed clover and decorated with pistachios, it is served at the New-Year festival in March – part of the ancient festival of 'No Rooz'.

I have borrowed the Persian idea of using chickpea flour and developed the Scottish technique of making shortbread for this recipe, which is flavoured with cardamom. I like to use whole cardamom pods for cooking, rather than ground cardamom powder, since the flavour is stronger. I always use green pods, not the inferior brown or bleached white ones. To split the pods, simply snip or cut off one end, then scrape out the seeds and grind with a pestle and mortar. Chickpea flour, also known as gram flour, can be found in either health-food shops or Indian specialists. In Indian cookery it is chickpea flour that binds onion bhajis together.

In this recipe, the shortbread is crisp and short in texture, yellow in colour because of the golden chickpea flour, and slightly scented from the cardamom. Serve it with a cup of morning coffee. Alternatively, serve it with Indian kulfi (ice-cream) for dessert.

■ 113 g / 4 oz chickpea (gram) flour ■ 57 g / 2 oz plain flour ■ 85 g / 3 oz caster sugar
■ 3 green cardamom pods ■ 113 g / 4 oz unsalted butter, softened ■ caster sugar, to dust

Pre-heat the oven to 150°C/300°F/Gas mark 2. Sift the flours into a bowl, then stir in the sugar.

Split the cardamom pods, scrape the black seeds into a mortar and grind with a pestle. Add to the bowl.

Incorporate the softened butter into the flour mixture with the back of a wooden spoon. You will know that the mixture is ready when there are no obvious lumps of butter.

Divide between 2 buttered 18 cm/7 in sandwich tins and press down with the back of a metal spoon to give a smooth, even surface.

Bake in the oven for 22–25 minutes, or until the edges are just beginning to turn a pale golden brown.

Mark into 8 wedges each, sprinkle with caster sugar and allow to cool in the tin before turning out. Store in an air-tight container. ❋

MINCEMEAT SHORTBREAD

Makes 16 squares

I love any recipe containing mincemeat – although I have to say that home-made is always best. The commercial ones can be 'doctored' by adding a drop of brandy, orange juice or whisky and some freshly grated apple, orange zest and chopped nuts. The result you can almost pass off as your own!
I like to make mincemeat shortbread not just at Christmas, but at any time of the year. The addition of semolina and custard powder might seem a little unusual, but it adds a nice short crispness to the finished biscuits. Mincemeat shortbread is good served on its own with a cup of tea, but it is also excellent served freshly baked and still warm for pudding, with a good dollop of crème fraîche, the acidity of which balances the sweetness of the mincemeat.

- 227 g / 8 oz plain flour ■ 28 g / 1 oz semolina ■ 28 g / 1 oz custard powder
- 57 g / 2 oz icing sugar ■ 198 g / 7 oz unsalted butter, cut into cubes
- about 4 tablespoons cold water ■ 397 g / 14 oz best mincemeat ■ caster sugar, to dust

Pre-heat the oven to 190°C/375°F/Gas mark 5. Sift the flour, semolina, custard powder and icing sugar into a bowl. Combine well. Rub in the butter until the mixture resembles breadcrumbs.

Add just enough cold water to bind the mixture together – start with 3 tablespoons and increase to 4, if necessary.

Press two-thirds of the mixture into a buttered 23 cm/9 in square tin, pressing down with the palms of your hands so it fills into all corners.

Spread the mincemeat on top, leaving a narrow margin all round.

Using your fingers, crumble the remaining shortbread mixture over the top. Then gently press down with your fingers to ensure an even coverage.

Bake in the oven for 30 minutes, or until golden brown on top. Cut into 16 squares while still hot. Allow to cool in the tin, then transfer to a wire rack to become completely cold. ❉

PARMESAN SHORTBREAD

Makes about 20 biscuits

Strange though it may seem, savoury shortbread really works. These little biscuits are crisp, cheesy and wonderfully savoury. They are the perfect accompaniment to pre-dinner drinks, since they are sufficiently salty to get those gastric juices going, but simple enough not to detract from the main event – the dinner. I find that over-elaborate canapés can take the edge off one's appetite too much. Make sure you use real – freshly grated – parmesan for the best flavour.

■ 85 g / 3 oz finely grated, fresh parmesan cheese ■ 85 g / 3 oz plain flour, sifted
■ ¼ teaspoon salt ■ 71 g / 2½ oz unsalted butter, creamed until very soft ■ 2 teaspoons olive oil

Pre-heat the oven to 150°C/300°F/Gas mark 2. Mix everything together in a bowl until well combined, then gather together with your hands. Roll out to a long sausage-shape, about 23 cm/9 in long. Try to make it as round a shape as possible. Set on a plate in the refrigerator for at least 30 minutes.

After this time, cut into thin slices using a very sharp knife and set on a very lightly buttered baking tray.

Bake in the oven for 20–25 minutes, or until pale golden brown.

Transfer to a wire rack and allow to cool before eating. ✳

MELTING MOMENTS

Makes 16–20 biscuits

So-called because they simply melt in the mouth and take only a moment to devour, these light buttery biscuits are quick and easy to make. They are rolled in crushed cornflakes before baking, which gives them a nice crunchy outside. If you prefer to use rolled oats, they make a very good substitute. You can decorate the biscuits with a glacé cherry just before baking, although personally I have never been a great fan of them. Once they emerge from the oven, the biscuits will still feel a little soft to the touch, but they soon firm up to give a crisp, crunchy bite.

■ 113 g / 4 oz butter, softened ■ 85 g / 3 oz caster sugar ■ half an egg, beaten
■ 1 teaspoon vanilla ■ 113 g / 4 oz self-raising flour ■ 28 g / 1 oz cornflour
■ about 4 heaped tablespoons cornflakes, crushed (or rolled oats)

Pre-heat the oven to 190°C/375°F/Gas mark 5. Cream the butter and sugar together until pale and fluffy. Beat in the egg and vanilla and stir well. Sift in the flours and combine thoroughly with a wooden spoon. Do not beat at this stage or the mixture will be tough.

With wet hands, shape into 16–20 little balls. Roll in crushed cornflakes (or oats) and set on a buttered baking tray.

Bake in the oven for about 15 minutes, or until light golden brown.

Transfer to a wire rack to cool. ✳

ANZAC BISCUITS

Makes 24–30 biscuits

These are traditionally eaten on Anzac Day (25th April) in Australia and New Zealand. They were introduced during the First World War as a tribute to the Australian and New Zealand forces, who fought in the invasion of the Gallipoli peninsula in 1915. 'Anzac' stands for Australian and New Zealand Army Corps. The biscuits are crunchy, buttery and crisp: delicious with a cup of frothy hot chocolate – my daughter Faith's favourite.

- 170 g / 6 oz unsalted butter
- 1 tablespoon golden syrup
- 1 teaspoon bicarbonate of soda
- 1 tablespoon boiling water
- 113 g / 4 oz rolled oats (jumbo oatflakes)
- 113 g / 4 oz plain flour, sifted
- 57 g / 2 oz desiccated coconut
- 113 g / 4 oz caster sugar

Pre-heat the oven to 160°C/325°F/Gas mark 3. Melt the butter and syrup in a large saucepan over a low heat. Dissolve the bicarbonate of soda in the water, then stir into the melted mixture.

Mix together the remaining ingredients in a separate bowl and turn into the saucepan. Stir well to combine.

Using dessertspoons, place small spoonfuls of the mixture on to a lightly greased baking tray.

Bake in the oven for 15–20 minutes, or until a light golden brown.

Cool for 2 minutes in the tin, then transfer to a wire rack to cool completely.

ANZAC BISCUITS

SHREWSBURY BISCUITS

Makes 25–30 biscuits

These delightfully crisp little biscuits come from the Midlands. In Shrewsbury, they are traditionally
baked for Easter. They come in many varieties – some are flavoured with caraway seeds
(about 1 heaped teaspoon is sufficient for this mixture); most contain currants, but some include raisins
and mixed peel too; others are spicier, with the addition of mixed spice. Although most
recipes stipulate the use of caster sugar, I sometimes make them with golden granulated sugar, which
gives them more of a crunch – not authentic, but delicious nonetheless.

■ 113 g / 4 oz unsalted butter, softened ■ 113 g / 4 oz caster (or golden granulated) sugar ■ 1 egg, beaten
■ 227 g / 8 oz plain flour ■ the grated zest of 1 lemon ■ 57 g / 2 oz currants ■ caster sugar, to dust

Cream the butter and sugar together until pale
and fluffy.

Beat in the egg, a little at a time, then sift in
the flour. Add the lemon zest and combine well
with the back of a wooden spoon, then stir in
the currants.

Flour your hands lightly and combine to a
firm – not sticky – dough with your hands. Do
not overwork the mixture or the biscuits will be
tough. Turn on to a lightly floured board and roll
out to a thickness of about 5 mm / ¼ in. Then,

using a small biscuit or pastry cutter, cut into
25–30 rounds.

Set on 2 lightly buttered baking sheets and
place in the refrigerator to harden for about 30
minutes. Pre-heat the oven to 180°C/350°F/
Gas mark 4.

Bake in the oven for about 15 minutes, or
until lightly browned and firm to the touch.

Transfer to a wire rack and sprinkle immediately with caster sugar. Leave to cool completely
before packing into air-tight containers. ❊

LIME AND BROWN SUGAR MERINGUE BISCUITS

Makes about 24 meringues

These are a great favourite with my daughter Jessica. She is invariably the one scouring for the last
meringue to devour at any buffet lunch. This recipe is not for high fluffy meringues, however.
These spread out more, to give a very light biscuit-cum-meringue that is nicely flavoured with tangy
lime zest. Although excellent on their own, with tea, they are also good for pudding:
sandwich a couple of them together with whipped cream flavoured with lime zest and serve with sliced
strawberries. Or serve them alongside a large bowl of summer fruits and clotted cream. Make
sure you line your baking tray with non-stick paper – or oil it extremely well – or the mixture will stick.

■ 198 g / 7 oz egg whites (about 4–5 eggs) ■ 170 g / 6 oz caster sugar
■ 85 g / 3 oz soft light brown sugar ■ 85 g / 3 oz ground almonds ■ the zest of 1 lime

Pre-heat the oven to 130°C/250°F/Gas mark ½. Whisk the egg whites until stiff, but not quite dry. Then gradually whisk in the sugars, a little at a time. (I use my electric beater for this, and lower the speed at this point.) Stop beating when the mixture looks smooth and glossy.

Using a metal spoon, fold in the almonds and lime zest.

Spoon small amounts on to 2 lined or greased baking trays. Bake in the oven for 45 minutes, then switch off the oven and leave to 'dry out' for a further hour. Cool on a wire rack. ✳

CHOCOLATE AND COCONUT MACAROONS

Makes 30 macaroons

Macaroons bring back memories of Enid Blyton's Famous Five. Prior to any of their ripping adventures, Anne, George, Julian and Dick would tuck into a massive plate of macaroons, all washed down with some jolly good lemonade. Even Timmy the dog was given some! Since I was a Famous Five 'groupie' as a child, I still get excited when I see macaroons. I am often disappointed, however, because the shop-bought ones are invariably too sweet and rather boring.
The following recipe is for coconut-flavoured macaroons, flecked with milk-chocolate chips. They are not too sweet. Try to find golden caster sugar, which gives them a golden-caramel colour. Otherwise regular caster sugar will do. It can be difficult to remove the cakes from the baking tray once cooked. If you wait too long, they become stuck and if you remove them too soon, they tend to collapse as you transfer them. I suggest waiting for 2–3 minutes, then sliding in a spatula or fish slice with a deft touch. Macaroons are great tea-time treats. I like them with a cup of tea, but ginger beer or pop will do!

■ 3 egg whites ■ a pinch of salt ■ 113 g / 4 oz golden caster sugar
■ 227 g / 8 oz desiccated coconut ■ 113 g / 4 oz milk-chocolate chips

Pre-heat the oven to 160°C/325°F/Gas mark 3. Whisk the egg whites with the salt until they form soft peaks. Then gradually incorporate the sugar, adding it a little at a time. With each addition, beat in the sugar with the whisk. (I always use an electric beater for this. You can use the fastest speed for the first stage, but switch to medium or low when you beat in the sugar.)

Gently fold in the coconut and chocolate chips.

Using 2 dessertspoons, drop spoonfuls of the mixture on to 2 well-greased baking trays. You should have about 30 macaroons in all. Set in the oven for about 15–20 minutes, or until the tops are golden brown.

Leave to cool on the tray for 2–3 minutes, then remove carefully to a wire rack to cool. ✳

JAMMY DODGERS

Makes 12–15 biscuits

Jammy Dodgers have always been a favourite with the children. Although the recipe below looks and tastes different from the commercial biscuits, they are still delightfully jammy. Those you buy usually have a heart-shape spot of jam on the top of 2 thin biscuits, which are sandwiched together with jam. My recipe is for one thicker biscuit that has a good crunchy texture – from the semolina – and an interesting spicy taste, from the addition of ground cinnamon and cloves. Be careful not to overdo the cloves, or you will be able to taste nothing else!
In order to obtain the most perfectly-shaped hole for the jam to fit in the biscuit, you should make the shape just before baking and fill it only halfway through cooking. Either use your thumb or the end of a wooden spoon to make the hole. Remove the biscuits after 10 minutes of cooking and fill with the jam, working as quickly as possible. My children prefer strawberry jam, but you could use apricot or raspberry.

■ 113 g / 4 oz plain flour ■ 28 g / 1 oz semolina ■ a pinch of salt ■ ¼ teaspoon ground cinnamon
■ a scant ¼ teaspoon ground cloves ■ 113 g / 4 oz unsalted butter, softened
■ 71 g / 2½ oz soft light brown sugar ■ 1 egg yolk ■ 1 teaspoon vanilla essence
■ 3–4 teaspoons strawberry jam

Pre-heat the oven to 180°C/350°F/Gas mark 4. Sift the flour, semolina, salt and spices into a mixing bowl.

In another bowl, beat together the butter and sugar until creamy and soft. Add the egg yolk and vanilla, and stir well.

Add the dry ingredients to the butter mixture and combine to a soft dough.

With floured hands, divide the mixture into 12–15 small balls (about the size of walnuts).

Place on a lightly buttered baking tray and flatten the tops slightly. Using the tip of your thumb or the handle of a wooden spoon, make a little depression on the top of each biscuit.

Set in the oven for 10 minutes, then remove and fill each little hole with a tiny amount of jam. Return to the oven for a further 10–12 minutes, or until golden brown. Transfer at once to a wire rack to cool completely before serving. Store in an air-tight container. ❋

GINGER BISCUITS

Makes about 36 biscuits

Ginger snaps, along with digestive and rich-tea biscuits, were the only commercial biscuits I can remember from my childhood. Since all other baked goodies were home-made – from scones and cakes to buns and Belgian biscuits – I used to love the treat of shop-bought biscuits. Children are notoriously contrary!
Ginger biscuits are still a regular in my biscuit barrel now, for my own children. I also love to use them in desserts – they make a welcome change from digestives in a cheesecake biscuit base, for example. Or they can be mixed with melted butter and layered with whipped double cream and crushed pineapple for a very simple, but delicious, pudding.
The mixture in my ginger biscuit recipe is loosely based on a Swedish one. The mixture should be made in advance and chilled in the refrigerator overnight. Then it is rolled out on the following day and cut into rounds. It can be difficult to roll out when it is cold, so I suggest cutting it into 4 pieces and rolling them out with a rolling pin. They should be chewy inside immediately after baking, but they harden up nicely as they cool.

■ 142 ml / ¼ pint double cream ■ 227 g / 8 oz black treacle ■ 57 g / 2 oz soft light brown sugar
■ 2 heaped teaspoons ground ginger ■ the grated zest of ½ lemon ■ 454 g / 1 lb plain flour
■ ¼ teaspoon salt ■ ½ teaspoon bicarbonate of soda

Place the cream, treacle and sugar in a small pan and melt over a low heat. Once the sugar has melted, beat well with a wooden spoon.

Add the ginger and lemon zest, then sift in the flour, salt and bicarbonate of soda. Combine to a stiff dough.

Wrap the dough in clingfilm and chill in the refrigerator overnight.

Next day, pre-heat the oven to 180°C/350°F/ Gas mark 4.

Roll out the dough as thinly as possible and cut into rounds, using floured cutters. Set on 2 lightly buttered baking sheets and bake in the oven for about 10 minutes, or until just firm to the touch.

Transfer to a wire rack to cool. ❋

VANILLA COOKIE SANDWICHES

Makes 8 biscuits

These are big cookies! Can you guess the country of origin? Yes, America – home of the ridiculously large but satisfying cookie. This recipe is loosely based on one called 'peach cookies' given to me by a Californian friend. When she described it to me I was intrigued. Her recipe calls for the cookies to be slightly undercooked, so that the insides can be scooped out and filled with vanilla pudding. Two cookies are then sandwiched together and dunked in sweet vermouth, before being rolled in sugar. After a quick spell in the refrigerator, they are decorated with tiny leaf shapes to make them look like peaches. That all seemed far too long and complicated for me – and anyway I like my peaches fresh from the fruit bowl – so I changed her recipe. My cookies are cooked through and then sandwiched together with Galliano-flavoured crème fraîche. Galliano liqueur is strongly flavoured with vanilla, so it complements the vanilla in the actual cookie. If you don't have any, you could subsitute vanilla essence. These are more of a dessert cookie than an afternoon tea cookie – dainty they are not, but delicious they most certainly are.

COOKIES

■ 3 eggs ■ 85 g / 3 oz caster sugar ■ 114 ml / 4 fl oz vegetable oil ■ 2 tablespoons baking powder
■ 1½ teaspoons vanilla essence ■ 284 g / 10 oz plain flour

FILLING

■ 284 ml / ½ pint crème fraîche ■ 1 tablespoon Galliano liqueur

Pre-heat the oven to 150°C/300°F/Gas mark 2. Using a balloon whisk, beat together the eggs, sugar, oil, baking powder and vanilla.

Once smooth, sift in the flour and fold gently together with a wooden spoon to combine.

Using 2 dessertspoons, drop 16 blobs of the mixture on to a lightly greased baking sheet. Bake in the oven for about 20 minutes, or until cooked through and a pale golden brown. Transfer at once to a wire rack and allow to cool.

Once cooled, prepare the filling. Stir the Galliano into the cream and beat well until smooth.

Sandwich 2 cookies together with the cream filling. They are best assembled just before eating, although they will hold well (without becoming too soggy) for about 1 hour.

ICE-CREAM SANDWICHES

Makes 12 biscuits

These are extremely popular for dessert at family Sunday lunch. They can, of course, be
served in the traditional way – a bowl of ice-cream and a plateful of cookies – but, served as a
combination, they make the whole experience really special.
The cookies can be made a couple of days in advance, but they should only be filled an hour or so
before serving. This way, the ice-cream is still hard, but the cookies do not have time to
freeze. If you do want to prepare the cookies in advance, make sure you remove them from the freezer in
order to soften up before serving. Use the best-quality chocolate for the cookies and whichever
flavour of ice-cream you like – I recommend chocolate, fudge, nut or toffee.

COOKIES

■ 170 g / 6 oz golden caster sugar ■ 170 g / 6 oz unsalted butter, softened ■ 1 egg
■ 170 g / 6 oz plain flour, sifted ■ 57 g / 2 oz porridge oats ■ a pinch of salt
■ 113 g / 4 oz quality milk chocolate, roughly chopped

FILLING

■ ice-cream (flavour of your choice)

Pre-heat the oven to 180°C/350°F/Gas mark 4.
Place the sugar, butter and egg in a food processor and process briefly until blended.

Add the flour, oats and salt, then process
again until well-mixed. Turn in to a bowl and
stir in the chocolate.

Using 2 teaspoons, place 24 mounds of the
mixture on to 2 buttered baking sheets. Bake in
the oven for 12–15 minutes, or until golden
brown, but still slightly soft in the centre.

Allow to cool in the tin for 2 minutes, then
transfer to a wire rack to cool completely.

Soften the ice-cream very slightly, then
assemble the cookies in pairs: spoon a little of
the ice-cream on to the flat side of one cookie
and sandwich together with the flat side of
another cookie. Press down gently so the ice-
cream is pushed out to the edges.

Once all the sandwiches have been filled, return to the freezer to firm up for 45–60 minutes.
❄ The unfilled cookies freeze well, but do not
freeze the filled cookies for more than 1 hour.

*Make these ice-cream sandwiches with other cookies,
such as Peanut Butter on page 144 or Rocky Road
on page 141.*

BROWNIES, FLAPJACKS & TIFFIN

Here are all sorts of baked goodies which are cut directly from the baking tray or tin – 'tray-bakes'. Firm favourites with children, they are also gloriously tempting for grown-ups. You too will yield to a slice of paradise cake, believe me.

CHOCOLATE FUDGE BROWNIES

Makes 20 brownies

Brownies are vintage North American. They are an integral part of America's culinary heritage, along with Mom's apple pie and Thanksgiving pumpkin pie. Rather like our biscuits and cakes, there are many variations. You can add nuts – pecans, walnuts, macadamias or hazelnuts – or white chocolate chips. You can even ice them with fudge icing or rich chocolate frosting. The basic brownie should be fairly dense in texture – moist and fudgey – although still fairly soft. They are delicious eaten freshly-baked, but they can also be reheated slightly and served for dessert with dollops of ice-cream and a drizzle of hot chocolate sauce. You can add 57 g / 2 oz chopped nuts to this basic recipe, if you wish. It is important not to overcook the brownies, or they will be dry inside.

■ 142 g / 5 oz plain chocolate (look for at least 50 per cent cocoa solids) ■ 113 g / 4 oz unsalted butter ■ 4 eggs, beaten ■ 142 g / 5 oz caster sugar ■ 113 g / 4 oz plain flour ■ 1 teaspoon baking powder ■ a pinch of salt ■ 1 teaspoon vanilla essence

Pre-heat the oven to 180°C/350°F/Gas mark 4. Melt the chocolate and butter together over a low heat, then allow to cool for about 5 minutes.

Beat the eggs and sugar together using a whisk, until light and creamy. Then sift in the flour and baking powder. Add the salt and vanilla and combine well.

Gently fold the warm chocolate mixture into the dry ingredients, until well-combined.

Pour into a buttered 23 cm / 9 in square tin. Bake in the oven for 20–25 minutes, or until a skewer inserted into it comes out barely clean.

Cut into squares at once, then allow to cool in the tin for about 5 minutes.

Using a fish slice, carefully transfer to a wire rack. Cool for about 15 minutes before eating. ❋

There is a fine line between undercooked and overcooked brownies. To test, insert a skewer into the centre. A tiny amount of the soft mixture should adhere to it. If it comes out clean – as for other cakes – the texture will be dry, not fudgey.

'NO MESS' CHOCOLATE BROWNIES

Makes 16 squares

Just read the instructions to this recipe – incredible, isn't it! Everything is mixed together in the cake tin used for the actual baking; it is rather like making mud pies. It is so easy – and, more importantly, so tidy! There is absolutely no mess, as you have no mixing bowls to wash up.

■ 170 g / 6 oz self-raising flour ■ a pinch of salt ■ 2 heaped tablespoons cocoa powder
■ 170 g / 6 oz caster sugar ■ 5 tablespoons sunflower oil ■ 1 tablespoon clear, distilled vinegar
■ 1 teaspoon vanilla ■ 227 ml / 8 fl oz cold water

Pre-heat the oven to 180°C/350°F/Gas mark 4. Grease a 20 cm/8 in deep square cake tin. Sift the flour, salt and cocoa into the tin, add the sugar and stir to combine.

Once it is mixed, mark out 3 grooves in the middle of the tin. Pour the oil into one groove, the vinegar into the second, and the vanilla into the third. Now pour over the water and, using a wooden spoon, stir everything together until it is thoroughly mixed. Do make sure you get into all the corners, to ensure there are no blobs of unmixed flour.

Bake in the oven for about 25 minutes, or until a little of the mixture adheres to a skewer when inserted into the centre.

Transfer to a wire rack and allow to cool in the tin for 5 minutes, before cutting into squares. Cool for a further 10–15 minutes, then transfer the squares to the wire rack. If you can wait, cool for a further 10 minutes before eating. ✳

WHITE CHOCOLATE CHIP BROWNIES

Makes 16–20 brownies

These are dangerously good brownies! They are also easy enough for children to make, but take care not to overcook them. Since the white chocolate topping is rather sweet and cloying, it is important to use a good-quality bitter dark chocolate. The addition of chopped nuts is optional. If you are making them for the children, it is probably wise to leave them out – few children seem to like nuts. Then again, it might be a good idea – more for you!

■ 198 g / 7 oz dark chocolate ■ 142 g / 5 oz unsalted butter ■ 85 g / 3 oz caster sugar
■ 2 eggs, beaten ■ 2 teaspoons vanilla essence ■ 227 g / 8 oz self-raising flour, sifted
■ a pinch of salt ■ 99 g / 3½ oz white chocolate chips ■ 57 g / 2 oz chopped walnuts (optional)

Pre-heat the oven to 180°C/350°F/Gas mark 4. Melt the dark chocolate and the butter, then stir in the caster sugar. Add the eggs a little at a time, beating well between each addition.

Add the vanilla extract, then fold in the flour and salt. Combine everything thoroughly, then gently fold in the white chocolate chips (and walnuts, if using).

Turn the mixture into a buttered, floured 20 cm/8 in square baking tin and smooth the top. Bake in the oven for about 25 minutes, or until a little of the mixture adheres to the very end of a skewer inserted into the middle.

Set on a wire rack, cut into squares and allow to cool in the tin for 30 minutes. Then transfer to the wire rack and cool completely. ✳

CHOCOLATE LEMON CHEESE SLICES

Makes 12–16 slices

This is a delightful combination – lemon curd and chocolate cake. While lemon curd is more commonly combined with sharp berries – blackcurrants, brambles or raspberries, for example – in pies, tarts and crumbles, it also works well in chocolate cake. Rather than spreading it 'neat' on to layers of cake, which concentrates its sharp flavour too greatly, I like to mix it with that most luscious and fattening of cream cheeses, mascarpone. The result is a finely textured chocolate cake, crumbly from the ground almonds, which is filled and topped with a mixture of lemon curd and mascarpone. See page 88 for my easy Lemon Curd recipe.

CAKE

■ 4 eggs ■ 142 g / 5 oz caster sugar ■ 113 g / 4 oz self-raising flour ■ 28 g / 1 oz cocoa powder
■ 57 g / 2 oz ground almonds ■ 28 g / 1 oz butter, melted

FILLING / TOPPING

■ 227 g / 8 oz mascarpone cream cheese ■ 2 heaped tablespoons (about 170 g / 6 oz) fresh lemon curd
■ edible flowers, such as pansies, heartsease and herb flowers, to garnish (optional)

Pre-heat the oven to 190°C/375°F/Gas mark 5. Lightly beat the eggs in a china or glass bowl, then add the sugar. Set the bowl over a pan of gently simmering water and, using a balloon whisk, beat together until thick, pale and creamy – this takes about 5 minutes.

Sift the flour and cocoa powder into the bowl, along with the ground almonds and gently fold together. Then stir in the melted butter and combine well.

Pour into a 20 cm / 8 in square baking tin and set in the oven for about 20 minutes, or until a skewer inserted into the middle comes out clean.

Invert carefully on to a wire rack and allow to cool. When cold, cut the cake in half.

To make the filling, beat the mascarpone and lemon curd together. Sandwich the cakes together with half the lemon cheese mixture and use what remains to ice the top. Cut into squares. Serve as it is, or decorate with edible flowers.

CHOCOLATE LEMON CHEESE SLICE

MINCEMEAT AND ORANGE FLAPJACKS

Makes 24 bars

Flapjacks are a family favourite. They are quick to make, very cheap and versatile – many ingredients can be added to the basic mixture. The secret of good flapjacks is to remove them from the oven while still slightly soft in the centre – they will harden up with cooling. If you leave them in the oven for too long, they become brittle. The perfect flapjack should be moist, rather chewy, but also slightly crumbly. The following flapjacks are wonderfully moist and packed full of flavour, especially if you use home-made mincemeat. I usually add whisky to my mincemeat, so the flapjacks are rather rich and boozy.

■ 227 g / 8 oz best mincemeat ■ 170 g / 6 oz butter ■ 284 g / 10 oz golden syrup
■ the grated zest of 1 large orange ■ 425 g / 15 oz porridge oats

Pre-heat the oven to 180°C/350°F/Gas mark 4. Warm the mincemeat, butter and golden syrup together until melted – either over a low heat or in a microwave (on High for 2–4 minutes), stirring often.

Once the butter has melted, stir in the orange zest. Then tip in the oats and combine well.

Pour the mixture into a buttered swiss-roll tin, 23 × 33 cm/9 × 13 in, and press down with the back of a spoon. Bake in the centre of the oven for about 25 minutes, or until golden brown.

Set the tin on a wire rack and cut into squares while still hot. Allow to cool in the tin until completely cold. ❋

BLACK BOTTOM FLAPJACKS

Makes 24 flapjacks

The following recipe is for plain flapjacks which are allowed to cool, then dipped into melted dark chocolate. Once cool, they can be stored for 2–3 weeks in an air-tight container. This recipe uses porridge oats, but you could use half porridge oats and half whole rolled oats for a rougher texture. For the black bottoms, use a good-quality chocolate – chocolate chips will do if they are not too sweet. It can be difficult to get an exact measurement for tablespoons of syrup – one cook's heaped tablespoon is another's level dessertspoon because so much adheres to the spoon. If you are confident of your syrup-measuring skills (and if you first dip the tablespoon into boiling water), then count on 6 rounded tablespoons for the weight given here. Otherwise, if weighing I recommend you flour the scales well first, then it will be far less messy.

FLAPJACKS

■ 198 g / 7 oz unsalted butter ■ 312 g / 11 oz golden syrup ■ a pinch of salt ■ 454 g / 1 lb porridge oats

TOPPING

■ 142 g / 5 oz dark chocolate

Pre-heat the oven to 180°C/350°F/Gas mark 4. Melt the butter and syrup together – either in a saucepan over a low heat or in a microwave for 2–3 minutes.

Once they have melted, stir well, then add the salt and the oats. Stir very well to combine.

Pour the mixture into a buttered swiss-roll tin, 23 × 33 cm / 9 × 13 in. Using the back of a metal spoon, level off the surface.

Bake in the oven for 25 minutes, or until golden brown. Remove and cut into squares at once, while still hot. Allow to cool in the tin, then transfer the squares to a wire rack.

Melt the chocolate: place in a bowl and set over a pan of simmering water. Dip the end of each flapjack into the chocolate, so that the bottom is completely covered. Return to the wire rack, chocolate side-up, to cool . ❄

BANANA OAT SQUARES

Makes about 24 squares

These are really a variation on flapjacks. They have a strong banana flavour throughout and are slightly softer than flapjacks, because of the banana. Like flapjacks, it is important to cut them while they are still hot and allow to cool in the tin. Although they are good served with a cup of tea or coffee, I would also recommend them as fillers for the children's lunch-boxes. Or, for a really substantial winter pudding, serve them alongside banana ice-cream, topped with a drizzle of maple syrup. Make sure you have a light main course first!

■ 142 g / 5 oz butter ■ 85 g / 3 oz soft light brown sugar ■ 142 g / 5 oz (about 3 tablespoons) golden syrup
■ 340 g / 12 oz porridge oats ■ ½ teaspoon ground cinnamon ■ ½ teaspoon ground ginger
■ ½ teaspoon baking powder ■ 2–3 bananas (about 198 g / 7 oz, peeled weight)

Pre-heat the oven to 180°C/350°F/Gas mark 4. Melt the butter, sugar and syrup together in a large saucepan over a low heat. Then pour in the porridge oats and stir. Add the spices and baking powder and continue to stir well.

Mash the bananas, then add to the mixture. Combine thoroughly, then turn into a buttered swiss-roll tin, 23 × 33 cm / 9 × 13 in. Smooth the surface with the back of a metal spoon.

Bake in the oven for 20–25 minutes, or until the edges are beginning to turn golden brown.

Cut into squares while still hot, then allow to cool in the tin before transferring to a wire rack to become completely cold. ❄

NUTTY CHOCOLATE TIFFIN

Makes 16 squares

There are many variations of this old favourite, which is also known as chocolate biscuit cake
or refrigerator cake. My mother-in-law makes a similar one to serve for pudding, called African Queen.
It is made with broken biscuits – not crumbs – and is generously doused with brandy or rum.
It is served in thin wedges with plenty of thick pouring cream.
My recipe is vaguely reminiscent of the chocolate snowballs we used to make in the Brownies, but
please do not let that put you off. I should perhaps add that in my mind's eye I see those
coconut-coated balls of chocolate fudge through rose-coloured spectacles. They were probably dreadful
– over-sweet and sickly – but to me, an eager 8-year old Brownie, they were a real treat.
And they helped me achieve my 'Cookery' badge. Luckily my own daughters have to bake proper buns
and cook bacon and eggs for their badge, so I need not reveal my latent chocolate
snowball-rolling skills to them!
The tiffin is very rich, so it should be cut into fairly small pieces. It keeps well, but I do
suggest you keep it in a cake tin at the back of the cupboard – not in a glass jar nestling temptingly
beside the coffee and kettle. You have been warned!

■ 227 g / 8 oz unsalted butter ■ 2 tablespoons golden syrup
■ 227 g / 8 oz plain chocolate (look for 50–60 per cent cocoa solids)
■ 284 g / 10 oz rich tea biscuits ■ 57 g / 2 oz blanched hazelnuts, roughly chopped
■ 57 g / 2 oz raisins ■ 57 g / 2 oz desiccated coconut

Melt the butter, syrup and chocolate together over a low heat, stirring often.

Crush the biscuits into fine crumbs with a food processor, then turn into the hot chocolate mixture. Add the chopped hazelnuts, raisins and coconut and stir well to combine. Once thoroughly mixed, turn into a very lightly buttered 20 cm / 8 in square tin and leave to cool.

Once the tiffin is set and completely cold, cut into squares. Store in an air-tight container. ❉

NUTTY CHOCOLATE TIFFIN

THICK CHOCOLATE COCONUT BARS

Makes 20 bars

It is essential to use good-quality milk chocolate for these – try to find some with at least 30 per cent cocoa solids. The regular brands contain only about 20 per cent, and far too much sugar. These bars have a coconut and biscuit crumb base and a thick chocolate topping. They are not baked, but you must leave them to set for a couple of hours – either in a cold larder or in a refrigerator – before serving. If you really like nuts, add 57 g/2 oz chopped walnuts to the base.

BASE
■ 113 g/4 oz butter ■ 57 g/2 oz caster sugar ■ 1 teaspoon vanilla essence ■ 4 tablespoons cocoa powder
■ 227 g/8 oz digestive biscuits, crushed into crumbs ■ 85 g/3 oz desiccated coconut

TOPPING
■ 284 g/10 oz best milk chocolate, chopped

Warm the butter, sugar, vanilla and cocoa in a saucepan until the butter melts. Remove from the heat and beat well.

Add the biscuit crumbs and coconut and stir well to combine.

Press into a buttered 25 × 18 cm/10 × 7 in tin, smoothing the top level.

Allow to set in the refrigerator or in a cool larder for about an hour.

Melt the chocolate (either in a double boiler or in the microwave) and pour over the base, again smoothing the surface level. Leave in a cold place to become completely hard, then cut into bars. ❈

BUTTERSCOTCH BARS

Makes 12 bars

These are reminiscent of brownies in texture – crisp on the outside, and moist and chewy inside – but their colour is nothing like the common chocolate brownie. This type of tray bake is sometimes called a blond brownie. The butterscotch flavour comes from the mixture of butter and soft brown sugar. These bars are perfect for children's lunch boxes or for picnics.

■ 142 g/5 oz soft light brown sugar ■ 57 g/2 oz unsalted butter ■ 1 egg, beaten
■ 85 g/3 oz self-raising flour, sifted ■ a pinch of salt ■ 57 g/2 oz pecans, roughly chopped
■ 1 teaspoon vanilla essence

Pre-heat the oven to 180°C/350°F/Gas mark 4. Melt the brown sugar and butter together in a saucepan over a low heat, then allow to cool for 15–20 minutes

Add the egg and stir well, then stir in the flour and salt.

Add the nuts and vanilla, and combine well.

Spoon into a buttered 18 cm/7 in square tin and bake in the oven for about 25 minutes. Transfer to a wire rack and cut into 12 bars.

Leave to cool in the tin for about 30 minutes, then turn on to a wire rack to cool completely. ❄

CHOCOLATE PEANUT BUTTER SLICE

Makes about 24 squares

The idea for this recipe comes from The Village Bakery in Melmerby, Cumbria. They bake not only the most wonderful breads – from deep, dark Russian rye to Greek olive – but also a range of delicious cakes and biscuits. Their 'peanutter' is a great favourite in The Village Bakery's restaurant. My recipe uses primarily self-raising flour, for a light texture, and also a small quantity of plain flour (only wholemeal is used at The Village Bakery). It is important to use sugar-free peanut butter and I personally prefer the crunchy variety, although use smooth if you wish. Some peanut butters from health-food shops are salt-free, in which case you must add a pinch of salt with the flour.

As for the covering, use only best-quality chocolate, milk or plain. Once the Chocolate Peanut Butter Slice has cooled, cut into squares and keep in an air-tight tin, ready to accompany a cup of morning coffee. It will certainly keep away those mid-morning hunger pangs!

BASE

■ 198 g / 7 oz wholemeal self-raising flour ■ 85 g / 3 oz plain flour, sifted
■ 227 g / 8 oz soft dark brown sugar ■ 113 g / 4 oz butter, softened
■ 113 g / 4 oz peanut butter (sugar-free) ■ 2 eggs, beaten

TOPPING

■ 142 g / 5 oz chocolate, milk or plain ■ 85 g / 3 oz peanut butter ■ 57 g / 2 oz desiccated coconut

Pre-heat the oven to 180°C/350°F/Gas mark 4. For the base, mix together the flours, sugar, butter, peanut butter and eggs. Spoon into a buttered swiss-roll tin, 23 × 33 cm/9 × 13 in, and level off the top with a spatula.

Bake in the oven for about 25 minutes, or until the edges are slightly firm and the centre is still slightly soft. Transfer to a wire rack and allow to cool for about 5–10 minutes

While it cools, prepare the topping. Melt the chocolate: place in a bowl and set over a pan of simmering water. Stir in the peanut butter and coconut and spoon over the biscuit base, carefully smoothing the surface.

Cut into squares and allow to cool in the tin for about 20 minutes. Then transfer to a wire rack and leave to become completely cold before hiding away in air-tight tins. ❄

PARADISE CAKE

Makes 12–16 squares

Paradise cake was a great favourite in my childhood. I used to love the rich filling of jam, coconut, dried fruit and cherries, all encased in rich shortcrust pastry. I have absolutely no idea where the name came from, but I can only assume it is something to do with the fact that it tastes so heavenly!

It is important to leave the cake to cool completely in the tin before decanting. Otherwise, it will be far too sticky – deliciously gooey, but far too difficult to handle.

PASTRY

- 227 g / 8 oz plain flour, sifted
- 113 g / 4 oz butter, cut into cubes
- 28 g / 1 oz caster sugar ▪ 1 egg

FILLING

- 170–227 g / 6–8 oz strawberry or raspberry jam
- 170 g / 6 oz caster sugar
- 57 g / 2 oz butter, softened
- 2 small eggs (size 4), beaten
- 113 g / 4 oz desiccated coconut
- 113 g / 4 oz sultanas
- 57 g / 2 oz glacé cherries, halved

First make the pastry: place the flour, butter and sugar in a food processor and process until the mixture resembles breadcrumbs. Add the egg through the feeder tube and process until combined. Wrap in clingfilm and chill for 1 hour.

PARADISE CAKE

Roll out the pastry to fit a lightly buttered 25 × 18 cm/10 × 7 in baking tin. Prick all over and chill for at least 1 hour – or, preferably, overnight – to help prevent shrinkage. Pre-heat the oven to 190°C/375°F/Gas mark 5.

Line the pastry with foil, fill with baking beans and bake 'blind' for 10 minutes. Remove the foil and beans and cook the pastry for a further 5 minutes.

Allow to cool. Reduce the oven to 180°C/350°F/Gas mark 4.

Once the base is cool, spread with jam. Cream together the sugar and butter, then beat in the eggs. Fold in the coconut, sultanas and cherries and combine well. Pour over the jam, ensuring the base is evenly covered.

Bake in the oven for about 30 minutes, or until golden brown and set. Allow to cool in the tin for about 20 minutes, then cut into squares with a sharp knife.

Leave to cool in the tin, then decant only when completely cold. ❄

RHUBARB STREUSEL SQUARES

Makes 16 squares

In Germany, we had many delicious Streusel cakes. These usually consisted of seasonal fruit – blackcurrants, cherries, pears or apples, for example – baked in a light cake and covered with a crumbly, crunchy topping. This topping is a near relation to our crumble, which we always serve as pudding, not cake. This recipe has a light almondy cake base, a filling of cooked rhubarb and a crumbly topping, which is made even more crunchy by the addition of oatflakes. Make sure you use jumbo (large) oatflakes, for a good coarse texture.

FILLING
■ 454 g / 1 lb rhubarb, washed and chopped ■ 57 g / 2 oz soft light brown sugar

BASE
■ 85 g / 3 oz ground almonds ■ 170 g / 6 oz self-raising flour, sifted ■ 85 g / 3 oz soft light brown sugar
■ 113 g / 4 oz butter, cut into cubes ■ 1 egg ■ ½ teaspoon vanilla essence

STREUSEL TOPPING
■ 2 heaped tablespoons jumbo oats ■ 2 tablespoons plain flour ■ 3 tablespoons soft light brown sugar
■ 1 heaped teaspoon ground ginger ■ 2 tablespoons sunflower oil

First prepare the filling: place the rhubarb in a saucepan with the sugar. Heat gently over a very low heat, stirring often, until the sugar has dissolved. Cover and cook for a further 10 minutes, shaking the pan occasionally, until tender. (Since no liquid is added, it is important to start the cooking over a very low heat indeed.) Remove from the heat and allow to cool.

Pre-heat the oven 180°C/350°F/Gas mark 4.

To make the base, place the almonds, flour, sugar and butter in a food processor and process until the butter is incorporated. Add the egg and vanilla, then process until blended.

Spoon into a buttered 20 cm/8 in square cake tin and smooth the top with a spatula.

Top with the cooled rhubarb, leaving a border all around the edges.

To make the topping, mix the oats, flour, sugar and ginger together, then stir in the oil.

Spoon over the rhubarb to form an even layer.

Bake in the oven for about 50 minutes, or until well-risen and pale golden brown around the edges.

Cut into squares and leave to cool in the tin before decanting. ❄

If using frozen rhubarb, drain it well both before and after cooking. Otherwise the mixture will be soggy.

FRUIT COCKTAIL SQUARES

Makes about 24 squares

Strange title, strange ingredients! In this cake mix is an entire tin of fruit cocktail – the type you used to have with custard for school dinners. Fortunately, nowadays, we can buy the fruit in fruit juice, not syrup, so the overall taste is not too sweet. It makes an interesting tea-time treat – a light sponge full of chopped fruit with a crunchy coconut and sugar coating. Serve cold with a cup of tea; or warm with creamy custard (preferably one that in no way resembles school custard).

CAKE

■ 2 eggs ■ 113 g / 4 oz caster sugar ■ 1 × 415 g tin of fruit cocktail in fruit juice, well-drained
■ a pinch of salt ■ 1 teaspoon baking powder ■ 227 g / 8 oz self-raising flour
■ 99 ml / 3½ fl oz vegetable oil

TOPPING

■ 28 g / 1 oz desiccated coconut ■ 28 g / 1 oz soft light brown sugar

Pre-heat the oven to 160°C/325°F/Gas mark 3. Stir together the 7 cake ingredients until well mixed. Do not beat too vigorously, or the fruit will break up.

Spoon into a buttered 25 × 18 cm/10 × 7 in tin and smooth the top.

Combine the coconut and sugar for the topping and sprinkle over the top.

Bake in the oven for about 25 minutes, or until crusty and golden on top.

Cool in the tin, then cut into squares and set on a wire rack to cool completely.

DATE AND GINGER SHORTBREAD SQUARES

Makes 16 squares

I have adapted these delightful shortbread squares from a recipe given to me by a friend who runs a small catering business in Edinburgh. I have added ginger and currants to Hilary's basic date mixture. The result is a light, buttery shortbread with a crunchy texture, given by the semolina, and a spicy filling of dates, honey, lemon and stem ginger.

FILLING

- 170 g / 6 oz pitted dates, roughly chopped
- 57 g / 2 oz currants
- 1 tablespoon stem ginger, chopped
- 1 tablespoon ginger syrup (from a jar of stem ginger)
- 1 tablespoon honey
- 3 tablespoons water
- 1 tablespoon lemon juice
- a pinch of ground cinnamon

SHORTBREAD

- 170 g / 6 oz self-raising flour, sifted
- 170 g / 6 oz semolina
- 170 g / 6 oz butter
- 85 g / 3 oz caster sugar

Pre-heat the oven to 190°C/375°F/Gas mark 5. To make the filling, place the 8 ingredients in a saucepan and slowly bring to the boil. Cover, then lower the heat and simmer for about 10 minutes, or until the dates are soft. Then turn into a food processor and purée until smooth.

To make the shortbread casing, place the flour and semolina in a bowl. Warm the butter and sugar in a small saucepan over a low heat until the sugar has dissolved. Pour into the flour mixture and stir well to combine.

Press two-thirds of the shortbread mixture into a buttered 20 cm/8 in square tin. Using a spatula, smooth the surface. Spoon the date mixture on top, leaving a margin all round.

Cover with the remaining mixture: I find it easiest to 'crumble' the shortbread over the top with my fingers, then to press down lightly with the palm of my hand.

Bake in the oven for about 25 minutes, or until golden brown. Cut into squares immediately, while still hot.

Leave to cool in the tin for at least 20–30 minutes before transferring to a wire rack to cool completely. (If you try to move the squares while they are still hot, they will collapse.)

DATE AND GINGER SHORTBREAD SQUARES

PINE-NUT CARAMEL SQUARES

Makes 8 large squares

I simply cannot resist these. The idea is that you make a whole tray batch and keep them to serve for dessert with either vanilla ice-cream or thick Greek yoghurt. But, invariably, the number you actually cut out of the tray to keep is 7 – not 8 – and a lot of the ends are 'trimmed up'! The pastry is a short, lemony one, the tang of the citrus fruit being essential to cut through the sweetness of the caramel filling. The pine-nuts can be toasted for added colour and better depth of flavour.

PASTRY CASE

■ 28 g / 1 oz caster sugar ■ the grated zest and juice of 1 lemon ■ 170 g / 6 oz plain flour, sifted ■ 85 g / 3 oz unsalted butter, cut into cubes ■ a pinch of salt

FILLING

■ 85 g / 3 oz unsalted butter ■ 170 g / 6 oz soft light brown sugar ■ 85 g / 3 oz thick honey ■ 142 ml / ¼ pint double cream ■ 113 g / 4 oz pine-nuts

For the pastry, place the sugar, lemon zest and flour in a food processor and process until combined. Add the butter and salt and process again until the mixture resembles breadcrumbs. Then add the lemon juice and process until the mixture comes together. Wrap in clingfilm and chill for at least 2 hours.

Roll out the pastry to fit a greased 18 × 25 cm / 7 × 10 in baking tin. Prick all over and chill overnight – or for at least 2 hours. Pre-heat the oven to 190°C/375°F/Gas mark 5.

Line the pastry with foil and baking beans and bake 'blind' for 15 minutes. Remove the foil and the beans and cook for a further 5 minutes. Cool slightly.

Meanwhile, prepare the caramel: place the butter, sugar and honey in a heavy-based saucepan and warm over a low heat, stirring often, until the butter is melted. Bring slowly to the boil and bubble fiercely for 1 minute without stirring. Then remove from the heat. Cool for 1 minute, then stir in the cream a little at a time, taking care it does not splutter.

Sprinkle the pine nuts evenly over the pastry base, then pour the caramel on top. Return to the oven for 15–20 minutes, or until the caramel is bubbling fiercely.

Set on a wire rack and allow to cool completely before cutting into large squares. Tempting though it might be, you must allow it to become quite cold before cutting, otherwise the caramel will be too soft. You can even refrigerate it for an hour or so to harden up, if you like. Serve cold with Greek yoghurt or ice-cream.

LAMINGTONS

Makes 16 squares

During a summer stay in Sydney, I often enjoyed lamingtons, which are as Australian as boomerangs. They consist of a light sponge coated in chocolate icing and then dipped in desiccated coconut. They are taken on picnics, or offered for afternoon tea or as a dessert at barbecues. The origin of the word lamington is interesting. Australian food writer Maureen Simpson claims they are named after Baron and Baroness Lamington, governor (and wife) of Queensland from 1895–1901. However, well-known British food historian Clarissa Dickson Wright, whose mother was Australian, has always known lamingtons as a corruption of 'lambing teas' – since these little cakes were served during the lambing season. Nowadays, in rural Australia, there are special 'lamington drives', where money is raised for charity by baking and selling dozens upon dozens of lamingtons. The etymology matters not, however. These cakes – plain and simple – taste exceedingly good. They are easier to ice if they are 24 hours old. Make sure the icing is fairly thin, for easier coating.

CAKE

■ 113 g / 4 oz butter, softened ■ 113 g / 4 oz caster sugar ■ 2 eggs ■ 1 teaspoon vanilla essence ■ 227 g / 8 oz self-raising flour, sifted ■ about 3 tablespoons milk

ICING

■ 57 g / 2 oz butter, softened ■ 170 g / 6 oz icing sugar, sifted ■ 1 tablespoon cocoa powder, sifted ■ 3 tablespoons warm water ■ 57–85 g / 2–3 oz desiccated coconut

Pre-heat the oven to 180°C/350°F/Gas mark 4. For the cake, beat together the softened butter and sugar until light and creamy. Then beat in the eggs, one at a time. Stir in the vanilla, then the flour, and just enough milk to combine to a soft, dropping consistency.

Spoon into a greased 20 cm/8 in square cake tin and smooth the surface. Bake in the oven for about 30 minutes, or until golden brown and springy to the touch.

Cool for about 5 minutes in the tin, then transfer to a wire rack to cool completely. When cold, cut into 16 squares.

For the icing, cream the butter and sugar together until light and creamy. In a separate bowl, mix the cocoa and water to a paste. Add to the butter mixture and beat until smooth. Pour the desiccated coconut into a saucer or bowl, ready for dipping.

Using 2 forks, coat all 4 sides of the cold cake squares in icing, then dip the iced squares in the desiccated coconut.

Set on a board to dry completely before serving. (If, towards the end of icing, the chocolate icing begins to look rather thick, simply thin it down with a spoonful or 2 of milk.)

FRUIT LOAVES

The main ingredient in these sweet loaves is fruit, fresh and dried – though some vegetables have had their say too, as in the popular carrot cake or more unusual courgette loaf. Their texture moist and flavour sublime, these are fruit cakes with a difference. They are ideal alternatives to heavy puddings. Try them warm with Greek yoghurt, clotted cream or ice-cream.

SWEET POTATO AND ORANGE LOAF

Makes 1 loaf

There are different types of sweet potato, depending on which tropical country they come from. In Britain, the 2 most common types are those with white flesh and those with orange flesh. The former are slightly milder – and obviously do not impart such a rich colour to your dish. The idea for a sweet potato cake comes from the Caribbean, where they make one that is strongly flavoured with rum. Since I have enjoyed the combination of oranges with sweet potatoes in Australia, as a vegetable, I thought it would work well in a cake. I have enhanced the flavours with cinnamon. The resulting cake, or loaf, is wonderfully moist and almost sticky – quite delicious. My recipe can double up as a pudding, when freshly baked and still warm. Do not cut it while still hot, however. Offer some cream or yoghurt with thick slices, or serve in thinner slices with a cup of tea.

■ 454 g / 1 lb sweet potato ■ 113 g / 4 oz butter ■ 4 tablespoons freshly squeezed orange juice
■ the zest of 1 large orange ■ 170 g / 6 oz soft light brown sugar
■ 3 eggs, separated ■ 170 g / 6 oz self-raising flour ■ 1 teaspoon ground cinnamon

Peel the sweet potatoes and cut into chunks. Place in a pan of lightly salted water and bring to the boil. Cook until tender – about 10 minutes – then drain. Using a potato masher, mash them with the butter. Set aside to cool completely. Pre-heat the oven to 180°C/350°F/Gas mark 4.

Place the orange juice, zest and sugar in a mixing bowl and whisk well, using a balloon whisk. Then add the egg yolks and beat well. Turn into the sweet potato and stir well to combine.

Whisk the egg whites until stiff. Fold 1 tablespoon into the sweet potato mixture, then gently fold in the remaining whites. Finally, lightly fold in the flour and cinammon.

Pour into a buttered 907 g/2 lb loaf tin and bake in the oven for 60–65 minutes, or until a skewer inserted into the middle comes out clean. If necessary, cover lightly with foil towards the end of cooking to prevent the top from burning.

Cool in the tin for 15 minutes, turn out on to a wire rack and serve the same day.

MARMALADE LOAF

Makes 1 loaf

The quality of the marmalade is crucial for this loaf – use a cheap, sugar-laden one and it will taste inferior. The best type is home-made, but otherwise use a thick-cut, good-quality commercial one. I have used commercial marmalades flavoured with brandy or whisky with excellent results.

■ 113g / 4oz unsalted butter, softened ■ 113g / 4oz caster sugar
■ 2 heaped tablespoons thick-cut marmalade ■ 284g / 10oz self-raising flour, sifted ■ a pinch of salt
■ 2 eggs, beaten ■ 1 tablespoon freshly squeezed orange juice

Pre-heat the oven to 160°C/325°F/Gas mark 3. Cream together the softened butter and sugar until light and fluffy. Mix in the marmalade, stirring well.

Add the flour and salt alternately with the beaten egg. Once it is all incorporated, stir in the juice.

Spoon into a buttered, base-lined 907 g/2 lb loaf tin. Smooth over the top. Bake in the oven for 1 hour, or until well-risen and golden brown. It should feel springy to the touch.

Leave to cool for about 20 minutes in the tin, then transfer carefully to a wire rack. Allow to cool completely before cutting. ✳

PEAR LOAF

Makes 1 loaf

This cake has a soft, moist texture and an absolutely intriguing flavour. The dried pears are soaked in the cold tea, then the tea is added to the actual cake mix. The flavour of the tea really comes through, so if you like a scented tea with a particular flavour, then do use that. Serve the cake in thick slices with a cup of hot tea. This will keep very well for several days.

■ 142g / 5oz dried pears, roughly chopped ■ 114ml / 4floz strong cold tea
■ 113g / 4oz unsalted butter, softened ■ 113g / 4oz soft dark brown sugar ■ 2 eggs
■ 142g / 5oz self-raising flour ■ ½ teaspoon baking powder ■ a pinch of salt
■ ½ teaspoon ground ginger

Soak the dried pears in the tea for at least 6 hours, or overnight.

After this time, pre-heat the oven to 180°C/350°F/Gas mark 4.

Cream the butter with the sugar until soft and creamy, then beat in the eggs one at a time. Once they are incorporated, sift in the flour, baking powder, salt and ginger. Pour in the pears

and their liquid, then fold everything together until completely blended.

Spoon into a 454 g/1 lb loaf tin and level the top. Place on a baking sheet in the oven for about 45 minutes. If necessary, cover loosely with foil for the final 10 minutes to prevent the crust from burning.

Cool completely in the tin before decanting.

SPICED BLUEBERRY LOAF

Makes 1 loaf

This loaf is a joy to behold! There is a thick layer of deep-blue/purple blueberries sandwiched between an orange-flecked, crumbly cake. Because it is crumbly, you must wait until it is completely cold before cutting. Once cold, serve in thick slices – either with a cup of tea, or with some orange mascarpone for dessert. Simply beat some freshly squeezed orange juice and the zest of an orange (or some home-made orange curd) into a bowl of thick, creamy mascarpone.
Before you add the cottage cheese to the cake mix, make sure you either strain it or mash it to remove all the little lumps. Ricotta can be used in its place, and since this already has a smooth, soft texture, there is no need to strain it. If you use frozen blueberries, make sure they are extremely well-drained – otherwise you will have a soggy cake.

■ 227 g / 8 oz self-raising flour ■ ½ teaspoon ground cinnamon ■ ½ teaspoon ground ginger
■ 57 g / 2 oz semolina ■ 113 g / 4 oz caster sugar ■ the grated zest of 1 small orange
■ 1 egg ■ 57 g / 2 oz cottage cheese, strained ■ 114 ml / 4 fl oz sunflower oil
■ 1 tablespoon freshly squeezed orange juice ■ 198 g / 7 oz blueberries, drained

Pre-heat the oven to 180°C/350°F/Gas mark 4. Sift the flour and spices into a bowl, then stir in the semolina, sugar and orange zest.

Whisk together the egg, cheese, oil and juice in a separate bowl, then stir into the dry ingredients. The mixture will be fairly stiff.

Spoon about two-thirds of the mixture into a buttered 907 g / 2 lb loaf tin. Using the back of a spoon, press the mixture down.

Place the berries on top, making sure they do not touch the sides of the tin. Sprinkle the remaining cake mixture over the top, then pat down gently with your hard, taking care not to bruise the berries and release a blue flood.

Bake in the oven for about 40 minutes, or until golden brown and cooked through.

Remove to a wire rack and allow to become completely cold before carefully turning out.

Always 'base-line' your fruit cake/loaf tins before use. First grease the insides, then line the base only with a lightly buttered piece of greaseproof paper.

SPICED BLUEBERRY LOAF
CRANBERRY PECAN LOAF (page 186)

CRANBERRY PECAN LOAF

Makes 1 loaf

This is a light fruit and nut loaf that has a delightful citrus tang. I like cranberries not only at Christmas, but also at other times of the year, so I usually store some in my freezer during the winter months. Frozen ones are fine for this cake, but make sure you defrost them completely first. This is a fairly rich loaf, with plenty of sugar, so it is best served on its own without any butter. It is nicely moist, because of the orange juice.

■ 170g / 6oz self-raising flour ■ 142g / 5oz caster sugar ■ a pinch of salt
■ 57g / 2oz unsalted butter, cut into cubes ■ the grated zest of 1 small orange
■ 3 tablespoons freshly squeezed orange juice ■ 1 egg ■ 113g / 4oz cranberries
■ 57g / 2oz pecans, roughly chopped

Pre-heat the oven to 180°C/350°F/Gas mark 4. Sift the flour into a bowl, then add the sugar and salt. Rub in the butter.

Stir in the orange zest, juice and the egg, and combine well. Add the cranberries and nuts and fold in gently.

Spoon into a buttered, base-lined 454 g/1 lb loaf tin. Set on a baking tray in the oven for about 1 hour, covering with foil towards the end of cooking to prevent the crust from burning.

Set on a wire rack and allow to cool in the tin. Once completely cold, turn out carefully.

DRIED APRICOT AND FRESH THYME LOAF

Makes 1 loaf

For this moist, action-packed loaf, I like to use Elvas apricots – those luscious Portuguese preserved fruits – but you can use ordinary dried apricots if you cannot find the Elvas ones. The fresh thyme lends an unusual flavour to this light, golden-coloured loaf, which has a nicely crunchy topping from the sugar crystals and thyme leaves. Serve this in thick slices with an espresso coffee or a glass of sweet white wine.

LOAF
■ 170g / 6oz dried apricots, roughly chopped ■ 142ml / ¼ pint dry white wine
■ 3–4 thick sprigs fresh thyme ■ 170g / 6oz self-raising flour ■ 57g / 2oz polenta
■ 1 teaspoon baking powder ■ ¼ teaspoon salt ■ 113g / 4oz unsalted butter, softened
■ 113g / 4oz caster sugar ■ 2 eggs

■ 1 heaped teaspoon sugar crystals ■ 1 teaspoon fresh thyme leaves

Combine the chopped apricots, wine and thyme in a small pan. Bring slowly to the boil, then remove from the heat the minute the bubbles appear. Cover and leave to infuse for 1 hour. Pre-heat the oven to 180°C/350°F/Gas mark 4.

Sift the flour into a bowl and combine with the polenta, baking powder and salt.

In a separate bowl, beat together the butter and sugar until light and creamy, then beat in the eggs a little at a time. Beat thoroughly for 1 minute, or until fluffy.

Strain the apricots through a sieve, reserving the liquid. Add the liquid to the butter mixture, then fold in the flour mixture. Stir in the apricots (discard the thyme sprigs). Mix well.

Spoon into a buttered 907 g/2 lb loaf tin. Combine the sugar crystals with the thyme and sprinkle over the top.

Bake in the oven for 50 minutes, or until a skewer inserted into the middle comes out clean. Cool in the tin for at least 30 minutes, then turn out on to a wire rack to cool completely. ❄

PUMPKIN LOAF

Makes 1 loaf

This is a really interesting loaf. It is sweet and spicy and packed with all things good. The pumpkin seeds add not only a welcome crunch but also a lovely green colour. The freshly grated pumpkin flesh gives a nice moist texture and rich flavour. Eat this loaf cold in thick slices – I think it is ideal to take on a picnic, for it is wholesome and exceedingly tasty. You will no doubt have to buy a whole – and incredibly heavy – pumpkin in order to have a mere slice for this recipe. But do not despair. You can cook the rest with onions and spices, such as turmeric, ginger or cumin, to make a thick vegetable soup; or roast chunks in olive oil, in a hot oven, to serve with Sunday lunch.

■ 284 g / 10 oz self-raising flour, sifted ■ 57 g / 2 oz All-Bran (or similar shredded bran cereal)
■ ½ teaspoon ground cinnamon ■ ½ teaspoon ground ginger ■ ½ teaspoon allspice
■ ¼ teaspoon salt ■ 170 g / 6 oz fresh pumpkin, grated ■ 57 g / 2 oz green pumpkin seeds
■ 142 g / 5 oz caster sugar ■ 1 egg ■ 227 ml / 8 fl oz vegetable oil

Pre-heat the oven to 180°C/350°F/Gas mark 4. Combine the first 6 ingredients in a bowl. Then stir in the grated pumpkin, the pumpkin seeds and the sugar.

Whisk together the egg and oil in a separate bowl, then add to the dry ingredients. Stir well.

Spoon into a buttered 907 g/2 lb loaf tin. Level the top.

Bake in the oven for about 1 hour, or until a skewer inserted into the middle comes out clean.

Allow to become completely cold in the tin before decanting.

BEETROOT CHOCOLATE LOAF

Makes 1 loaf

Beetroot in a cake? Yes, and delicious it is too!
The colour is just right for chocolate
cake and the grated beetroot gives the cake a
beautiful moist texture.
Although I have seen recipes using cooked,
puréed beetroot, I prefer to use raw
grated beetroot, which gives a coarser texture
and fresher flavour. Since you have to
peel and grate the beetroot for this recipe, I
would advise wearing rubber gloves –
otherwise your fingernails will be stained for
days! As for the chocolate, look for
dark chocolate with at least 55 per cent
cocoa solids.
You can either eat the loaf slightly warm, with
a dollop of sour cream or Smetana
(flavoured with brown sugar); or serve it
plain and quite cold with a cup of
strong tea.

- 227 g / 8 oz self-raising flour
- 28 g / 1 oz cocoa powder
- 1 teaspoon baking powder
- 113 g / 4 oz caster sugar ■ a pinch of salt
- 85 g / 3 oz dark chocolate
- 85 g / 3 oz unsalted butter
- 113 g / 4 oz raw beetroot
(this is the peeled weight)
- 2 eggs, beaten

BEETROOT CHOCOLATE LOAF

Pre-heat the oven to 180°C/350°F/Gas mark 4. Sift the flour, cocoa and baking powder into a bowl, then stir in the sugar and salt.

Melt the dark chocolate and butter in a saucepan over a low heat, then leave to cool for at least 5 minutes.

Grate the beetroot, using a fine grater.

Beat the eggs into the chocolate mixture, then stir in the grated beetroot and the flour mixture. Stir well to combine.

Spoon into a 907 g/2 lb buttered loaf tin. Bake in the oven for about 50 minutes, or until a skewer inserted into the middle comes out clean. Allow to cool in the tin. ❋

COURGETTE LOAF

Makes 1 loaf

This loaf is a great favourite of mine. It is light in texture and has a very interesting flavour. The courgettes add not only a lovely moist texture, but also a very unusual and striking green colour. It is important not to peel the courgettes, so there are flecks of bright green throughout. Eat this cake in thick squares – either freshly baked or warmed in a low oven after a few days – and serve with a dollop of whipped cream.

■ 227 g / 8 oz caster sugar ■ 3 eggs ■ 227 ml / 8 fl oz vegetable oil
■ 1 teaspoon vanilla essence ■ 227 g / 8 oz grated courgettes, unpeeled (this is the prepared weight)
■ 340 g / 12 oz plain flour ■ 1 teaspoon baking powder ■ 1 teaspoon bicarbonate of soda
■ ½ teaspoon salt ■ 1 level teaspoon ground cinnamon
■ ¼ teaspoon grated nutmeg ■ 85 g / 3 oz walnuts, roughly chopped

Pre-heat the oven to 180°C/350°F/Gas mark 4. Whisk together the sugar, eggs, oil and vanilla until thick.

Stir in the grated courgettes.

Sift the dry ingredients into the bowl, then add the nuts. Stir well.

Spoon into a 25 × 18 cm/10 × 7 in buttered tin. Bake in the oven for 40–45 minutes, or until a skewer inserted in the centre comes out clean. Allow to cool in the tin for at least 30 minutes, then cut into squares and transfer to a wire rack to become completely cold.

LINCOLNSHIRE PLUM LOAF

Makes 1 loaf

Like any regional breads, there are many variations. When I lived in Lincolnshire, the most typical loaf was similar to my recipe – a fruit loaf made with self-raising flour. The type of dried fruit varies, but I like the authentic recipe which uses prunes – hence the name, Plum Bread.
A less typical type of bread nowadays, but one which I like very much, is yeast-based: it is a mixture of a Selkirk Bannock and a Cornish Saffron Cake (without the saffron). This is the classic Lincolnshire Plum Bread. A perfect example of this yeasted bread is found at Mr Phipps', one of the best butchers in Lincolnshire, who has a little, old-fashioned-looking shop in the village of Mareham le Fen, near Coningsby. I love making a rum-soaked bread and butter pudding with the yeasted variety.
Both loaves are equally delicious, but the following recipe is very easy to make and takes very little time – apart from an overnight soak. It is perfect sliced thickly and taken on picnics.

■ 113 g / 4 oz prunes, pitted ■ 227 g / 8 oz raisins ■ 284 ml / ½ pint warm tea
■ 113 g / 4 oz unsalted butter ■ 113 g / 4 oz demerara sugar ■ 2 eggs ■ 1 tablespoon brandy
■ 255 g / 9 oz self-raising flour ■ a pinch of salt ■ 1 tablespoon marmalade
■ 28 g / 1 oz mixed peel, chopped (optional)

On the night before, chop the prunes, then mix them with the raisins in a bowl. Pour over the warm tea and leave to stand, covered, overnight.

On the following day, pre-heat the oven to 150°C / 300°F / Gas mark 2. Cream together the butter and sugar until fluffy. Beat in the eggs, one at a time, then add the brandy. Sift in the flour and salt and fold together.

Drain the prunes and raisins (discarding the liquid) and add to the bowl with the marmalade (and chopped mixed peel, if using). Stir everything together until thoroughly combined.

Spoon the mixture into a buttered 1 kg / 2 lb loaf tin. Bake in the oven for about 1½ hours, or until a skewer inserted into the middle comes out clean. Cover with foil for the last 15 minutes if the crust becomes too dark.

Allow to cool in the tin on a wire rack. Turn out only when completely cold. ❊

Most large fruit cakes / loaves should be 'decanted' from their tins only when completely cold.

TEISEN LAP

Makes 1 loaf

The ingredients in this typical Welsh cake are very similar to those in griddle-baked Welsh Cakes. 'Teisen Lap' – which means 'moist cake' – is baked in a round, shallow cake tin in the oven. Welsh food writer Gilli Davies suggests that this cake has always been the ideal snack for miners to take down the pits, in south Wales. It is very quick to prepare and is good eaten warm or cold.

■ 227 g / 8 oz self-raising flour ■ 1 heaped teaspoon mixed spice ■ 113 g / 4 oz butter, cut into cubes
■ 85 g / 3 oz caster sugar ■ 113 g / 4 oz raisins and currants (mixed) ■ 2 eggs, beaten ■ 1 tablespoon milk

Pre-heat the oven to 180°C/350°F/Gas mark 4. Sift the flour and spice into a bowl. Rub in the butter, then stir in the sugar and dried fruit.

Add the eggs, then the milk. Stir until it is a softish consistency. Spoon into a 20 cm/8 in buttered sandwich tin. Level the surface.

Bake in the oven for about 35 minutes, or until a skewer inserted into the middle comes out clean.

Allow to cool in the tin for 2–3 minutes, then carefully turn out on to a wire rack. Cool for at least 15 minutes before cutting. ❄

CARROT AND NUT LOAF

Makes 1 loaf

This is a very different carrot cake from the next recipe. Equally moist and delicious, this one is bulging with fruit and nuts. One bite and you suddenly feel terribly healthy. This is not a cake for icing, since it stands perfectly well by itself. It will keep for a couple of weeks in an air-tight container. I like to add either hazelnuts or walnuts, but you could try pecans or brazils.

■ 114 ml / 4 fl oz sunflower oil ■ 3 eggs, beaten ■ 1 teaspoon vanilla essence
■ 198 g / 7 oz grated carrots (this is the peeled weight) ■ 99 g / 3½ oz desiccated coconut
■ 99 g / 3½ oz raisins ■ 99 g / 3½ oz nuts, roughly chopped ■ 227 g / 8 oz plain wholemeal flour
■ 142 g / 5 oz soft light brown sugar ■ a pinch of salt ■ 1 teaspoon bicarbonate of soda
■ 1 teaspoon baking powder ■ 1 heaped teaspoon ground cinnamon

Pre-heat the oven to 180°C/350°F/Gas mark 4. Beat the oil with the eggs and vanilla, whisking well until combined.

Stir in the grated carrots, coconut, raisins and nuts. Add the flour, sugar, salt, bicarbonate of soda, baking powder and cinnamon. Mix well.

Pour into a buttered, base-lined 907 g / 2 lb loaf tin. Level the top with the back of a spoon.

Bake in the oven for about 1 hour, or until a skewer inserted into the centre comes out clean. (After 45 minutes or so, you might need to cover the top of the loaf loosely with foil to prevent it from burning.)

Set on a wire rack and leave to cool in the tin for 20 minutes. Then transfer to the wire rack until completely cold. ✳

CARROT CAKE WITH ORANGE CREAM CHEESE ICING

Makes one large cake or 16–20 squares

There are so many varieties of carrot cake in this country. Some are deeply healthy and packed with fruit, nuts and seeds; some are ordinary sponge cakes that are far too dry and only thinly coated with white icing. My recipe gives a wonderfully moist cake (that is, after all, the whole purpose of the carrots in the cake – to keep it moist). The topping is a rich, creamy icing – nicely flavoured with orange – and there is plenty of it. I love cakes which are iced with a really thick layer of good butter-cream or cream cheese icing.

CAKE
■ 227 ml / 8 fl oz sunflower oil ■ 227 g / 8 oz caster sugar ■ 3 eggs
■ 227 g / 8 oz self-raising flour, sifted ■ 1 heaped teaspoon ground cinnamon ■ a pinch of salt
■ 255 g / 9 oz grated carrots (about 5 large peeled carrots)

ICING
■ 57 g / 2 oz unsalted butter ■ 113 g / 4 oz cream cheese ■ 284 g / 10 oz icing sugar, sifted
■ the grated zest of 1 small orange ■ 1 tablespoon freshly squeezed orange juice

Pre-heat the oven to 180°C/350°F/Gas mark 4. For the cake, whisk the oil and sugar together with a balloon whisk.

Whisk in the eggs, one at a time. Then sift in the flour, cinnamon and salt and gently fold together. Finally, stir in the grated carrots.

Spoon into a buttered 25 × 18 cm/10 × 7 in square tin and smooth the top. Bake in the oven for about 45 minutes, or until a skewer inserted into the middle comes out clean.

Carefully transfer to a wire rack and allow to cool in the tin.

For the icing, beat together the softened butter and cream cheese until light and fluffy. Add the sugar and orange zest and juice. Beat everything together until really thoroughly mixed.

Once the cake is completely cold, turn on to a wire rack – I suggest you divide it into 4 and remove each quarter with a large spatula.

Spread thickly with icing and leave on the wire rack until completely set, then cut into small squares.

✳ Freeze fully iced: first open freeze, then wrap once frozen.

ORANGE AND HAZELNUT CAKE

Makes 1 cake

In Claudia Roden's book on Middle Eastern food, she explains that there are a minority of dishes in the Middle East which are Sephardic Jewish in origin. The Spanish and Portuguese influences are evident in these dishes. Although the Jews left Spain and Portugal in the 14th and 15th centuries, during the time of the Inquisition, there are still dishes – cakes, in particular – that closely resemble those cooked in Spain and Portugal today. Examples of these are cakes baked for the Jewish Passover using ground almonds or fine matzo meal instead of flour.

Claudia Roden's fine examples of sephardic cakes include a cake of oranges and almonds, both ingredients being popular in Spanish kitchens today. I have adapted this idea to produce an orange and hazelnut cake, since ground hazelnuts are becoming just as easy to find in Britain these days as ground almonds. The oranges are cooked whole, then, after the pips are removed, they are whizzed to a pulp in an electric blender or food processor. The flavour of the orange is, therefore, not just a hint, but the prime constituent. The resulting cake is very moist indeed. Although it can be cooled and served in thick slices as a cake, I prefer to serve it as a pudding. Allow it to cool until barely warm, then serve in wedges with thick Greek yoghurt.

■ 2 large oranges, washed ■ 5 eggs ■ 170 g / 6 oz caster sugar
■ 170 g / 6 oz ground hazelnuts ■ 1 heaped teaspoon baking powder

Place the oranges in a large saucepan, then half-fill the pan with water. Bring to the boil, then cover and simmer for about 1¼–1½ hours, or until completely soft. Allow to cool. Pre-heat the oven to 190°C/375°F/Gas mark 5.

When cold, cut into quarters and remove any pips. Place in a food processor or electric blender and process to a pulp, making sure no large pieces of skin escape the blades.

In a large bowl, whisk the eggs until thick, then slowly add the sugar, beating well. Fold in the ground nuts and baking powder and combine thoroughly.

Then fold in the orange pulp, and stir well.

Pour into a loose-bottomed, greased and floured 23 cm/9½ in tin and smooth the surface.

Bake in the oven for 55–60 minutes, or until a skewer inserted into the middle comes out clean.

Cool in the tin for about 15 minutes, then carefully remove the sides. Allow to cool on a wire rack until just warm before removing the base and cutting into wedges.

ORANGE AND HAZELNUT CAKE

DATE AND WALNUT LOAF

Makes 1 loaf

Unlike many date loaves, which are heavy, dark and sticky in texture, this is light both in texture and in colour. It is very good cut into thick slices and spread with butter. A touch of honey would also go well. If you like to enhance the flavour of the walnuts even more, give them a quick toasting under the grill, before chopping.

■ 284g / 10oz plain flour ■ 1½ teaspoons baking powder ■ 142g / 5oz caster sugar
■ 2 teaspoons thick honey ■ 2 tablespoons milk ■ 85g / 3oz butter
■ 2 eggs, beaten ■ 113g / 4oz stoned dates, chopped ■ 85g / 3oz walnuts, roughly chopped

Pre-heat the oven to 180°C/350°F/Gas mark 4. Sift the flour and baking powder into a bowl. Add the sugar and stir well.

Heat the honey, milk and butter, just until lukewarm, then add to the bowl with the eggs, dates and walnuts. Stir everything together.

Spoon into a buttered 907 g/2 lb loaf tin and level the top. Bake in the oven for about 1 hour, or until a skewer inserted into the middle comes out clean.

Cool on a wire rack and only turn out when completely cold. ❈

BANANA BREAD

Makes 1 loaf

If you cannot persuade those fussy fruit-eaters to peel those very ripe, brown-speckled bananas which linger in the fruit bowl, you must convert the bananas into a pudding or cake. I have tried many local recipes in Bermuda. There is a banana chutney flavoured with dates and ginger; banana custard, with honey and vanilla; and the heavenly fluffy and creamy banana pie. The following recipe is based on Bermudian banana bread. The nutmeg should be freshly grated.

■ 255g / 9oz plain flour ■ 1 teaspoon salt ■ 1 teaspoon bicarbonate of soda ■ ½ teaspoon grated nutmeg
■ 170g / 6oz soft light brown sugar ■ 85g / 3oz butter, softened ■ 2 eggs, beaten
■ 2 large bananas (about 340g / 12oz unpeeled weight), mashed ■ 57g / 2oz walnuts, chopped

Pre-heat the oven to 180°C/350°F/Gas mark 4. Sift together the flour, salt, bicarbonate of soda and nutmeg.

In another bowl, cream together the sugar and butter until light and fluffy. Add the eggs, one at a time, beating thoroughly each time.

Beat in the mashed bananas, stirring well to combine. Fold in the dry ingredients, then stir in the walnuts.

Pour into a greased, base-lined 907 g/2 lb loaf tin. Bake in the oven for 1 hour, or until a skewer inserted into the middle comes out clean. I usually cover the cake loosely with foil for the last 20 minutes of baking, but this depends on your oven. If the loaf looks very brown and well-risen, but is not yet ready, cover with foil and bake for a further 10 minutes.

Allow to cool for about 20 minutes in the tin, then invert on to a wire rack. Cool completely before cutting into thin slices. ❄

RUSSIAN SPICE BREAD

Makes 1 loaf

This cake is called 'pryanik' in Russian, from *pryanost* meaning spice. Lesley Chamberlain, in *The Food and Cooking of Russia*, explains how it was originally made with only the simplest ingredients – rye flour, honey, berry juice and, later, spices – but these have now been supplemented by eggs, milk or baking powder to transform an otherwise dense, unleavened loaf into a light, springy cake. Although the rye and/or wholemeal flour and the spices are indispensable, the other ingredients vary enormously today and include any of the following: cinnamon, cardamom, nutmeg, ginger, coriander, allspice and star anise. Lesley Chamberlain mentions also that its sweetness has been reduced to suit modern tastes. My interpretation of a Russian pryanik is not dissimilar to the French 'pain d'épice' in texture, for neither contains any fat. The texture is not one we are familiar with in Britain, but it is light and nicely moist from the honey and sour cream. Chopped nuts or peel are optional; I prefer the loaf plain.

■ 57 g / 2 oz rye flour ■ 227 g / 8 oz wholemeal self-raising flour ■ ½ teaspoon ground ginger
■ ½ teaspoon ground cinnamon
■ ½ teaspoon crushed cardamom (remove husks from 6 pods and grind seeds in a pestle and mortar)
■ the grated zest of ½ lemon ■ 4 tablespoons honey ■ 142 ml / ¼ pint milk
■ 142 ml / ¼ pint sour cream ■ 2 eggs ■ 28–57 g / 1–2 oz chopped nuts or mixed peel (optional)

Pre-heat the oven to 180°C/350°F/Gas mark 4. Place the first 6 ingredients in a bowl and stir together. Warm the honey and milk in a small pan, just until the honey has melted.

Whisk together the sour cream and eggs, then pour into the dry ingredients, with the honey and milk. Add the nuts or peel, if using.

Stir everything together until well-mixed, then turn into a buttered 907 g/2 lb loaf tin.

Bake in the oven for 45 minutes, or until a skewer inserted into the centre comes out clean.

Leave to cool in the tin for 2–3 hours, then turn out on to a wire rack and allow to become completely cold. ❄

TARTS & PASTRIES

What is a cinnamon nablab? Can you really put Sangria
in a tart? Is impossible coconut pie truly impossible?
Find out in this chapter on savoury and sweet pies, pastries, tarts and cheesecakes. The myth that special skills
are required to produce good pastry is dispelled here. All
you need is a rolling pin, butter, flour and eggs. Most
importantly, you need hungry guests. Enjoy!

RHUBARB AND WHITE CHOCOLATE TART

Serves 8

The flavours in this tart are exquisite. The tart taste of the rhubarb works very well with the
wonderfully cloying sweetness of the white chocolate. The rhubarb is also flavoured
with Pernod – a combination I first tasted years ago in a chocolate truffle and have been enamoured
with ever since. It is important to cook the rhubarb only until it is just done. Do not let it
become mushy or the whole look of the tart will be ruined. Since the tart has a lattice top, you can see
the fruit though the pastry strips, so the rhubarb should look nice and chunky – not like a soft
purée. Make sure you use the very best quality white chocolate – Milky Bar will not do in this instance!
Offer the tart with a bowl of double cream, lightly whisked and splashed with a
little Pernod. Serve warm in small slices.

PASTRY

■ 227 g / 8 oz plain flour ■ a pinch of salt ■ 28 g / 1 oz caster sugar
■ 113 g / 4 oz unsalted butter, cut into cubes ■ 1 egg ■ 1 tablespoon double cream

FILLING

■ 680 g / 1½ lb young rhubarb, cleaned and chopped ■ 2 tablespoons Pernod ■ 57 g / 2 oz caster sugar
■ 113 g / 4 oz white chocolate, grated or finely chopped

GLAZE

■ 1 tablespoon double cream ■ 2 teaspoons caster sugar

Make the pastry: place the flour, salt, sugar and butter in a food processor and process until the mixture resembles breadcrumbs. Mix together the egg and cream and slowly add through the feeder tube while the machine is still running. Switch off and gather together with your hands. Knead for a couple of seconds, then wrap in clingfilm and refrigerate for at least 1 hour.

Roll out two-thirds of the pastry and use to line a deep 23 cm / 9 in fluted, loose-bottomed flan tin. Prick the base all over with a fork. Roll out the remaining pastry to from a rectangle, approximately 28 × 20 cm / 11 × 8 in. Cut into 8 strips (I like to use a fluted pastry cutter, but a knife will do), place on a board and refrigerate for at least 1 hour. Pre-heat the oven to 190°C / 375°F / Gas mark 5.

Line the pastry case with foil and baking beans and bake 'blind' for 15–20 minutes. Remove the foil and beans and cook for a further 5 minutes. Remove from the oven and cool for 10–15 minutes.

Prepare the filling: place the rhubarb, Pernod and sugar in a saucepan and slowly bring to the boil, stirring occasionally. Cook for 5 minutes, or until the rhubarb is just cooked but still firm. Drain at once through a sieve, reserving the liquid. Return the liquid to the pan and boil rapidly for about 5 minutes, or until there is 1–1½ tablespoons liquid remaining.

Sprinkle the grated white chocolate over the pastry case, then spoon over the rhubarb. Drizzle with the Pernod-flavoured juices.

Remove the pastry strips from the refrigerator and arrange in a lattice on top (see page 213). Trim any ragged edges, then, using a pastry brush, glaze the top with double cream and sprinkle with caster sugar.

Bake in the oven for 30 minutes, or until the pastry is golden brown. Allow to cool for at least 20 minutes before removing from the tin. Serve with Pernod-flavoured cream.

SANGRIA TART

Serves 6–8

Sangria is a great favourite of mine in summertime. Much cheaper to make than Pimms, it can be equally refreshing and fruity on a warm sunny day. Although sangria is also made in Spain with white wine, it is far more common made with red. Do not feel obliged to use your best vintage red, but on the other hand, do not use inferior wine. A full-bodied one is best. I like to use a hearty Rioja. The flavour of the tart is undeniably of sangria, for the essential flavourings – red wine, lemon and orange – are all there. This is an unusual but really good dessert to offer at dinner, for it is refreshing and tangy but also very satisfying. For the sweet pastry, I suggest you use either the recipe given for Prune and Chocolate Tart on page 206, or the one for Rhubarb and White Chocolate Tart, opposite.

■ 198–227 g / 7–8 oz sweet pastry, chilled ■ 113 g / 4 oz golden caster sugar
■ the grated zest of 1 large orange ■ the grated zest of 1 large lemon ■ 14 g / ½ oz plain flour
■ 142 ml / ¼ pint red wine ■ 7 g / ¼ oz butter

Roll out the pastry thinly to fit a shallow 20 cm/ 8 in buttered, loose-bottomed tart tin. Do not prick. Chill for at least 1 hour. Pre-heat the oven to 200°C/400°F/Gas mark 6.

Line the pastry case with foil and baking beans and bake 'blind' for 20 minutes. Remove the foil and beans and allow to cool.

Mix together the sugar, the grated orange and lemon zests and the flour. Then stir in the red wine. Whisk until well-mixed.

Place the tart tin on a baking sheet near the oven, then pour in the liquid. (This is so it does not overflow.) Dot with the butter.

Very carefully transfer to the oven and bake for about 25 minutes, or until the pastry is golden brown and the filling has set around the edges (the centre might still be a little 'wobbly', but this will firm up on cooling). Allow to cool completely before serving at room temperature.

Roll any left-over pieces of shortcrust pastry into balls, wrap in clingfilm and freeze (labelled sweet or savoury). Once you have 3 or 4 balls, you can produce a good base for a whole tart or pie.

DUTCH APPLE TART

Makes 1 large tart (serves 8–10)

'Appel Taart' is a family favourite in Holland and is brought out on special occasions. My recipe is based on one from my Dutch friend, Mary-An. Her father Cornelius, one of 13 children, remembers it as a particular treat during the War years. As there were never fewer than 18 people at each meal, an 18th of a (rationed) tart was never enough!

PASTRY

■ 284 g / 10 oz self-raising flour, sifted ■ 170 g / 6 oz unsalted butter (cold), cut into cubes
■ 99 g / 3½ oz / caster sugar ■ 71–85 ml / 2½–3 fl oz cold water

FILLING

■ 2 teaspoons semolina ■ 1.134 kg / 2½ lb large cooking apples ■ 85 g / 3 oz caster sugar
■ 2 heaped teaspoons ground cinnamon
■ 57 g / 2 oz raisins (optional) ■ egg white and caster sugar, to glaze

For the pastry, combine the flour, butter and sugar in a food processor. Process until the mixture resembles breadcrumbs. Then add sufficient water for it to combine to a firm dough – start with 71 ml / 2½ fl oz, and increase if necessary. Combine with your hands in a ball, wrap in clingfilm and refrigerate for about 1 hour. Wash your food processor – you will need it again. Preheat the oven to 200°C/400°F/Gas mark 6.

Roll out two-thirds of the pastry, on a floured board, and use it to line the base and sides of a buttered 24 cm / 9½ in loose-bottomed, deep baking tin. Sprinkle the semolina over the base.

Prepare the apples: first peel and core them, then slice thinly.

Combine the sugar and cinnamon in a bowl.

Fill about a third of the tin with apples, pressing down gently. Add the raisins, if using, then top with a third of the sugar mixture. Continue layering the fruit and sugar to fill the tin.

Roll out the remaining pastry to a large rectangle. Set aside a quarter of the pastry. Cut out 8 long, fairly thick strips and use them to make a simple lattice over the top of the apples: lay one strip over the apples, then place another at right angles, and so on. Roll out the remaining pastry to make another long strip, and lay it around the circumference of the tin to neaten the edges. Brush with egg white and sprinkle with sugar to glaze.

Bake in the oven for 10 minutes, then reduce the heat to 180°C/350°F/Gas mark 4 and continue cooking for a further 40–45 minutes, or until the pastry is golden brown and the apples are tender. Cover with foil towards the end of cooking if the top becomes too dark. Once cooked, remove from the oven and allow to cool in the tin for about 20–30 minutes, before very carefully decanting.

Serve the tart warm with plenty of thick cream or Greek yoghurt. ✱

DUTCH APPLE TART

CHOCOLATE AND WALNUT TART

Serves 8

This is a very rich tart, which is all too difficult to resist. The pastry is a crumbly nutty one, flavoured with walnuts. Pecans can also be used. The richness of the chocolate cream filling is balanced nicely by the addition of tangy lemon zest. I use a chocolate with between 50 and 60 per cent cocoa solids, as it is not too bitter for this dish. Offer pouring cream with the tart.

PASTRY

■ 113g / 4oz plain flour, sifted ■ a pinch of salt ■ 57g / 2oz golden caster sugar
■ 57g / 2oz walnuts ■ 71g / 2½ oz unsalted butter, cut into cubes ■ 2 egg yolks

FILLING

■ 284ml / ½ pint double cream ■ 284g / 10oz dark chocolate, chopped
■ the grated zest of 1 large lemon

For the pastry, place the flour, salt, sugar and walnuts in a food processor. Process briefly, just until the walnuts are roughly chopped.

Add the butter and process until the mixture resembles breadcrumbs.

Add the egg yolks, a little at a time, through the feeder tube and process briefly until the mixture comes together.

Gently press into a fluted, loose-bottomed, buttered 23 cm/9 in tin. Press the mixture up the sides and all over the base. Prick all over with a fork and either chill for 2 hours or freeze for 15 minutes. Pre-heat the oven to 190°C / 375°F / Gas mark 5.

Bake in the oven (without baking beans or foil) for 20 minutes, or until cooked through.

For the filling, bring the cream to boiling point in a saucepan. Immediately the bubbles appear, remove from the heat and stir in the chopped chocolate. Leave to cool for about 30 minutes, stirring occasionally.

Stir in the lemon zest and pour into the pastry case. Refrigerate for at least 2 hours, or until set, before serving.

PEAR TARTE TATIN

Serves 8

The original 'tarte tatin' is made with apples, but I like to use pears for a change. Sometimes I add chopped stem ginger and a little ginger syrup to the pears, but only if it is for adults. (I know of no child who appreciates stem ginger!) In France, 'reinette' apples are used, which are fragrant eating apples. Our British Cox give the best results, should you prefer to use apples.

For pears, make sure you use slightly under-ripe fruit. I recommend Conference, Comice or William's Bon Chrétien pears. Some tarte tatins are made with puff pastry, but this is by no means authentic; anyway, I far prefer a well-made shortcrust to puff pastry.

The origins of the French tarte are interesting. The story goes that there were 2 sisters – 'les Demoiselles Tatin' – who created a caramelised apple tart in their small hotel in the town of Lamotte-Beuvron, in the wooden area of the Sologne, south of Paris. I had always been led to believe that the upside-down tart was the result of trying (successfully!) to correct an error in the baking of an apple tart. But food writer Nigel Slater, in his delightful book *Real Good Food*, points out that it was simply a means of cooking a tart on top of the stove's burners (covered completely by a metal dome), since the sisters' wood-burning stove did not possess an oven. This explains far more plausibly how this rustic tart – with its sticky, caramelised fruit and light, buttery pastry – came into being.

PASTRY

■ 227 g / 8 oz plain flour, sifted ■ a pinch of salt ■ 28 g / 1 oz icing sugar, sifted
■ 142 g / 5 oz unsalted butter, cut into cubes ■ 1 egg ■ 1–2 tablespoons cold water

FILLING

■ 57 g / 2 oz unsalted butter ■ 85 g / 3 oz caster sugar ■ 1.134–1.247 kg / 2¼–2½ lb pears

First make the pastry. Place the flour, salt and sugar in a food processor. Add the butter and process until the mixture resembles breadcrumbs. Add the egg and just enough cold water to form a stiff dough (start with 1 tablespoon and increase, if necessary). Wrap in clingfilm and refrigerate for 1 hour.

For the filling, you need a round, heavy, ovenproof pan (I use one 25 cm / 10 in in diameter and 5 cm / 2 in deep). Place this over a medium heat and melt the butter, then add 57 g / 2 oz of the sugar. Stirring constantly, cook for 4–5 minutes, or until golden brown. (Do watch out, since the mixture will burn very quickly if you do not stir it.)

Remove from the heat. Pre-heat the oven to 190°C / 375°F / Gas mark 5.

Peel the pears and slice thickly. Lay these on top of the caramelised sugar, either neatly in concentric circles, or at random. Sprinkle over the remaining sugar.

Roll out the pastry to a circle 5 cm / 2 in bigger than the pan. Lay over the pears, tucking the edges carefully between the pears and the tin (these form the tart's sides, once inverted).

Using a fork, prick the pastry lid 2 or 3 times, then bake in the oven for 40–45 minutes, or until golden brown.

Remove from the oven and allow to cool for at least 5 minutes. Then carefully run a knife around the edges of the pan. Place a large plate over the top and, grasping the plate and the pan, turn the tart upside down with one rapid turning action. (This is definitely a case of 'he – or she – who hesitates is lost'.) Remove the pan and underneath you should have a perfectly inverted tarte tatin. Serve while still warm, with clotted cream or Greek yoghurt.

PRUNE, CHOCOLATE AND LEMON TART

Serves 6–8

Prunes have always suffered from bad press in Britain. Indeed, their wizened, wrinkled appearance does nothing to enhance their appeal. But the plump, tenderised, 'no-soak' ones now available are a revelation. They are succulent and moist, and can be eaten as they are – straight from the packet – or chopped, without soaking, into a myriad of dishes. This recipe combines prunes with 2 flavours which, on their own, are classics in tarts – lemon and chocolate. The hint of lemon is just enough both to sharpen the sweetness of the chocolate and to cut through the richness of the prunes. This tart should be eaten warm, while the chocolate is still melting into the prunes and the filling is still soft and sticky. It will elevate prunes above the level of merely being good for you!

PASTRY

■ 113 g / 4 oz plain flour, sifted ■ 28 g / 1 oz caster sugar ■ 57 g / 2 oz ground almonds
■ 85 g / 3 oz unsalted butter, cut into cubes ■ 1 egg

FILLING

■ 113 g / 4 oz 'no-soak' tenderised prunes, pitted
■ 113 g / 4 oz plain dark chocolate (look for 60–70 per cent cocoa solids) ■ 2 eggs
■ 57 g / 2 oz soft light brown sugar ■ 52 g / 2 oz unsalted butter, melted and cooled for 5 minutes
■ the zest and juice of 1 lemon

To make the pastry, place the flour, sugar, almonds and butter in a food processor. Process until the mixture resembles breadcrumbs. Add the egg through the feeder tube and process briefly, just until combined. Gather together with your hands and wrap in clingfilm. Chill for at least 2 hours.

Roll out the pastry to fit a shallow 20 cm / 8 in tart tin. Prick all over with a fork and chill again (to prevent shrinkage) – preferably overnight, or for at least 2 hours. Pre-heat the oven to 190°C / 375°F / Gas mark 5.

Line the pastry case with foil and baking beans and bake 'blind' in the oven for 15 minutes. Then remove the baking beans and foil and cook for a further 5 minutes. Remove and allow to cool.

Roughly chop the prunes and chocolate and place in the cooled tart. Beat together the eggs, sugar, melted butter and lemon zest and juice. Pour over the filling in the tart.

Bake in the oven, at the same temperature, for about 25 minutes, or until golden brown. Remove and allow to cool for a short time, before cutting into slices. Serve warm. ❄

To bake pastry 'blind', fill the foil with baking beans, to prevent the sides of the tart collapsing.

MELKTERT

Serves 8

This traditional South-African tart has been around for many years. Some South-African cookery books suggest it arrived during the 17th or 18th centuries, when the Cape Malays introduced spices (usually cinnamon or nutmeg is sprinkled over the top of the tart). Whatever the history, it is a delightful tart – not dissimilar to our custard tart. Many South-African recipes stipulate the use of puff or flaky pastry for the case, but I like to use sweet shortcrust, which is equally good served warm or cold. (I find puff pastry is not nearly as good when served cold.) The filling should be cooked for long enough to thicken, but not too long, or it will stick to the base of the saucepan. The top can be sprinkled with freshly grated nutmeg, or with a little cinnamon and sugar.

PASTRY

■ 227 g / 8 oz plain flour ■ 85 g / 3 oz icing sugar ■ a pinch of salt
■ 113 g / 4 oz unsalted butter, cut into cubes ■ 1 egg, beaten ■ 1–1½ tablespoons cold water

FILLING

■ 540 ml / 19 fl oz milk ■ 99 g / 3½ oz caster sugar ■ 2 eggs ■ 57 g / 2 oz plain flour
■ 28 g / 1 oz cornflour ■ 1 teaspoon vanilla essence ■ 14 g / ½ oz butter ■ whole nutmeg, to grate

For the pastry, sift the flour and sugar into a food processor. Add the salt and butter and process until the mixture resembles breadcrumbs. Add the egg and just enough water, through the feeder tube, to combine to a firm dough. Then gather it with your hands, wrap in clingfilm and chill for 1 hour.

Roll out the pastry to fit a 23 cm / 9 in flan tin, prick the base and chill for at least 2 hours. Preheat the oven to 190°C / 375°F / Gas mark 5. Line the pastry case with foil, fill with baking beans and bake 'blind' for about 20 minutes. Then remove the foil and beans and continue to cook for a further 5–10 minutes or until just cooked through.

For the filling, place the milk in a heavy-based saucepan and bring to the boil. Beat the sugar and eggs together in a separate bowl, then sift in the 2 flours, beating until smooth. Pour about a quarter of the boiling milk into the mixture, whisking all the time. Then pour the mixture back into the saucepan containing the remaining milk. Whisking or stirring constantly, cook over a medium to low heat until thick. (This should take about 3–4 minutes.) Then remove from the heat and beat in the vanilla and butter.

Pour the mixture into the baked pastry case (it should still be warm). Grate some nutmeg over the top (or sprinkle with cinnamon, if you prefer). Return to the oven for 15–20 minutes, or until set. Serve warm or cold.

Although it is quicker to make pastry in a food processor, you must be careful not to overblend the dough. Use the pulse button. Overworking the dough will result in brittle pastry.

CHOCOLATE SWIRL CHEESECAKE

Serves 8

This recipe combines 2 of my favourite foods: cheesecake and chocolate. The base is crunchy and nutty, with the addition of hazelnuts. Toasting the nuts in advance makes the flavour more pronounced. The topping consists of a curd cheese filling and a chocolate-flavoured one. The 2 are swirled together for an attractive marbled effect – no further decoration is needed.

BASE

■ 198 g / 7 oz digestive biscuits ■ 57 g / 2 oz blanched hazelnuts, toasted (see page 74)
■ 85 g / 3 oz butter, melted

FILLING

■ 454 g / 1 lb curd cheese ■ 2 heaped tablespoons crème fraîche ■ 2 eggs ■ 57 g / 2 oz caster sugar
■ 113 g / 4 oz bitter chocolate ■ 57 g / 2 oz soft light brown sugar

Pre-heat the oven to 180°C / 350°F / Gas mark 4. Crush the biscuits and nuts in a food processor. Mix with the melted butter. Press into a buttered 23 cm / 9 in, loose-bottomed, deep fluted flan tin. Bake in the oven for 10 minutes, then allow to cool. Reduce the oven temperature to 150°C / 300°F / Gas mark 2.

Beat the curd cheese and crème fraîche together, then mix in the eggs and caster sugar. Beat everything together really well.

Pour half the mixture into a separate bowl. Melt the chocolate and brown sugar together, stirring until well-mixed. Pour into one of the bowls containing the cream cheese mixture and mix well.

Pour the plain cream cheese mixture into the flan tin. Top with the chocolate mixture, then, using the tip of a sharp knife, swirl the two flavours together to create a marbled effect.

Bake in the oven for about 40 minutes, or until just set. Switch off the heat and leave the cheesecake in the oven for about 1 hour, before removing and allowing to become completely cold. Serve in small wedges with pouring cream.

BAKEWELL PUDDING

Serves 8

Bakewell pudding is usually called Bakewell Tart, because it is made in a pastry case, but the original Derbyshire dish was in fact a pudding – and one with a most interesting story.
In the middle of the 19th century, a cook at The Rutland Arms in Bakewell mistook her mistress' instructions and, from this apparently grave error, a great dish was created. In his book,

Traditional Dishes of Britain, Philip Harben explains how a Mrs Greaves, the owner of the Rutland Arms, had instructed her new cook on how to cook the meal for some important guests. She planned a rich jam tart, the pastry enriched with plenty of melted butter and beaten eggs. Mrs Greaves thought nothing more about the recipe until afterwards, when the guests thanked her for the meal and, in particular, for the pudding. Why 'pudding', when she had left instructions for a 'tart' as the final dish? After interrogation, the new cook confessed she had forgotten about the enriched pastry which was to be topped with jam. She had therefore made ordinary puff pastry and spread it with jam. Having the mixture of melted butter and eggs left over, she simply poured them over the top and baked the pudding as normal, for fear of retribution if her mistress found the mixture left over. Her state of contrition changed at once when Mrs Greaves insisted she must do the same pudding again, for it was such a great success. This, therefore, is the tale of how a small Derbyshire town gave its name to a traditional dish.

Now, of course, there are many variations of Bakewell pudding, but the most common one – with an almond-flavoured cake mix – is not only inauthentic, but also more of a tea-time treat, to be served cold with afternoon tea, than a pudding to be served at the end of a meal. My version uses a crisp shortcrust instead of puff pastry and is made in a round, instead of the traditional oval.

PASTRY

■ 142 g / 5 oz plain flour, sifted ■ a pinch of salt ■ 57 g / 2 oz ground almonds
■ 85 g / 3 oz unsalted butter, cut into cubes ■ 1 egg, beaten

FILLING

■ 2–3 tablespoons strawberry jam ■ 85 g / 3 oz unsalted butter
■ 85 g / 3 oz caster sugar ■ 3 eggs

For the pastry, place the flour, salt and almonds in a food processor with the butter. Process until the mixture resembles breadcrumbs.

Add the beaten egg through the feeder tube as the machine is running. Bring the pastry together with your hands and wrap in clingfilm. Chill for about an hour.

Roll out the pastry to fit a buttered 20 cm / 8 in fluted flan tin. Prick the base with a fork and chill for at least 2 hours, or (preferably) overnight. Pre-heat the oven to 190°C / 375°F / Gas mark 5.

Line the pastry case with foil and baking beans and bake 'blind' for 15 minutes. Then remove the foil and beans and bake for a further 5 minutes. Allow to cool. Increase the oven temperature to 200°C / 400°F / Gas mark 6.

Once the case is cool, spread with strawberry jam. Melt the butter and sugar together in a small saucepan, then beat in the eggs. Whisk together until thoroughly combined.

Pour over the jam and bake in the oven for 20 minutes, or until the top is a light golden brown. Serve warm or at room temperature.

SUNDAY PLUM PIE

Serves 8

This pie is called Sunday Plum Pie because it is
based on a Finnish recipe called
'Sunnuntai Piirakka' or Sunday Pie. This
consists of a wholewheat cake base,
topped with berries – usually lingonberries – and
a cheesecake-like mixture. And yes –
you guessed – it is usually served on Sundays.
I have adapted the idea into a plum pie.
Use either fresh plums, if they are in season,
or those wonderfully sticky Elvas
(preserved) plums, which are an unusual
green colour (they are actually
preserved greengages).
Serve this for pudding with a little
pouring cream, or, as they do in Finland, as a
cake with a strong cup of coffee.

BASE
- 99 g / 3½ oz butter, softened
- 57 g / 2 oz caster sugar
- 57 g / 2 oz self-raising flour
- 57 g / 2 oz wholemeal self-raising flour ■ 1 egg

FILLING
- 5–6 plums (fresh or preserved)
- 142 ml / ¼ pint sour cream ■ 1 egg
- ½ teaspoon vanilla essence
- 57 g / 2 oz caster sugar

SUNDAY PLUM PIE

Pre-heat the oven to 200°C/400°F/Gas mark 6. Place all the ingredients for the base in a food processor and process until blended.

Spoon into a buttered 18 cm / 7 in square cake tin, smoothing the top with the back of a spoon.

Stone and halve the plums and arrange over the top of the base. Then beat the cream, egg, vanilla and sugar together and pour over the top.

(Do not worry if the mixture spills down the sides – provided the tin is well-buttered, it should not stick.)

Bake in the oven (not too near the top) for about 30 minutes, or until the edges are a deep golden brown and the filling is just set (it will firm up as the pie cools).

Transfer to a wire rack and cut into squares. Serve warm.

IMPOSSIBLE COCONUT PIE

Serves 6

I first spotted a recipe for Impossible Pie in a collection of favourite recipes sold in aid of The Girls' Brigade some years ago. I have altered the original a little, but the basic concept is the same. The reason it is impossible is because all the ingredients look a complete mess – sloppy and liquid – when they are mixed together and poured into the tin. After around 50 minutes' baking time, however, a miracle takes place – the pie divides into 3 layers. In the original recipe book, it describes these layers as pastry base, egg-custard middle and coconut-sponge topping. I prefer to describe them as a thin pastry-like crust, a creamy custard middle and a crunchy coconut-sponge topping. Whichever way you wish to describe them, it is truly amazing to see the transformation from a globby batter to a three-layered pudding. This recipe can be served warm for pudding or cold as a cake. There is surely no more versatile – or mysterious – pie around.

■ 4 eggs ■ 170g / 6oz caster sugar ■ 57g / 2oz butter, softened ■ 85g / 3oz plain flour, sifted
■ ¼ teaspoon salt ■ ½ teaspoon baking powder ■ 426ml / ¾ pint milk
■ 113g / 4oz desiccated coconut ■ ½ teaspoon vanilla essence

Pre-heat the oven to 180°C/350°F/Gas mark 4. Place all the ingredients in a large mixing bowl, then beat or whisk together until everything is really well combined.

Pour into a deep, greased 25 cm/10 in pie dish (I use the same one I use for the Pear Tarte Tatin on page 204). Bake in the oven for about 50 minutes, or until it is puffed up and a crunchy golden brown.

Allow to cool for at least 5–10 minutes (during which time the pie will deflate slightly), then cut into wedges and serve warm or cold.

LINZERTORTE

Serves 8

Sachertorte and Linzertorte are probably the best-known of Austrian 'tortes'. Sachertorte is a rich chocolate cake laced with apricot jam which was supposed to originate at the Hotel Sacher in Vienna. Linzertorte is really the ultimate jam tart. It has a rich sweet pastry and is filled with best-quality raspberry jam. The pastry topping is layed out in a lattice pattern, which can seem very complicated to do. You are meant to place half the strips over the tart, then fold back every other one halfway and place the remaining strips across the unfolded strips before unfolding them. Then you should fold back the alternate strips and continue until the lattice is finished. Since I do not possess a degree in geometry, I simply cheat and place one strip across the top edge of the tart, then another at right angles over the first strip. Then I continue until they are all finished, starting at alternative sides of the tart each time. The result, although not authentically 'woven', looks really rather good.

■ 57 g / 2 oz caster sugar   ■ 113 g / 4 oz ground almonds   ■ 113 g / 4 oz plain flour, sifted
■ ¼ teaspoon ground cinnamon   ■ 113 g / 4 oz unsalted butter, chilled and cut into cubes
■ 1 large egg yolk (size 1)   ■ the grated zest of 1 lemon   ■ the juice of ½ lemon
■ 284 g / 10 oz best-quality raspberry jam   ■ icing sugar, to dust

Mix together the sugar, ground almonds, flour and cinnamon in a food processor, then add the butter and process until the mixture resembles breadcrumbs. Add the lemon zest and process briefly. Add the egg yolk and lemon juice and process briefly until the mixture combines to a dough. Gather together in your hands, wrap in clingfilm and chill for at least 1 hour.

Grease and flour a 20 cm / 8 in fluted (deep) flan tin. Roll out two-thirds of the pastry and use to line the tin. Chill for 30 minutes.

Now pre-heat the oven to 180°C / 350°F / Gas mark 4. Prick the base all over, then spread with the jam. Roll out the remaining pastry, cut into strips and arrange in a lattice pattern, over the top.

Bake in the oven for 35–40 minutes, or until the pastry is crisp and golden brown. Dust while still warm with icing sugar. ❄

The quicker you can make pastry the better; the longer the dough is worked, the more elastic it becomes as the gluten in the flour is developed. This results in tough pastry which shrinks during cooking.

CINNAMON NABLAB

Makes about 20 squares

At the But'nBen restaurant in Auchmithie, near Arbroath, some of the finest traditional home-cooking is to be found. Margaret Horn, now with her son Angus, has cooked there for years. She uses the best of local produce, such as the marvellous fresh shellfish and fish, especially Arbroath Smokies.

One of my favourites from the cake trolley is a speciality which Margaret has grown up with; Cinnamon Nablab – a pastry base with a currant filling, light cake topping, then cinnamon-flavoured icing. The bakers in Arbroath usually display 3 types of nablab: one with brown (cinnamon) icing, one with white icing, and a special pink-iced nablab which used to have sixpences wrapped up inside. The etymology of *nablab* is interesting. In north-eastern Scots dialect, *nab* – sometimes written knab – means a morsel of food, or a bite. *Lab* (*leb* or *laib*) means to lick or gobble up. Perhaps nablabs were – after the famous Smokie – Arbroath's first 'fast food'!

PASTRY

- 227 g / 8 oz plain flour, sifted - 57 g / 2 oz ground almonds or hazelnuts - 28 g / 1 oz caster sugar
- 113 g / 4 oz unsalted butter, cut into cubes - 1 egg yolk - approximately 4 tablespoons cold water

FILLING

- 198 g / 7 oz currants - 4 tablespoons water - 71 g / 2½ oz soft light brown sugar
- 1 heaped teaspoon ground cinnamon - 14 g / ½ oz cornflour, slaked in 2 tablespoons water

CAKE

- 227 g / 8 oz butter, softened - 227 g / 8 oz caster sugar - 4 eggs - 227 g / 8 oz self-raising flour, sifted
- 1 teaspoon ground cinnamon

ICING

- 198 g / 7 oz icing sugar, sifted - 2 heaped teaspoons ground cinnamon - about 2 tablespoons water

First make the pastry. Place the flour, ground nuts and sugar in a food processor, then add the butter. Process until the mixture resembles breadcrumbs.

Add the egg yolk and just enough water to combine to a firm pastry dough. Roll into a ball, wrap in clingfilm and chill in the refrigerator for 30 minutes. Then roll out to fit a lightly greased swiss-roll tin, 23×33 cm/9×13 in. Prick all over with a fork.

If time permits, chill in the refrigerator overnight. (If not, chill for at least 2 hours.)

For the filling, place the currants and water in a small saucepan. Bring slowly to the boil, then stir in the sugar and cinnamon. Reduce the heat slightly and add the slaked cornflour. Stirring constantly, bring to the boil and cook for a couple of minutes, or until thick. Allow to cool for a least 10 minutes. Pre-heat the oven to 200°C/400°F/Gas mark 6.

For the cake, beat the butter in a mixing bowl with a wooden spoon until soft, then add the sugar and beat until creamy and light. Add the eggs, one at a time, beating well after each addition. Fold in the flour and cinnamon.

Spread the filling over the chilled pastry base. Then top with the cake mix, spreading it out well to cover the filling completely. Bake in the oven for about 30 minutes, or until well-risen and a skewer inserted into the middle comes out clean. Leave to cool completely.

Cut into 4 large sections and, using a fish slice, transfer carefully to a wire rack. Beat all the icing ingredients together until smooth, then spread over the cooled cake. Leave to set, then cut into squares. ❄

RICHMOND MAIDS OF HONOUR

Makes 12 tarts

In Philip Harben's book on the traditional dishes of Britain, he explains that the story behind these dainty little curd-cheese tarts began around the year 1525. One day, Henry VIII came across a group of Queen Catherine of Aragon's Maids of Honour – including his future wife, Anne Boleyn – eating some cakes with obvious gusto. He tried one himself, was smitten (by the tart, not Anne Boleyn) and made the Court pastry cook rustle up some himself. Lost for an appropriate name, the King called them 'Maids of Honour' tarts.
They became firm favourites at Court, but their recipe was a well-kept secret . . . until smuggled out, some 200 years later, by a lady of the Court. She passed it on to a gentleman, who set up shop selling nothing but Maids of Honour tarts. The secret was out – and now we too can enjoy them. You can add a drop or two of vanilla essence, or sprinkle a little grated nutmeg over the top for added flavour, but just remember that these additions do not make the authentic tarts which so beguiled the King. I confess I have added lots of grated lemon zest, to counteract the richness of the curd filling. May the curse of Henry VIII be upon me.

■ 227 g / 8 oz puff pastry (preferably 'ready-rolled') ■ 227 g / 8 oz curd cheese
■ 1 egg ■ the grated zest of 1 large lemon ■ 14 g / ½ oz butter, melted ■ 57 g / 2 oz caster sugar

Either roll out the pastry as thinly as possible, or take a piece of 'ready rolled' pastry. Cut out 12 × 8 cm / 3 in rounds, using a fluted cutter.

Place in a deep, buttered muffin / bun tin, pressing a little up the sides to form an edge.

Refrigerate for 1 hour. Pre-heat the oven to 200°C / 400°F / Gas mark 6.

Beat together the cheese, egg, zest, butter and sugar. Divide between the 12 pastry 'shells'.

Bake in the oven for 25–30 minutes, or until the filling is puffed up and golden brown on top and the pastry is cooked through.

Remove to a wire rack and allow to cool. Serve warm.

CHORLEY CAKES

Makes 6

Everyone has heard of Eccles cakes, but very few people outside Lancashire know anything about
Chorley cakes, which I happen to prefer. Trying to find an authentic recipe for them posed rather
a problem. Locals would divulge merely that the filling should consist only of currants (not other dried
fruits, as in Eccles Cakes) and the pastry should be shortcrust, never puff. I have devised
this recipe, which, although not exactly authentic, is a good imitation of the Chorley cakes I have
tasted in the Chorley area, including the excellent ones from Morris' Bakers in Coppull.
A Chorley cake is egg-washed, whereas the Eccles cake is dipped in sugar to give it a crunchy glaze and
is eaten 'au naturel', without a spread of butter. Eccles cakes puff up as they bake, whereas
Chorley cakes are flatter. And lastly, Eccles cakes are finished with 3 parallel cuts in their surface, while
Chorley cakes have 2. Pedantry aside, the following recipe is very easy and is worth trying.

PASTRY

■ 227 g / 8 oz plain flour ■ 113 g / 4 oz strong white flour ■ 1 teaspoon baking powder
■ 28 g / 1 oz caster sugar ■ a pinch of salt ■ 170 g / 6 oz unsalted butter, cut into cubes
■ approximately 114 ml / 4 fl oz milk ■ egg white or beaten egg, to glaze

FILLING

■ 227 g / 8 oz currants ■ 57 g / 2 oz soft light brown sugar ■ 28 g / 1 oz butter, melted

Sift the flours and baking powder into a food
processor. Add the sugar, salt and butter. Process
until the mixture resembles breadcrumbs, then
slowly pour in just enough cold milk to form a
fairly stiff dough. Wrap in clingfilm and either
chill in the refrigerator for 30 minutes, or pop in
the freezer for 10 minutes. Pre-heat the oven to
190°C/375°F/Gas mark 5.

Meanwhile, combine the currants, sugar and
melted butter in a bowl.

Roll out the pastry to a thickness of about
5 mm / ¼ in. (As this is quite a lot of pastry to
work with, I usually divide it into 2 and roll out
each half separately.)

Using a large saucer or small plate as a guide,
cut out 6 rounds of pastry, each with a diameter
of about 20 cm / 8 in. Spoon a little filling on to
the centre of each pastry circle and spread out
slightly (allow about 2 tablespoons each).

Moisten the edges of the pastry all round with
a little water, then draw the edges together to
form a small round parcel. Turn upside down, so
that the edges are tucked underneath, then roll
out very gently with the rolling-pin, just until
the currants show through. Your rounds should
now have a diameter of about 10 cm/4 in.

Brush the tops with egg wash, then set on a
lightly buttered baking sheet. Using a sharp
knife, make 2 short parallel cuts in the surface of
each. Bake in the oven for 30 minutes, or until
golden brown, and the pastry is cooked through.
Transfer to a wire rack and allow to cool for at
least 10–15 minutes before serving. Or serve
completely cold, spread with butter. ❊

CHRISTMAS STARS

Makes 8 pastries

These are Finland's answer to our mince pies – ubiquitous and delicious, a real festive treat. They are puff-pastry stars, filled with prune jam. Although many Finnish cooks make their own puff pastry, I am happy to substitute it with the ready-rolled variety.

The stars are filled with prune (or sometimes plum) jam or purée. Prune jam can be bought in all the food shops in Finland, so very few cooks make their own. However, since we seldom see prune jam in this country, I have given my Finnish friend Ritva's recipe, with the addition of a little brandy to add to the festive cheer!

These tarts or 'Joulutortut' are served in most Finnish homes around Christmas time with strong coffee and spicy little ginger biscuits. They also serve a lethal drink or 'glogi' – reminiscent of a Glühwein – which is made with red wine, cardamom, cloves, cinnamon, raisins and sugar. This is all heated together, then a good slug of vodka is added just before serving. Drunk piping hot, it certainly helps expel the freezing Arctic cold! I like to serve the Christmas tarts straight from the oven, while still warm. They also make a good alternative to Christmas pudding, reheated and served with some good vanilla ice-cream.

■ 340 g / 12 oz 'ready-rolled' puff pastry ■ 227 g / 8 oz pitted prunes ■ cold water ■ 57 g / 2 oz sugar
■ 1 cinnamon stick ■ 2 tablespoons brandy ■ egg white and caster sugar, to glaze

Defrost the puff pastry.

To make the jam, place the prunes and 142 ml / ¼ pint cold water in a pan with the sugar and cinnamon. Bring slowly to the boil, stirring until the sugar is dissolved. Reduce the heat and simmer, covered, for 15–20 minutes.

Once the water has evaporated, add a further 71 ml / 2½ fl oz water and the brandy. Simmer, uncovered, for about 10 minutes, or until most of the liquid has evaporated. You should have only about 2 tablespoons of liquid left.

Remove from the heat and turn into a food processor. Process until it becomes a thick purée. Allow to cool. Pre-heat the oven to 230°C / 450°F / Gas mark 8.

Meanwhile, prepare the pastry. Cut out 8 × 8 cm / 3 in squares. Split all 4 corners of each square, by cutting diagonally from the tip of the corner to about half-way towards the centre. Place a dessertspoon of the prune jam in the centre of each square.

Fold over every other split corner to form a windmill-like tart. To do this, take one split end in your fingers and fold this on to the prune filling. Then do the same with the other 3 alternate corners to create the windmill shape. Seal all the ends firmly together in the centre with a little water.

Place the tarts on a buttered baking sheet, then brush with egg white and sprinkle with caster sugar.

Bake in the oven for about 10 minutes, or until puffed up and golden brown. Remove to a wire rack and serve warm. ❄

FORFAR BRIDIES

Makes 4 turnovers

Bridies are to Forfar what pasties are to Cornwall. Both are all-in-one meals – shortcrust pastry surrounding a hearty meat filling – but the pasty is a half-moon shape while the bridie is a horseshoe shape and filled with beef (or venison) and onion only. Bill McLaren, whose family-run bakery in Forfar makes some of the best bridies around, has used the same recipe since they opened in 1893. I have altered Bill's recipe (he uses plain flour, margarine and dripping), since I prefer the firm texture given by strong white (bread) flour. I also use white (vegetable) fat and butter, for added flavour. The important procedure of 'dunting' and 'nicking' seals the filled bridies. The 'dunting' is done with the heel of the hand, pressing down on the edges; the 'nicking', which finishes the sealing process, is done with the forefinger and thumb. Unlike the pasty, the bridie is pricked with a characteristic hole prior to baking. Forbar bridies are at their best served warm, but are also good cold.

PASTRY
■ 255g / 9oz strong white flour ■ 85g / 3oz plain flour ■ a pinch of salt
■ 85g / 3oz unsalted butter, cut into cubes ■ 85g / 3oz white fat, cut into cubes
■ 2½–3 tablespoons cold water

FILLING
■ 454g / 1lb shoulder or rump beef ■ 85g / 3oz beef suet, grated
■ 1 small onion, peeled and finely grated ■ salt and pepper, to season

For the pastry, place the flours and salt in a food processor. Add the fats and process until incorporated. Then add just enough cold water to bind to a stiff dough. Gather in your hands, wrap in clingfilm and chill for at least 1 hour.

For the filling, roughly chop the beef – I use the 'pulse' action on my food processor. Alternatively, mince very coarsely. Mix together the beef, suet, onion and plenty of seasoning – the texture should be that of a fairly stiff paste.

Divide the pastry into 4 and roll each piece into an oval-shape. Divide the filling into 4 and spoon on to one half only of the pastry ovals, leaving a border all round.

Dampen the edges and fold the top half of the pastry over the filling to enclose it. Using a sharp knife, trim the edges into a neat 'horseshoe' shape. Now 'dunt' and 'nick' – by pressing down the edges to seal and by crimping all around, to give a nicely finished look. Place on a lightly greased baking tray and chill for 1 hour. Pre-heat the oven to 200°C/400°F/Gas mark 6.

Bake in the oven for about 35–40 minutes, or until golden brown. Serve warm. ❊

FORFAR BRIDIES
SPINACH EMPANADAS (page 220)

SPINACH EMPANADAS

Makes 6

Empanadas are those little pies, made from shortcrust or puff pastry, or (and this is the most authentic) a yeast-based bread dough. The fillings can range from meat – minced lamb or chopped chorizo sausage – to vegetables such as mushrooms, peppers or artichokes. These empanadas are filled with spinach, flavoured with garlic and bound together with some grated mature cheese. To be truly traditional you should use Manchego, which is a mature ewe's milk cheese from the central region of Spain. But a nicely matured, traditionally-made Cheddar will do just as well.
Serve the empanadas either for lunch at home, or take on a picnic. Or, in true Spanish style, as canapés – or should I say, tapas – with a pre-dinner drink. Serve either warm or cold, preferably with a chilled Fino sherry.

DOUGH

■ 227 g / 8 oz strong white flour ■ 1 teaspoon easy-blend dried yeast ■ ½ teaspoon salt
■ 1 tablespoon olive oil ■ 99–114 ml / 3½–4 fl oz warm water

FILLING

■ 284 g / 10 oz frozen spinach, defrosted ■ 1 tablespoon olive oil ■ 3 garlic cloves, peeled and chopped
■ 85 g / 3 oz grated cheese ■ salt and pepper, to season

For the dough, place the flour, yeast and salt in a bowl. Make a well in the centre and pour in the oil and just enough warm water to combine to a stiff dough. Knead for about 10 minutes, or until smooth. Then place in a lightly oiled bowl, cover with clingfilm and leave to rise in a warm place for about 1 hour.

Now make the filling: squeeze out any excess water from the spinach. Heat the oil in a frying pan and gently fry the chopped garlic. Add the spinach after a minute and fry for about 5 minutes, or until cooked through and fairly stiff in consistency. It is important that it is not at all liquid. Remove from the heat and leave to cool.

Then stir in the cheese and season well with salt and pepper. Pre-heat the oven to 220°C/425°F/Gas mark 7.

Divide the dough into 6 and roll out fairly thinly to circles of about 15–18 cm / 6–7 in.

Place a spoonful of the spinach filling on one half of each circle of dough, then wet the edges and fold over to seal. Using your forefinger and thumb, crimp round the edges. Then, using kitchen scissors, snip little 'air-vents' in the top. Place on a lightly oiled baking tray.

Bake in the oven for about 15 minutes, or until golden brown and cooked through. Serve warm or at room temperature.

CHEESE AND MUSTARD GOUGÈRES

Makes about 10 buns

Gougère is a Burgundian speciality – cheese-flavoured choux puffs which are joined together in a ring. These are typically eaten with a glass of local Burgundy, either as a pre-dinner appetiser or as a cheese course in itself – the ideal way to finish off a glass of red wine after the main course and before the dessert. The gougères in this recipe are individual little choux buns which I like to eat plain. They are also good filled with herby cream cheese or lightly smoked fish pâté. As long as you follow some basic rules, you cannot go wrong with any choux pastry recipe. First you must weigh out the ingredients precisely. Only a heavy-based saucepan will provide perfect results. You must tip in all the flour at once, after the butter and water mixture has come to the boil. If you pour it in gradually, lumps will form. By contrast, the eggs should be added one at a time and the mixture beaten extremely vigorously between each addition. Only stop beating when the mixture looks smooth and shiny. To test whether the buns are cooked through after the suggested baking time, look at the sides – not the top or bottom. The sides brown last, so only when they are golden will your buns be ready. After transferring the buns to a wire tray, pierce the side with a sharp knife to allow the steam to escape. This prevents them going soggy.

■ 57 g / 2 oz unsalted butter, cut into cubes ■ 142 ml / ¼ pint cold water
■ 78 g / 2 ¾ oz plain flour, sifted ■ 2 eggs ■ 71 g / 2 ½ oz mature Cheddar, grated
■ 1 rounded teaspoon wholegrain mustard ■ salt, pepper

First weigh out all the ingredients in advance. Pre-heat the oven to 200°C / 400°F / Gas mark 6. Place the butter and water in a heavy-based saucepan and heat slowly until the butter melts. Now bring to a rapid boil and remove immediately from the heat.

Immediately tip in all the flour and return to a low heat. Beat vigorously until the mixture comes away clean from the sides of the pan. (This should take about 1 minute.)

Remove again from the heat and cool for 1–2 minutes. Add one egg, beating hard to ensure it is incorporated completely before adding a second egg. Beat vigorously until the mixture is smooth and shiny. (It should be firm enough to hold soft peaks when lifted with a spoon.)

Stir in the cheese, mustard, salt and pepper and combine well.

Using 2 dessertspoons, spoon about 10 blobs of the mixture on to a lightly buttered baking tray. (Or you can pipe the mixture, if you prefer). Space fairly well apart.

Bake in the oven for 22–25 minutes, or until puffed up and golden brown on all sides. Transfer to a wire rack and, using a sharp knife, pierce a tiny hole in the side of each to release any steam.

Allow to cool before eating.

✳ It is best to freeze choux pastry unbaked. Spoon the mixture on to the baking tray, then set in the freezer. Once frozen, wrap the uncooked buns in plastic bags. Bake from frozen, adding at least 5 minutes to the cooking time.

INDEX

almonds: Bakewell pudding, 208–9
poppy seed and almond cake, 72
Anzac biscuits, 153
apples: apple gingerbread, 83
apple scones, 115
Dutch apple tart, 202
Somerset apple cake, 97
apricots: dried apricot and fresh
thyme loaf, 186–7
rosemary and apricot muffins, 64
Aztec cookies, 142

baguettes, 38–9
Bakewell pudding, 208–9
bananas: banana bread, 196–7
banana oat squares, 167
banana pizza, 31
banana upside-down cake, 73
chocolate banana cake, 93
dosa with banana soufflé, 132–3
barley and sunflower bread, 46
barm brack, 16
Bath buns, 30
beef: Forfar bridies, 218
beetroot chocolate loaf, 189–90
biscuits, 139–59
Anzac biscuits, 153
Aztec cookies, 142
chickpea and cardamom
shortbread, 149
chocolate and coconut macaroons,
155
chocolate chunk cookies, 144–5
chocolate shortbread, 148
Christmas cookies, 140–1
ginger biscuits, 157
ice-cream sandwiches, 159
jammy dodgers, 156
lime and brown sugar meringue
biscuits, 154–5
melting moments, 151
mincemeat shortbread, 150
Parmesan shortbread, 150–1
peanut butter cookies, 144
petticoat tails, 147
pine-nut cookies, 145
rocky road cookies, 141
Shewsbury biscuits, 154
speculaas, 146
vanilla cookie sandwiches, 158
black bottom flapjacks, 166–7
black bun, 84–5

blackberries: yoghurt and bramble
scones, 110
blinis, 136–7
blueberry loaf, spiced, 184
bread, 33–55
brioche, lemon, 27
brownies, 162–3
butteries, 54–5
butterscotch bars, 170–1

caramel squares, pine-nut, 178
cardamom chocolate cake, 92
carrots: carrot and nut loaf, 192–3
carrot cake with orange cream
cheese icing, 193
passion cake, 70
chapatis, 134
cheese: cheese and mustard
gougères, 221
cheese sauce scones, 111
Parmesan shortbread, 150–1
cheese, soft: carrot cake with orange
cream cheese icing, 193
chocolate lemon cheese slices, 164
paskha, 24–5
Richmond maids of honour, 215
cheesecakes: chocolate cheese-
swirled squares, 77
chocolate swirl cheesecake, 208
Chelsea buns, 12–13
chestnut and pine-nut cake, 69
chickpea and cardamom shortbread,
149
chocolate: beetroot chocolate loaf,
189–90
black bottom flapjacks, 166–7
bulging chocolate muffins, 65
cardamom chocolate cake, 92
chocolate and coconut macaroons,
155
chocolate and walnut tart, 204
chocolate banana cake, 93
chocolate bread rolls, 14
chocolate cheese-swirled squares,
77
chocolate chunk cookies, 144–5
chocolate fudge brownies, 162
chocolate lemon cheese slices, 164
chocolate mud cake, 76
chocolate peanut butter slice, 171
chocolate shortbread, 148
chocolate swirl cheesecake, 208

'no mess' chocolate brownies,
162–3
nutty chocolate tiffin, 168
polenta chocolate cake, 75
prune, chocolate and lemon tart,
206
rhubarb and white chocolate tart,
200–1
thick chocolate coconut bars, 170
white chocolate and basil sauce,
96
white chocolate chip brownies,
163
cholla, 48
Chorley cakes, 216
Christmas cookies, 140–1
Christmas stars, 217
cider cake, 96–7
cinnamon nablab, 214–15
clafoutis cake, rhubarb, 68
coconut: chocolate and coconut
macaroons, 155
impossible coconut pie, 212
lamingtons, 179
macadamia, coconut and
pineapple cake, 61–2
thick chocolate coconut bars, 170
cookies: see biscuits
corn bread, Portuguese, 39
cottage loaf, 34–5
courgette loaf, 190
cranberries: cranberry pecan loaf,
186
cranberry scone round, 102
crepes, Breton, 130
crumpets, 123

dampers, 55
dates: date and ginger shortbread
squares, 176
date and walnut loaf, 196
dosa with banana soufflé, 132–3
drop scones, 118
Dundee cake, 80
Dutch apple tart, 202

empanadas, spinach, 220

fat rascals, 107
fatty cutties, 119
fennel seeds: seed cake, 90
Finnish oven pancake, 137

flapjacks: black bottom, 166–7
  mincemeat and orange, 166
flowerpot bread, 36–7
Fochabers gingerbread, 80–1
Forfar bridies, 218
fougasse, 50
fruit cakes: black bun, 84–5
  boiled fruit cake, 84
  Dundee cake, 80
fruit cocktail squares, 175
fruit loaves, 181–97

gâteau Basque, 58–9
ginger: apple gingerbread, 83
  date and ginger shortbread squares,
    176
  Fochabers gingerbread, 80–1
  ginger biscuits, 157
  gingerbread ice-cream, 99
  gingertorte, 62–3
  hot gingerbread pudding, 81
  Orkney broonie, 82–3
  parkin, 82
gooseberries: hot cobbled fruit,
  104–5
gougères, cheese and mustard, 221
Greek Easter bread, 13
griddle cakes, Northumberland, 120
griddle cakes, Italian, 129
griddle cookery, 117–37

hazelnuts: orange and hazelnut
  cake, 194
  roasted hazelnut cake, 74

ice-cream: gingerbread ice-cream,
  99
  ice-cream meringue cake, 98
  ice-cream sandwiches, 159
  shortbread ice-cream, 19
  Italian griddle cakes, 129

jam: jammy dodgers, 156
  Linzertorte, 213
Johnny bread, 133

Kentish huffkins, 35
kulich, 24–5

lamingtons, 179
leeks: leek granary scones, 114
  rice and leek bread, 47
lemon: chocolate lemon cheese
  slices, 164
  crusty lemon cake, 59
  lemon brioche, 27

lemon curd, 88
lemon curd polenta cake, 87
prune, chocolate and lemon tart,
  206
lime and brown sugar meringue
  biscuits, 154–5
Lincolnshire plum loaf, 191
Linzertorte, 213
Lucia rolls, 21–2

macadamia, coconut and pineapple
  cake, 61–2
macaroons, chocolate and coconut,
  155
Madeira cake, 89
maids of honour, Richmond, 215
marmalade breakfast muffins, 63
marmalade loaf, 182–3
mealie bread, 44
melktert, 207
melting moments, 151
meringues: ice-cream meringue
  cake, 98
  lime and brown sugar meringue
    biscuits, 154–5
Mexican-style tortillas, 131
mincemeat: mincemeat and orange
  flapjacks, 166
  mincemeat shortbread, 150
muffins, 126–7
  bulging chocolate, 65
  crunchy-topped raspberry and
    cinnamon, 66
  marmalade breakfast, 63
  rosemary and apricot, 64

nablab, cinnamon, 214–15
'no mess' chocolate brownies,
  162–3
nutty chocolate tiffin, 168

oats and oatmeal: Anzac biscuits,
  153
  banana oat squares, 167
  black bottom flapjacks, 166–7
  mincemeat and orange flapjacks,
    166
  oatcakes, 122
  Orkney broonie, 82–3
  parkin, 82
  Staffordshire oatcakes, 126
olive bread, 40
olive oil scones, 106–7
orange: mincemeat and orange
  flapjacks, 166
  orange and hazelnut cake, 194

sweet potato and orange loaf, 182
Orkney broonie, 82–3

pain d'épice, 94
pancakes: blinis, 136–7
  Breton crepes, 130
  dosa with banana soufflé, 132–3
  Scotch pancakes, 118
pannukakku (Finnish oven
  pancake), 137
Paradise cake, 173–4
parkin, 82
paskha, 24–5
passion cake, 70
peanut butter slice, chocolate, 171
peanut butter cookies, 144
pears: pear loaf, 183
  pear tarte Tatin, 204–5
pecan nuts: cranberry pecan loaf,
  186
  pecan bread, 37
petticoat tails, 147
pikelets, 128
pine-nuts: chestnut and pine-nut
  cake, 69
  pine-nut caramel squares, 178
pineapple: macadamia, coconut and
  pineapple cake, 61–2
pizza, banana, 31
plum pie, Sunday, 211–12
polenta: lemon curd polenta cake,
  87
  polenta chocolate cake, 75
poppy seeds: poppy seed and
  almond cake, 72
  poppy seed bread ring, 28
Portuguese corn bread, 39
potatoes: potato and tarragon
  rieska, 43
  potato scone round, 114–15
  potato scones, 121
prunes: Christmas stars, 217
  Lincolnshire plum loaf, 191
  prune, chocolate and lemon tart,
    206
  prune, lemon and hazelnut bread,
    26
pulla, 22–3
pumpkin loaf, 187

raspberry and cinnamon muffins,
  crunchy-topped, 66
rhubarb: hot cobbled fruit, 104–5
  rhubarb and white chocolate tart,
    200–1
  rhubarb clafoutis cake, 68

rhubarb streusel squares, 174–5
rice: rice and leek bread, 47
  rice cake, 74–5
Richmond maids of honour, 215
rieska, potato and tarragon, 43
rocky road cookies, 141
rosemary and apricot muffins, 64
rum, raisin and rye scone ring, 104
Russian spice bread, 197
rye bread, 42

saffron: Lucia rolls, 21–2
salami and sage scones, 112
Sally Lunn, 17
sangria tart, 201
sauce, white chocolate and basil, 96
scones, 101–115
Scotch pancakes, 118
seed cake, 90
Selkirk bannock, 18
Selkirk bannock pudding, 19
shortbread: chickpea and
  cardamom, 149

chocolate, 148
  date and ginger, 176
  mincemeat, 150
  Parmesan, 150–1
shortbread ice-cream, 19
Shrewsbury biscuits, 154
singin' hinnies, 120
soda bread, 48–9
Somerset apple cake, 97
sour skons, 106
speculaas, 146
spice bread, Russian, 197
spinach empanadas, 220
squash scones, 108
Staffordshire oatcakes, 126
stottie cake, 53–4
streusel squares, rhubarb, 174–5
Sunday plum pie, 211–12
sweet breads, 11–31
sweet potato and orange loaf, 182

tarts: chocolate and walnut tart,
  204

Christmas stars, 217
Dutch apple tart, 202
Linzertorte, 213
melktert, 207
pear tarte Tatin, 204–5
prune, chocolate and lemon tart,
  206
rhubarb and white chocolate tart,
  200–1
Richmond maids of honour, 215
sangria tart, 201
teisen lap, 192
tomato bread, fresh, 51
tortillas, Mexican-style, 131
treacle scones, 103

vanilla cookie sandwiches, 158

walnuts: chocolate and walnut tart,
  204
Welsh cakes, 124

yoghurt and bramble scones, 110

BIBLIOGRAPHY

BROWN, Catherine Scottish Cookery (Richard Drew Publishing, 1985)

CAMPBELL, Susan English Cookery New and Old (Consumers' Association and Hodder & Stoughton, 1981)

CHAMBERLAIN, Lesley The Food and Cooking of Russia (Penguin Books, 1983)

COLLISTER & BLAKE, Linda and Anthony The Bread Book (Conran Octopus, 1993)

DAVID, ELIZABETH English Bread and Yeast Cookery (Penguin Books, 1979)

DAVIDSON, Silvija Loaf, Crust and Crumb (Michael Joseph, 1995)

FITZGIBBON, Theodora A Taste of Scotland (Pan Books, 1971)

GREENBERG, Florence Florence Greenberg's Jewish Cookery Book (Jewish Chronicle 7th Edition, 1963)

GRIGSON, Jane English Food (Penguin Books, 1977)

HARBEN, Philip Traditional Dishes of Britain (The Bodley Head, 1953)

McNEILL, F. Marian The Scots Kitchen (Mercat Press, 1993)

MILLIKEN and FENIGER, Mary Sue and Susan Mesa Mexicana (William Morrow, 1994)

NORMAN, Jill The Complete Book of Spices (Dorling Kindersley, 1990)

PATERSON, Judy Scottish Home Baking (Judy Paterson & Lindsay Publications, 1993)

RODEN, Claudia A New Book of Middle Eastern Food (Viking, 1985)

SHAIDA, Margaret The Legendary Cuisine of Persia (Penguin Books, 1994)

SIMPSON, Maureen Australian Cuisine (ABC Enterprises, 1990)

SLATER, Nigel Real Good Food (Fourth Estate, 1995)

TANTTU, Anna-Maija and Juha Food From Finland (Otava Publishing Co, 1989)

WIDENFELT, Sam Swedish Food (Esseltes Goteborgsindustrier AB, 1948)